SANCTUARY

THE POND

© 1980, Anderson Isometric Maps

◆ SEEING THE REAL ◆
NEW YORK

Translated from German
by Roger and Gerda Marcinik

BARRON'S
Woodbury, New York • London

Frontispiece: A view of the southern tip of Manhattan

First U.S. Edition © 1981 by Barron's Educational Series, Inc.,
113 Crossways Park Drive, Woodbury, New York 11797.

© 1978 DuMont Buchverlag, Köln

All rights for all countries reserved by DuMont Buchverlag
GmbH & Co. Kommanditgesellschaft, Cologne, West Germany.

The title of the German Edition is *Richtig reisen: New York*

Library of Congress Catalog Card No. 80-28127

International Standard Book No. 0-8120-2242-4

Library of Congress Cataloging in Publication Data

Von Arnim, Gabriele.
  Seeing the real New York

   Translation of Richtig reisen: New York.
   Bibliography: p.
   Includes index.
1. New York (City) — Description — 1951–   — Guide-
books. I. Mayor, Bruni, joint author. II. Title
F128.18.V6613   1981   917.47′10443   80-28127
ISBN 0-8120-2242-4

Contents

Foreword

by Ruth Gilbert
New York Magazine

I once put up in my guest room an acquaintance from France who was visiting New York for the first time. She was here for two weeks—a long time to have anyone in your guest room—but I hardly ever saw her except for two trips to the ballet together. She was out of the house first thing every morning, out all day and out all evening. The next morning, before she dashed out again, she'd tell me where she'd been the previous day, all the things she'd seen and the people she'd met. She seemed to hit every museum, gallery (she was an artist), neighborhood, shopping district, landmark, nightclub, and tourist attraction there was. When, after two whirlwind weeks, it was over and she was about to leave, I asked her how her visit had been. "Well," she said, "it's been wonderful, but I don't think I've really seen the city yet."

That's the problem. No matter how long you stay in New York, you're likely to leave unsatisfied. But that's also what makes visiting New York more exciting, in a way, than visiting anywhere else. There is always more to see. You even feel that way after living here all your life. Every street you walk down is full of discoveries, novelty, variety. Every street offers a panorama of the human condition. You'll never be bored. New York is almost infinite.

It is a city of extremes. Two types of people move to New York, as I see it. The first type consists of the most ambitious people in America. They are here to become rich and famous, be it as actors, dancers, chefs, musicians, merchants, bankers, brokers, businessmen, politicians, writers, artists, or whatever. They are here because this is the place to rise to the top of it all. They are here because New York is the most exciting and challenging place in America, and their presence keeps it that way.

The other type is the down and out, the destitute, helpless immigrants from helpless nations, and impoverished natives of our own. They move to New York simply because it will accept them, because it seems to offer at least a chance. They are struggling just as hard as the people on top.

There is also a New York of more typical Americans—family people with good steady jobs and communities, people like schoolteachers, policemen, firemen, storekeepers, cabdrivers. Their ancestors were immigrants here, most likely from Ireland or Italy or Eastern Europe. They are the oft-overlooked backbone of the city, it almost seems to be passing them by as it grows ever richer and ever poorer. They do not have it easy.

For all these people, New York is a constant challenge. Just staying afloat in this powerful and expensive place is difficult, and getting ahead is what it's all about here for the great mass of New Yorkers.

It's a challenge for the visitor, too. So much to choose among, so much to see, so much to know about what to see. And so much to avoid—not only street crime, which is vastly overrated, but getting taken by unscrupulous merchants, getting lost on the Byzantine subway system, and various lesser worries that confront us all daily. It's all part of the adventure. New York wouldn't be New York without noisy, dirty, and labyrinthine subway lines any more than it would be New York without the Rainbow Room and the Statue of Liberty and the City Ballet.

A book like this, that goes beyond the usual sketchy tourist handbook and imparts some of the real character of the city, that contains real inside knowledge, is your best start. Now it's up to you. Immerse yourself in this city. You won't feel the same afterwards, I promise.

Preface

To organize this fascinating, bombastic city into carefully arranged information seems a daring undertaking. No one could consider all expectations and notions, nor would one want to. We can only make personal selections, as we have here. In *Seeing the Real New York* we have given you some first impressions: what has surprised, touched, or disgusted many; where people have been bored; and what they found exciting and fun. We were concerned not only with pointing out New York's façade — and it alone is impressive enough as it is — but also with discovering and conveying the "heart and countenance" of this city — as V. S. Pritchett calls it. The book is about sightseeing too, but there is not too much emphasis on the compulsory tourist exercises. *Seeing the Real New York* deals with practical tips, but even more with the feeling that one must develop for New York so as to understand it.

New York lays itself open to the visitor only superficially. The Empire State Building or the World Trade Center are not to be overlooked or left out of your tour. Even a section like SoHo, which was unknown only a few years ago, presents itself as a tourist mecca without the slightest embarrassment. However, the visitor usually does not find right away the Jewish and Puerto Rican Lower East Side, for example, and the integrated Upper West Side or the city's small parks and plazas. The fact that New York is not only a city of contrasts, but also the home of average citizens is often overlooked. We have attempted to show both sides of this city. New York is a gathering of neighborhoods whose sum does not make up the whole, but does modify and humanize the general impression. We hope to make this city accessible to you and let you draw your own conclusions. New York was and is a personal experience; that is just what it should be for you too.

We would like to thank a few people who made this book as complete and informative as it is: Peter Figlestahler for his information on pop and rock music; Douglas Blair Turnbaugh for his material on dance; and Irena von Zahn for her description of SoHo. We also thank the Downtown Lower Manhattan Association, Inc., for allowing us to reprint their walking tour of lower Manhattan, the "Heritage Trail."

Using this book: This book is divided basically into two parts. In the first half, the white portion, the information presented is to help you decide where to go and what to do. These are suggestions only, and the omission of a museum, or restaurant, or shop, for example, is not meant to imply anything negative. There is just so much to see and do in New York that we couldn't mention everything here. On the other hand, the Key to the City, as we call the second half of the book, is a reference for you. The listings are again not complete; that would be impossible. But they do include the major items or spots for each category and provide you with the fundamentals you will need as a tourist. We suggest that you read the white section to get a feel for what you wish to do in New York, then consult the Key for details.

Introducing New York, The Big Apple

New York is not known as a city for romantics or quiet observers longing for beauty. Hardly anyone expects to find charm and intimacy here; on the contrary, they seek sensation and the thrill of the big-city jungle. Indeed, many come with preconceived notions and forget about discovering the heart and countenance of this city. They are fascinated by the mass of stone and the crowds of people, by the skyscraper canyons and the concrete deserts. They want to be overwhelmed and impressed, rather than touched and moved. Everyone expects the monumental and bombastic, although the esthetic charm and peculiar beauty of the raised colossus may be surprising; but the small-town face, the many streets lined with low houses and rows of trees, and the small buildings wedged in between skyscrapers are astonishing. The visitor is just as prepared for ''the monoliths of mass dwellings'' (Pritchett) as for the ''teeming accommodations of the little people'' (Zuckmayer), but the sight of normality or the ambiance of civic bustle against the background of an ordinary city scene create confusion; those views do not fit the picture. Nothing and nobody can open up this city for you. You have to do that by yourself.

But one thing is sure: New York is a city that provokes. No person remains indifferent here. If you fall into confrontation, then it is not easy to keep your head; you alternate between euphoria and depression, between enthusiasm and disgust. At times New York appears to be a shattered wreck of a person, whose arm has been pierced by the heroin cannula and who has computer tape in his mouth for a tongue, as one journalist characterized it, while, as another observer said: ''If there were no New York, it would have to be invented instantly.''

New Yorkers have the international reputation of being discourteous, even rude and brusk; yet almost every guest who comes here is enthused and surprised by the helpfulness of friendly New Yorkers. You can, if you have bad luck and are not careful, be assaulted twice in one block, but there are also days when a taxi driver, on finding the purse you left in his car, brings it untouched to your home the next day.

New York has some of the greatest concentrations of wealth in the world on Park Avenue, but on that same avenue farther uptown is one of the most pathetic slum areas. In New York, you can rent a closed subway station for a party, be driven in a Rolls-Royce for $35 an hour, subscribe to a weekly delivery of a bouquet of flowers, or have a continental breakfast in bed delivered every day. Here they talk to green plants, hum merry melodies to ferns and palms, and whisper sweet nothings to cacti — the plant doctor is available twenty-four hours a day, seven days a week.

In New York you can eat homemade marmalade from oranges grown on a balony, be escorted on shopping trips by a fashion consultant, rent a partner for conversation, or take a seminar on restaurants in Chinatown in the academically high-standing New School. Here you can plunge into hectic activity, and will no doubt do that too at first — in any case it is hard to set priorities. If in most cities you have to take care not to miss anything, then here, conversely, you have to learn to let some things slip by.

New York is both a metropolis and a province, a "village suffering from delusions of grandeur," said German writer Wolfgang Koeppen. This is a city noted more for its contradictions than its harmony, for its antagonism than its conciliatoriness, for its anonymity than its solidarity. After a year in the same apartment, many New Yorkers still do not know the people using their elevator, but they may give a friendly greeting to people along their child's school block a few streets away. They are likely to be friendlier to their butcher than to their upstairs neighbor, simply because they see their butcher more often.

To understand New York, or better yet, to be able to respect and enjoy it, then you have to beware of clichés. New York is a city full of sensations, but at the same time it is also where the average citizen pursues everyday habits just like everywhere else. It is a city in which a one-sided view is perhaps more misleading than in most other cities. New York is neither one nor the other; it is always both.

"The good and the bad," writes Sabina Lietzmann, "is thrust together into the view, and hardly anyone is spared perceiving the glory clouded by the threat. Only the naïve and the insincere can deny that a declaration of love for New York can be ventured only by those who have seen the beloved as a Medusa as well."

The Typical
New Yorker?

The Melting Pot Gives Way to the Tossed Salad

"The story of New York," writes Anthony Burgess, "is a story of immigrant battling with immigrant, leaving to battle with immigrant but always ready to battle with a new immigrant." Each newcomer had to make his way against the establishment at the time: the Irish against the Teutonic Protestants (Germans, Scandinavians, English, Scots, and Dutch), the Italians against the Irish, the Jews against the Italians, and the blacks and Puerto Ricans since time immemorial against all of them. The Protestants had it easier from the start; their religion meant diligence, cleanliness, puritanical discipline and upbringing. "The faith of Dante and Michelangelo, on the other hand," once again according to Burgess, "was associated with shiftlessness, squalor, indolence and ignorance."

In 1640 New York's several hundred inhabitants spoke eighteen languages; even today the diversity of languages in this city is self-evident. In New York, the minorities seem to be the majority: almost 2 million Jews live here, blacks and Puerto Ricans make up about a third of the population, Italians constitute just under 10 percent, and Irish are about 7 percent. Almost 100,000 Chinese and some 300,000 Germans, Austrians, and Swiss also are here. On top of that, there are the Hungarians (about 100,000), the Greeks (about 60,000), the Armenians (50,000), the Filipinos (35,000), and those from India (3,500).

On closer examination, the well-known, much-quoted description of the melting pot can hardly be upheld — and less than ever for the last five to ten years. Mr. and Mrs. America are no longer accepted without reservations as models worthy of imitation. The desire for assimilation, to be as American as apple pie is less important. Earlier, the Jewish immigrants cut off their temporal locks and named their sons Jim and John. Today children named Joshua and Aaron play in the park with others called Maria or Juan.

Italian-Americans not only cook traditional pasta, but also take language courses to learn their mother tongue. And more and more blacks go by the motto: "To know where we are going, we have to know where we came from," in the search for their identity, for a historical continuity. The longing for spiritualism that embraced many Americans in the sixties and seventies is also revealed in this ethnic consciousness of the past. Some hope to find themselves while lying on a psychiatrist's couch or sit-

ting cross-legged with a guru, but others listen to grandmother's stories by the fireside. The newly discovered roots give support and help each to find his or her individuality, for which respect and tolerance are demanded.

By way of example, this development toward ethnic consciousness is quite clearly observable with the Chinese in New York's Chinatown. While the older generations strove less to conform than to be inconspicuous, they never learned English, and they wanted no say in their lives, the younger people have begun loudly to demand their rights. "Somehow the Chinese have been forgotten," a city official says; today that is no longer permitted.

Every tourist has to walk once through the Chinese, Italian, and Jewish neighborhoods on the Lower East Side to grasp what it means to go from one world to another, from one culture to the next, within a few blocks and yet to remain in New York. These different cultural and ethnic impressions are almost always visible, yet the New Yorker atmosphere dominates everything.

It is this pronounced ethnic consciousness, coupled with an unavoidable cosmopolitanism, that makes up the fascination of this city. When blacks and Jews don green caps and wave little green flags, singing "When Irish Eyes are Smiling" on St. Patrick's Day, then you might think you can understand the intention or the hope of the melting-pot theory. But predominant in everyday New York life is the consciousness of *not* being melted in that pot; it is the idea of blending flavors

Chinese in Chinatown;
Puerto Ricans in Harlem;
and Orthodox Jews
in the Lower East Side

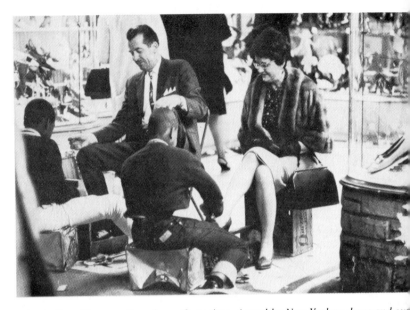

Above: Shoeshiners on Broadway. Opposite: A wealthy New Yorker; down and out on the Bowery

but retaining separate identities. *Tossed salad* would be a better term than *melting pot,* an observer of the scene once said, for each leaf of lettuce in the large bowl may taste different.

The Wealthy and the Poor Live Side-by-Side

Although they come from different backgrounds, is there a typical New Yorker? Is it possible to describe a representative citizen? Are New Yorkers more alert, agile, open-minded — conditioned by the restless, perpetually changing scenery of this city? Are they arrogant, callous, and calculating — disciplined by the relentlessly competitive struggle? Can someone — as a tourist once asked — tell just by looking whether a person lives in New York or in Chicago?

New York, known as the city of contradictions, has countless typical New Yorkers, but there is no such thing as *the* typical New Yorker. The banker who every morning fights for a seat on the subway to get to his Wall Street office belongs here as much as Norman Mailer, Jackie Onassis, or the doorman who guards the entrance to the large apartment buildings. The resident of a spacious apartment on Park Avenue at 65th Street is just as much a New Yorker as the resident of a dilapidated brownstone on Park Avenue at 119th Street. And both know next to nothing about each other.

An unpublicized number of millionaires reside in New York. They live in suites or

18

Fifth and Park avenues. Behind more or less anonymous façades, they collect art treasures of immeasurable value. "I always thought the English were rich," a staff member of a large auction house remarked, "yet what I have seen here surpasses simply everything." An admirer of Versailles had a fifty-five-foot-long hall of mirrors installed in his fourth-floor apartment on Fifth Avenue. The salons adjacent to it are decorated with original furniture. And already hanging in the checkroom on the 31st floor of a new building, where one expects nothing spectacular in the typical boxlike rooms with low ceilings, is the first Delvaux, which fills the entire wall.

There are also over a million welfare recipients. Some — the poor and the elderly, the unemployed and the "flipped-out" — in contrast often live in squalid buildings in run-down neighborhods. Many elderly people live in deteriorating apartments, often relics of a neighborhood once middle class but now a slum. Behind multiply locked doors they spend their much-quoted golden years in fear. The collecting point for the social outsiders, for those who are no longer making it or have never made it, are the so-called welfare hotels — the breeding ground for crime in this city. In such buildings, which offer furnished single rooms and apartments for permanent residents and transients, live drug addicts and alcoholics, people mentally ill, petty criminals, and panhandlers crowded together with innocent pensioners and others living only on social security. "In some of these hotels," a police officer explained, "just as many crimes are committed as in a normal small town."

The gap between rich and poor is very seldom bridged by interpersonal contact. Those on welfare are at best a factor for statistics or subjects for a human interest story. But as individuals — as personalities — they remain unimportant persons of no political and social interest. Ideas about the daily course of their lives remain vague; slum residents are a category, not human individuals.

This realization may seem harsh, and yet it explains why some travelers feel that New Yorkers are cold or indifferent. But New York can be electrifying and cruel. To keep up with the pace, a person needs stamina and endurance. Anyone going through this city with his or her eyes open rapidly becomes sensitized to the sufferings. The result is that you either are crushed by it, or you close your eyes and shut yourself off — both are typical New Yorker reactions.

Everyday New Yorkers

New Yorkers include the influential banking figure David Rockefeller, as well as countless other top-level executives. But on the streets of this city are other New Yorkers: construction workers, messengers, diplomats, actors, artists, and bookkeepers. There are also the shopping bag ladies — women who make their home on door sills and who carry their few personal belongings in innumerable shopping bags.

Here is where you'll see the art patrons and antique dealers. It is where chauffeured limousines stand in front of Tiffany's, Van Cleef & Arpels, or Elizabeth Arden, ignoring traffic regulations. A few blocks away, careworn old people scrounge in garbage cans for something to eat. New Yorkers are the indefatigable

A Park Avenue businessman

Scenes of the city: Nightlife; an afternoon's stop at Rockefeller Center; escape in the park

violinist fiddling for tips in front of Broadway's theaters, allegedly to finance his music studies, or the painter who does portraits of sneakers for $40 apiece. The site of the world's largest stock exchange and countless banks, New York is the home office for calculating, worldly business executives and clever lawyers. Yet it is also the workplace of fastidious, accurate, competent, and considerate clerks, waiters, secretaries, and shopkeepers.

You'll find some New Yorkers at poetry readings and gallery openings, while others prefer exclusive private parties and illegal after-hours clubs. The city's museums and concert halls are usually full, as are the theaters and movie houses. New Yorkers eagerly watch the newspapers and magazines for exhibit openings and new places to go. They have an almost insatiable appetite for the novel and exotic, whether it be in regard to food, art, or theater. Thousands of New Yorkers are experimenting in pseudopsychological and pseudoreligious groups with all sorts of psychotherapeutic techniques. The search for their own selves drives them into the arms of gurus, yogis, swamis, parapsychologists, quasitherapists, and other enlightened ones who proclaim salvation and promise healing. The traveler not visiting California — the cradle of the psychotherapeutic subculture — can also get his or her money's worth in New York. Every week the *Village Voice* has at least a page of advertisements for suitable courses, lectures, or meetings.

East Side/West Side

As in other cities, your address is of considerable importance. An artist or writer residing on the Upper East Side would be labeled bourgeois by his circle, while a banker living on the Upper West Side would be viewed as adventurous by his colleagues. Fifth or Park avenues, Beekman or Sutton places are the prestige addresses in the city. Here New Yorkers either have the money for a lovely suite or they squeeze into a small apartment with a view of someone else's backyard. On the West Side, for usually less rent, a person can have a spacious, if somewhat deteriorating apartment in an old building that may likely not be impenetrable. Debates about the East Side or West Side rarely deal with questions of amenities, like public transportation, good restaurants, movies, or shops. Someone does not merely live on the East Side or West Side — he or she is a West Sider or an East Sider.

The Upper East Side is smart, elegant. Doormen are everywhere and often there are several in the same place. There are very beautiful brownstones and apartment buildings from the twenties, but also many ugly high-rise apartment houses. There are high-class restaurants, first-run movie theaters, Yves St. Laurent, Bloomingdale's, Van Cleef & Arpels, Tiffany, the Metropolitan Museum of Art, the Guggenheim, and so on. Along First Avenue, there are the many, many singles' bars and pubs.

The Upper West Side, in contrast, is faded splendor, with doormen every so often and surely never two at a time. There are welfare hotels, dirty supermarkets, and winos in doorways. But there are also chic boutiques, interesting faces, magnificent brownstones, and very beautiful apartment buildings whose pillars and reliefs form a remarkable contrast. And of course, there is Lincoln Center and the American Museum of Natural History.

Naturally, everything is not quite that simple. The West Side is becoming fashionable, as more and more shops and restaurants open along Columbus Avenue. Soon Amsterdam Avenue will undergo this rejuvenation as well, and the hitherto less expensive, more casual West Side will change, as does everything else in New York.

Opposite: The Flatiron Building, New York's first skyscraper. Above: The more casual West Side

27

Mannahatta

I was asking for something specific and perfect for my city,
Whereupon lo! upsprang the aboriginal name.

Now I see what there is in a name, a word, liquid, sane, unruly,
    musical, self-sufficient.
I see that the word of my city is that word from of old,
Because I see that word nested in nests of water-bays, superb,
Rich, hemm'd thick all around with sailships and steamships,
    an island sixteen miles long, solid-founded,
Numberless crowded streets, high growths of iron, slender, strong,
    light, splendidly uprising toward clear skies,
Tides swift and ample, well-loved by me, toward sundown,
The flowing sea-currents, the little islands, larger adjoining
    islands, the heights, the villas,
The countless masts, the white shore-steamers, the lighters,
    the ferry-boats, the black sea-steamers well-model'd,
The down-town streets, the jobbers' houses of business, the
    houses of business of the ship-merchants and money-brokers, the
    river-streets,
Immigrants arriving, fifteen or twenty thousand in a week,
The carts hauling goods, the manly race of drivers of horses,
    the brown-faced sailors,
The summer air, the bright sun shining, and the sailing clouds
    aloft,
The winter snows, the sleigh-bells, the broken ice in the river,
    passing along up or down with the flood-tide or ebb-tide,
The mechanics of the city, the masters, well-form'd, beautiful-
    faced, looking you straight in the eyes,
Trottoirs throng'd, vehicles, Broadway, the women, the shops and
    shows,
A million people — manners free and superb — open voices — hospitality —
    the most courageous and friendly young men,
City of hurried and sparkling waters! city of spires and masts!
City nested in bays! my city!

Walt Whitman, *Leaves of Grass*

Color Photographs

3

4

35

36

for the
martini
BEEFEATER
LONDON DISTILLED
DRY GIN
IMPORTED FROM ENGLAND
GIN
ONE WAY
W 46
Coca-Cola
ELPINE
HAMBURGERS - FRUIT DRINKS
FRUIT DRINKS
TOW AWAY ZONE

8

9

10

11

12

13

What does Grand. Say?
Your answer is he

CORNER
HOUSE

THE
RAT
OPPEL
OPPEL
OME
LET

STU-
PENDIS
SALADS
&
SAND
WICH

FABULOUS

RESTAUR
ANT

FOUNTAIN
FEATURES

15

OFF-TRACK BETTING

17

Schaefer
BEER

19

21

22

24

25

26

28

30

31

The Quality of Life

Certainly it is easier to visit or live in many other cities. In terms of a tourist town, New York has always attracted visitors; now it is beginning to really welcome them. But living in this city can be an exasperating experience. The little conveniences or nice touches that make some other cities sometimes more comfortable places to live are often lacking here. Buses do not always run on time, garbage is often spilled from trucks as it is picked up, public officials are frequently less than sympathetic or helpful.

New York has 7 million people. About 1.5 million are over sixty — a number that indicates the unhealthy development of New York's population structure. The exodus of the middle class — both black and white — is among New York's biggest problems. Will New York become the city of only the poor and the super-rich? Is the middle class, irrespective of color and race, turning its back on the city? The future of life in New York will to a large extent depend on whether its government succeeds in overcoming the financial crisis that gradually developed over the years. The world's richest city is time and again on the brink of bankruptcy, and a city in financial straits can be uncomfortable to live in. Less money available to spend on mass transit means dirtier, less efficient service; fewer teachers in the schools implies larger classes and poorer education for all; cuts in sanitation services often lead to an overall deterioration of a neighborhood.

In the long run, no city can afford to pay garbagemen $17,000 a year or to train police cadets for nine months at an annual salary of $12,000 without a contract specifying a minimum number of years of service, to subsequently pay them up to $20,000 per year, and to give them the opportunity to retire after twenty years with the right to a pension based on their last year's earnings including overtime. Under the circumstances, it is not surprising that even the laziest workers become dynamic in their twentieth year of service. New York pays out some $1 billion in pensions annually. Owing to the financial crisis, fire houses have been closed, police and teachers let go, hospitals closed down, garbage collection reduced, and library hours curtailed.

New York's citizens, long dissatisfied with municipal services, are now resorting more and more to self-help. They are replacing thousands of discharged police with hundreds of private police and security guards who patrol office buildings, private houses, and even entire blocks. They are often engaged by block associations — self-help organizations of citizens against neglect and crime. The yearning of every New Yorker for the small-town atmosphere finds its expression in these neighborhood associations: the members know each other and help one another. Block associations are buying brighter street lights and large mirrors for entrance hallways so that someone can better see if anyone is following when entering a building; they are persuading landlords that not only the second door, but also the first, should be fitted with a spring-bolt lock; they are planting trees and flowers; they are organizing clean-up parties and selling whistles (which, used in an emergency, bring all other whistle owners to their windows and into the street, making such a concert of whistle noise to drive any criminal away). Block-watchers also have a code number which gets

...eople live in crowded conditions, where they make do with what they have

...iority attention for their call to the police. This job is commonly done by pen-
...oners; they often sat for hours at the window before, anyhow, so now their idle
...atching has become an important assignment. They report anything suspicious, any
...ranger behaving peculiarly.

...Citizen initiatives have helped make the streets cleaner, prettier, and safer, but the
...timate responsibility remains nevertheless with the city. This is true to an even
...eater extent for hospitals, schools, kindergartens or playgrounds, and other ser-
...ces where reality often looks depressing. If on the other hand, bankruptcy is
...erted in the long term, the soundness of city finances restored, Central Park is
...eaned up, the rivers run clear, the neighborhoods preserved from decay, and the
...ees and bushes protected against air pollution, then New Yorkers will be able to
...eathe again, and resident and tourist alike will enjoy the opportunities this city has
...offer.

Getting Around Town

Once you understand the basic gridlike pattern of Manhattan's streets — and the exceptions to that pattern — you will find traveling from one place to another is quite easy. This criss-cross pattern does not apply to the other boroughs, and as a tourist, you will need help in getting to most places outside of Manhattan. Let's consider a few basics:

Manhattan is divided into three parts: lower Manhattan is the area roughly south of 34th Street, also generally referred to as downtown. Midtown is, reasonably, the area extending from 34th to 86th streets. Upper Manhattan is anywhere from 86th Street all up to the Bronx. Likewise, Manhattan is divided lengthwise, and Fifth Avenue separates the East Side from the West Side, from Washington Square Park northward.

Streets in New York run east and west. Generally, even-numbered streets are eastbound and odd-numbered ones are westbound. Avenues usually run alternatively north and south, although Broadway, New York's longest street, runs on a diagonal, starting on the East Side downtown, crossing Fifth Avenue at 23rd Street, and continuing to the West Side all the way uptown. All the avenues in Manhattan are busy thoroughfares, but the main streets going crosstown are 14th, 23rd, 34th, 42nd, and 57th. Above 59th Street, there are transverses through Central Park at 65/66th, 79/80th, and 96/97th streets.

You can tell from a Manhattan address approximately where that business or residence is located, by using the formula given on page 258. The system is a bit complicated, but once you are familiar with the mechanics, you'll have no trouble finding the places you wish to go.

Public Transportation

By far the best way to get around the city is to use public transportation. Do not attempt to drive in New York unless you are very familiar with the traffic patterns. Since there is a major traffic problem, and since parking in the city is limited and costly, you are better off using other means.

Buses will take you most anywhere in the city that you wish to go. About 4,500 of them go up and down the avenues and crosstown on the most important streets, along two hundred different routes. For 60¢ (for the moment) you can travel on any one of them as far as you like, and for another half fare you can get a transfer for a bus going at a right angle to yours.

Buses normally stop every two blocks, but if the driver does not stop because no ne is waiting to board, ring the bell. You get in in front, put your money — exact hange or subway token — into the receptacle next to the driver, and get out again at ne rear. Most buses operate all night long but at less frequent intervals. Drivers do ot give change and do not accept dollar bills. There is a city bus map included in this ook, or you may obtain a larger version of it at the city's Visitor Center.

New York's **subway** system is the largest in the world and carries the greatest umber of people every day. It runs twenty-four hours, although service late at night s much curtailed. You buy your tokens (60¢) and put one in the turnstile slot. Wait or your train on the proper platform, designated downtown or uptown, like the en-rance above ground. Both local and express trains often run on the same track, so be ure to check the sign on the first car as the train pulls into the station, or read the igns posted along the sides of the cars. The paths that the trains take are compli-ated, so be sure to check the subway map included in this book. If possible, avoid iding the subway late at night and if you have to take it, travel in the car with a oliceman or the conductor who opens and closes the doors.

The buses and subways are pretty dirty and during rush hours they creep along vhile the people are packed in like sardines. Off-hours, however, are usually better, vith faster service as well.

Taxis cruise the city's streets continually, but obtaining one can often be difficult, specially on rainy days, at rush hours, and in crowded areas, such as the theater dis-rict when shows break. They are popular, and are an easy way to get about town, but hey are becoming more and more expensive. There are few taxi stands, but the best vay to get a cab is to stand at a street corner (especially major intersections) and vave. The sign atop the car's roof indicates whether it is vacant and on duty. For onger trips you can call a taxi company, such as the Minutemen (899-5600), listed in he telephone yellow pages. Tips should be 15 percent of the fare.

Sights to See

What you choose to do in New York depends entirely on your own interests, how-ver this city is most noteworthy for its historic buildings and modern skyscrapers, as center for business and finance, for its varied entertainment offerings, and as a cul-ural center for the nation. But here you'll also discover colorful and quaint alley-vays, idiosyncratic people, and an endless array of ethnic restaurants. Special sights re listed in the Yellow Pages, as are also some sightseeing tours.

If your stay is long enough, also consider crossing the boundaries that separate Manhattan from the rest of the city. The other boroughs have their own character and istory, often neglected by Manhattanites as well as out-of-towners. These areas are escribed on pages 209-219. And if you really have the extra time, visit the city's uburbs as well. Although they are not technically part of the city, Long Island and Westchester — or even parts of New Jersey — owe their existence to this metropolis. This is where many of New York City's working population live; they spend their lays in the active, electric air of New York, then retreat to the quiet greenery of out-ying regions. Excursions are listed in the Key to the City as well.

Times Square at night

Fear

Travelers taking in Manhattan's standard tourist sites via a taxi hailed by a door man from an elegant hotel are perhaps choosing the safest, but without doubt also th most boring way to get to know the city. Naturally, Manhattan between 42nd an 80th streets, from Fifth to Lexington avenues, should by all means be on the program but a tourist who wants a true impression of New York has to go through it on a bu and subway — and walk it as well. This is — contrary to all the rumors — still pos sible. While it is true that crimes are committed in all parts of the city, daily life i New York is not nearly as dramatic as suggested by the sensationally exploited crim statistics. New York is, of course, not a city to be discovered by aimless saunterin either. You have to take care and be more cautious in some sections than others. Bu the fear that some people have is completely uncalled for and of little help. On th contrary, anyone who walks through New York in constant fear and anxiety is easil recognizable and a prey worthy of consideration.

Security is a combination of caution and information. That is why you shoul examine a city map before arriving here and walk through the city in your imagina tion; it is a waste of time and nerves to wait until you are in a hotel room to start plan ning. Incidentally, to reassure you somewhat: New York is only in seventeenth plac in U.S. crime statistics.

Naturally as a newcomer you cannot recognize at first sight whether an area of th city is passable or not and where it will be unpleasant. Too many streets appea equally dirty and run-down and too many people so exotic that they are difficult t classify according to the usual rules. Tourists may not know that the newly plante trees and the flower boxes on balconies and windowsills are mostly a sign of well-le block associations — groups of citizens who strive for security, cleanliness, an beauty in their block. You should be warned of the so-called welfare hotels. Crime are the order of the day in many of them, and you might consider crossing to th other side of the street if you see a SINGLE ROOM OCCUPANCY sign. A newcomer i startled when a police car makes its rounds in the park and suspects a crime behin the next bush. New Yorkers are thankful for any patrol that they see only remotel at all.

You can run around alone during the day, and in groups of two or more in th evening, in almost any part of Manhattan. In doing so though, you should choos busy streets, avoid blind building entrances, and look around when footsteps com closer from behind. Women should carry purses with clasps facing inward. It is bes to carry money in small bills in different coat and trouser pockets. Taxi drivers chang only $5 bills anyway, and subway stations a $10 note at most. For bus trips, yo must keep on hand sixty cents or a token. It is careless to look for coins or small bill in a crammed-full wallet on the street or in accesses to subway stations.

"Don't invite crime" is a common saying of New Yorkers. Should you actuall be held up, just don't resist. On the other hand, try to satisfy the assailant; the rat lies between $25 and $50.

Muggings, mostly holdups to take dollars for the next shot, are the most frequer street crime in New York. Drug traffic is booming here like never before. The hard

Glittering Times Square area involves some danger too

core heroin addicts in New York are estimated at 200,000 (some 400,000 in the whole country). The largest amount of drug traffic occurs on 116th Street in Harlem. Everyone knows this: pushers, addicts, and beginners as well as the police. At almost any time of the day and night, hundreds of people throng to the garbage-littered street and the dilapidated building entrances. Time and again groups disappear into one of the buildings to shoot up or into one of the neighboring bars to deal. That is where the bosses, the black drug mafia, sit. The latest models of European and American luxury cars in front of the door are their easily recognizable calling cards. Hardly any whites venture here into the pits, as the street corners are called in police jargon. Whites wait in the surrounding blocks and hope for honest middlemen to bring back some good stuff for them. This scenery, just so absolutely no doubt arises, can be safely observed only from a police car; a tourist has to restrain his or her curiosity and keep away from there. (By the way, marijuana is available — especially since possession of small amounts has been decriminalized — on many harmless street corners in the Village or in bars as well.)

Yet not every mugging is attributable to drug addiction; often it is strictly need. Almost 20 percent of New York's youth is unemployed and the figure for black teenagers is estimated at over 60 percent. Each dollar extorted and robbed, each camera stolen and purse snatched helps in getting by and surviving. Others however want to

Contrasting styles: Puerto Rican youths and East Side shoppers

et even with a society that has no room for them, that on the one hand emphasizes striving for a career and puts material success at the top, but on the other hand does not give them the slightest chance to prove themselves in this competitive struggle. Pent-up desperation and bottled-up rage lead to senseless brutality and cruel sadism. Thus, by way of example, thousands of helpless old people every year are beaten, raped, deceived, locked up in closets, and tied to bedposts, no matter whether they are over ninety, handicapped, crippled, or just simply weak. Earlier the police organized youth programs. They ran some baseball games on school sites, competitions, and trips. They gave the young people who habitually loaf around the opportunity to let off steam in a suitable way. Almost all the money for these programs has been depleted and more often the youths are joining gangs that terrorize their immediate neighborhoods.

Those are the facts and developments that you should know without being frightened by them. They are not meant to discourage you from discovering New York unconventionally, but just to warn you against acting cocky, careless, or venturesome.

Some Tips for Travelers

Traveler's checks should be deposited in your hotel safe, and the room door must always be securely locked. The subway has become safer at night; an armed policeman keeps a check in almost every train (unless still more officers are let go due to economy measures). Only the first three cars of a train are open in quiet periods (for example, between 8 and 10 PM). However, nobody guards the generally dark subway exits. If you are traveling in pairs and know the way, this is no problem. Tourists would be better off on the bus in the evenings. Even though that takes a little longer, you see more and get lost less often as well.

Many may regard some of these warnings superfluous, yet one hears time and again of tourists who either go to bed at nine out of total fear or who stroll through a deserted Central Park in the dark out of sheer ignorance. The latter takes a resident's breath away. It is delightful to rent a bicycle and ride through Central Park during the day, especially during the posted times when the park roads are closed to cars. Naturally, here too you have to again be careful to avoid the deserted "peaceful" paths and not ride beyond 100th Street. In the evening, you can go into Central Park only when the Metropolitan Opera, theater, pop groups, or the New York Philharmonic move their performances there in the summer. During such opportunities, a hundred thousand music enthusiasts rest in Sheep Meadow and picnic by candlelight with wine while listening to a concert directed by Zubin Mehta or other notables. That is an unforgettable as well as a safe way to spend an evening in Central Park.

So, to repeat once more: Both rashness and exaggerated caution are inappropriate. You can enjoy this city and take care of yourself at the same time. While you may have to keep reminding yourself on the first day what you may and may not do, it will already be routine on the second day. By the third or fourth day, you probably will think that everything has just been exaggerated and become careless — "be careful, don't invite crime!"

For Women Especially

As in any other big city, a man can go just about anywhere in New York with the proper caution and consideration. He does not have to run away from the exhibitionist next to him in the movies or ignore an irritating whistle on the street. Naturally, he too can be assaulted and therefore may not be careless. But since rape is one of the most frequent crimes in New York, a woman has to behave differently from a man here. She has to always be quick and let no insecurity show. A self-confident manner is a part of the strategy of deterrence (along with flat shoes; an assailant, according to one study, preferred women with high-heeled shoes since they could not run away so fast). The other strategy is bruskness: "be rude, not raped." In fact, helpful women are especially endangered. A study in New York showed that nurses, social workers, and teachers are frequent victims. And so some additional precautions are essential for female tourists.

Women should always check the convenient mirror in the top left-hand corner in almost every elevator to see who is in the elevator. Never ride alone with a strange man. If you suddenly find yourself alone with a strange man in an elevator, place yourself right next to the control panel and always know exactly where the alarm button is.

Women should not strike up a conversation, no matter how innocent, with someone on the street or in a park, to avoid possibly giving the impression to others that he is an acquaintance. Otherwise, in case of need, passers-by think they are seeing a fight and not an assault.

A woman should not give out her address to the "nice student" at a restaurant or let him bring her home. Give him your telephone number and then arrange to meet him at a safe place.

Walk down all streets assertively and with determination. You will give anyone watching you the impression that you know exactly where you are going and even perhaps that you are expected there at a certain time. Avoid dimly lit streets and, if you find that you must walk down such a street at night, stay away from the doorways; if necessary, walk straight down the middle of the street. If you suspect that someone is following you, cross over to the other side and determine if he crosses with you. If you are being followed, go immediately to any store or coffee shop that might be open. If no businesses are open and your pursuer is getting close, walk up to a house with lights on and knock on the door, yelling "I'm home, George." This implies that there is a waiting husband in that house to help you.

Carry your purse firmly. If you use a shoulder bag, slip the strap over your head, rather than dangling the purse on just your shoulder. If you wear a gold chain around your neck, protect yourself from the latest rash of "chain snatchings" by covering it with a sweater or coat, or even just a scarf.

These are just a few tips; many more are available in other books. The idea is that you should be "street-wise." Naturally one hears again and again of those women who have engaged in conversation and then had the best of times. But as said before, caution is imperative.

Women in the city need to be especially careful

New York's Past

Early Settlers

Along with America, New York owes its discovery to the search in the Middle Ages for a new way to the riches of the Indies and China, because the old route had for so long been barricaded by the Moslem empire. In 1524, Giovanni da Verrazano — born in Genoa as was Christopher Columbus — sailed into New York Harbor, and, as he was in the service of Francis I of France, he simply declared all the land he saw before him as belonging to the French crown. A few months later, Portuguese ships tried to land but were chased away by icy winds and blizzards. Finally Henry Hudson, an Englishman sent by the Dutch East India Company, sailed up the river now bearing his name, hoping to find India around the next bend.

The Puritans really should have landed in Manhattan as well, because then the whole coast from Virginia to Massachusetts would have been English, but they landed at Plymouth Rock inadvertently, thus allowing the Dutch East India Company to buy Manhattan from the Indians for knick-knacks worth sixty guilder (the famous $24) and to settle it with their own people.

The Dutch called their small settlement at the southern tip of the island New Amsterdam and bordered it to the north with a wall, later to become Wall Street. Soon there was a ferry to Longe Eyelandt, a windmill, a canal, and such a cosmopolitan group of inhabitants that eighteen different languages were spoken. As a director of the Dutch West India Company in New Amsterdam, Peter Stuyvesant was responsible for the well-being of his colony. Surrounded by English settlers, he tried unsuccessfully during the Anglo-Dutch wars to get money from Holland for fortifications, to enforce law and order, and to keep his citizens out of the taverns. Some New Yorkers say that on quiet Sundays they can hear the tack-tack sound of his wooden leg on Wall Street.

When the Duke of York, brother of Queen Anne and new owner of British land in the new world, arrived with all his battle ships, he brought the war to the colony. After some shilly-shallying — and once William of Orange was firmly ensconced on the British throne — the small settlement became English. The citizens were not very upset, convinced that they had made a good deal by keeping Suriname (Dutch Guiana) instead. The English established themselves: Breetweg became Broadway, the city government saw a number of changes and now boasted a mayor, and the pigs

Wall Street in 1859

shared the streets with everybody else. In 1683, the first city council meeting took place with the result that the government was now entitled to levy tolls for bridges, ferries, and the use of the harbor. During the next hundred years the Royal envoys and the inhabitants squabbled over control of the government. Governors and mayors changed rapidly and were only rarely able, or willing, to do something for the common good during their short reigns. These were unsettling times, and brought with them two Negro uprisings among other troubles, in 1712 and 1741.

During the middle of the eighteenth century, New York became an important participant in the resistance to English dominance. The leading citizens of the city, especially the descendants of the first Dutch settlers, were reasonably loyal, but had no illusions about the abilities of their governors. One of these, Francis Lovelace, apparently had a hole broken into the wall of the Stadhuis courtroom in order to get to the rum in the tavern next door without having to move. Another, Lord Cornbury, dressed up as a woman for one month of the year in order to show the gaping multitude how much he resembled his cousin, Queen Anne — proof for us that one has always been able to do just what one pleases in New York. A third governor was found hanging by the neck in his garden the morning after assuming his job. A fourth did something useful for a change by signing the founding document for King's College, which later became Columbia University.

New York grew at a fast rate. Around 1760 there were 14,000 inhabitants; twenty years later the number had doubled, and a fifth of them were blacks from Africa and the West Indies. A few years after the foundation of the first newspaper, the *New York Gazette,* German immigrant John Peter Zenger started his *New York Weekly* in 1733 and promptly attacked the governor in its pages. As a result, the offending

Broadway in the nineteenth century

copies were burned on Wall Street and Zenger went to jail. But he continued to publish his paper, and his release a year later was an important step toward establishing the freedom of the press. While New York continued to grow and increase in commercial importance, groups like the Sons of Liberty (demanding not only home rule but complete independence) and the British soldiers stationed in the city found plenty of opportunities for skirmishes. After a British ship with tea was prevented from entering the harbor and a few cases even landed at the bottom of the sea, the die was cast and things happened very quickly. On July 9, 1776, people in New York heard about the Declaration of Independence. In no time at all, ''American'' soldiers had tipped George III's equestrian statue from its pedestal in Bowling Green and destroyed it pretty thoroughly, although there was a rumor that the head turned up in England after a while. The War of Independence continued in and around New York. In September a fire raged through the southern tip of the island. Old Trinity Church burned like a torch, and it was only by a miraculous shifting of the wind that St. Paul's Chapel and King's College were saved. On the evening of that same day, Nathan Hale, who had penetrated the English lines dressed as a Dutch schoolteacher, was sentenced to death and hanged at the corner of 45th Street and Second Avenue. Every schoolchild in America knows his famous last words: ''I only regret that I have but one life to lose for my country.''

New York was in British hands until almost the end of the war and used as a hospital and prison. These were bad times for the city. The situation improved, however, with the evacuation in November of 1783. On April 30, 1789, George Washington swore his presidential oath on a borrowed Freemason bible at the corner of Broad and Wall streets, a spot marked today by Federal Hall and his statue.

City Hall, past and present; it was restored in 1956

A Growing Metropolis

Although New York remained the capital only until August of 1790, it was well on its way to developing into a metropolis of the first order. During the war between England and France both sides tried unsuccessfully to draw the new United States into their conflict. It insisted on its neutral position, which suited New York very well as it was much too busy growing. Since 1783 the population had doubled; the first steamship had to be tried out, the first stock exchange to be founded, people like John Jacob Astor had to make money. When he died in 1848, at the age of eighty-five, he left $20 million, which had grown to $450 million by the end of the century. The present City Hall was completed in 1812, and since there was not much going on to the north of it, the builder decided to save the marble facing on that side. The War of 1812 and the English blockade slowed the progress of the new metropolis some-what, but the opening of the Erie Canal in 1825 gave it a new lease on life: New York became an important export and transit port. Slavery was abolished and mass immi-gration began, especially by the Irish fleeing the failure of their potato crops and by the Germans fleeing the turmoil of '48. The water supply was insufficient, and yel-low fever epidemics decimated the population; yet the city continued to increase. New schools were founded, including New York University. Four newspapers ap-peared, among them the *New York Times*. Soon there were theaters, enthusiastic audiences, and sold-out performances. The fight between the American actor Edwin

Forrest and his English colleague William C. Macready over the role of Macbeth at the Astor Place Opera House turned into a riot which brought the police and the military to the scene and resulted in twenty-two dead and many wounded.

The city grew rapidly; shops and their owners moved north. Union Square became the best residential quarter, though beyond it were still open fields. In 1853, a copy of London's Crystal Palace became the site of New York's first world's fair, on the spot where today you will find the New York Public Library at Fifth Avenue and 41st Street. Three years later the 840 acres of land for Central Park were bought by the city for $5.5 million. A short but rather dangerous depression caused so much unrest that a modern municipal police force had to be organized. Fortunately, by the beginning of the Civil War the city had recovered financially, because it had to contribute heavily though with much protest — the citizens had to pay $1 million to the Union cause. The year 1863 saw the famous draft riots against military conscription during which fifty houses were burned down and many people died. At the end of the war the mayor claimed that New York had given $300 million and 80,000 men to the war effort.

When Charles Dickens came to visit he found that pigs were still cavorting in the streets, replacing the garbage removal crews. This was just as well, because the city could not have afforded them. Boss Tweed, a Tammany Hall politician (Tammany was an organization of the Democratic party, founded originally to protect the interests of the immigrants, especially the Irish), and his famous (or infamous) ring had managed to relieve the city purse of hundreds of millions of dollars.

The City Becomes Glamorous

New York continued to spread northward. Fifth Avenue became a millionaire's row of palatial townhouses; the wives of the "robber barons," the early industrialists, outdid each other with conspicuous parties and expensive dresses from Paris, while on the Lower East Side the new immigrants lived in indescribable squalor. By 1910, a million and a half Jews had arrived; after 1881 came the Italians, the Russians, and the Rumanians. In 1860, Columbus Circle was still an open field. When an enterprising man built a neo-Tudor apartment house on 72nd Street and Central Park West, he was told he might as well have put it up in the Dakotas among the Indians; so it was named The Dakota and is famous today for its past inhabitants and as the scene of Roman Polanski's film *Rosemary's Baby.*

Anthony Trollope's widely traveled mother came to America as well. She had quite a lot to say about American customs and manners ("the gentlemen eat noisily and spit on the floor"), and reported that New Yorkers are always moving from one abode to another — a habit they have not changed. One of the more spectacular events was the opening in 1883 of the Brooklyn Bridge, among fireworks and much ceremony. It took John A. Roebling, a German immigrant, and his son Washington and a firm of specialized engineers, almost ten years to build the "steel harp."

Fifth Avenue, which Chiang Y, "The Silent Traveller in New York," called the "white satin rope" in 1946, might have remained a residential street had it not been for B. Altman, who built his department store in 1906 on the corner of 34th Street. Despite much neighborly protest, he managed to affix a small sign with his name on the door; others followed suit.

A typical and much beloved sight of nineteenth-century New York were the "Els" (elevated railways). They ran on elevated tracks above the street, pulled by steam engines and emitting sparks, soot, and a great deal of noise. When the subway was built between 1900 and 1904, with money advanced by the Rothschilds, the Els were gradually torn down one by one and the face of the city changed irrevocably.

At 23rd Street and Madison Avenue, Fifth Avenue and Broadway cross to form a square which is a perfect site for the Flatiron Building, New York's first skyscraper. Built in 1902, its steel skeleton is faced with limestone in the manner of an Italian palazzo. In 1930, the Chrysler Building shot up on 42nd Street; its cupola is made of Krupp steel with diamond splinters, apparently the toughest steel ever made. A few months later it was no longer the tallest building in the world — the Empire State Building with its 102 stories had been completed. Until the crash of the *Hindenburg*, it proudly bore a landing rod for such dirigibles.

Prohibition presumably had a lot to do with turning the twenties into the "roaring twenties," F. Scott Fitzgerald's Jazz Age. Moonshine or liquor smuggled by the famous gangsters was drunk from coffee cups to the sound of jazz bands in smoky speakeasies in Harlem, the Village, or the East Fifties, known as the "wettest streets." The musicians came from Chicago and Kansas City, and New York became the Big Apple — *the* place for a jazz man to make it. New York jazzed along happily during the next decade until it was brought back to reality with the crash of 1929 and the miseries of the ensuing depression.

Jefferson Market, Greenwich Village

With their four-year term, New York's mayors change much too often, which can also be an advantage, of course. Only few in the long chain have stood out for excellence, although some of them — Jimmy Walker, for instance, with his barely disguised gangster practices — were reluctantly admired by their citizens. Much loved and evoked to this day is Fiorello La Guardia. He was the nephew of a Garibaldi partisan, tenderly called ''the Little Flower'' by all. He cleaned up a number of slums, fought against deep-rooted corruption in the city government, and during war blackouts read stories to the children over the radio.

During the war, New York had to be dark too. People were given food coupons, butter and sugar were hard to find, and gasoline was rationed. Trains were full to bursting and tickets not easily come by. Heating oil was scarce, and the icy winter wind was kept out with sandbags. But those days were soon forgotten. With the erection in the fifties of the Lever, Seagram, and Pan Am buildings on Park Avenue, and the United Nations Headquarters on the East River, Manhattan assumed its present shape. During the sixties the old, unpractical Metropolitan Opera House was torn down and the controversial Lincoln Center for the Performing Arts was put up. For eight years Mayor John Lindsay brought liberal attitudes and a goodly pinch of glamour to the city government. Financially, Bagdad-on-the-Hudson may totter atop its bedrock throne and power failures, looting, bombings, and strikes may make life very difficult for its citizens, but New York is a tough, determined, and flexible city that will survive these crises too.

Architecture

A Mixed Bag

New York's architecture is a mad mixture of all possible styles (mostly neo-), from the cast-iron façades of the old warehouses in SoHo, to the checked or striped skyscrapers in midtown and downtown Manhattan, to the New York Yacht Club on 44th Street, which looks not unexpectedly like a galleon. In the years of rapid industrial expansion during the latter part of the last century, architectural inventiveness seemed to know no bounds.

You will get your first impression of modern New York architecture if you arrive at John F. Kennedy International Airport in Queens. This is one of the largest and busiest airports in the world. New York's LaGuardia Airport is also in Queens, but it handles primarily domestic flights. The **International Arrivals Building** at Kennedy (Skidmore, Owings, and Merrill, a popular group of New York architects, built it for roughly $30 million) has a spectator terrace with a good view. A number of airlines have their own terminals: **TWA**'s is a pleasing yet functional design by Eero Saarinen, which looks from above like a large bird with its wings spread.

Manhattan is connected to the other boroughs by a series of bridges and tunnels. The most beautiful bridge is the **Brooklyn Bridge,** connecting Brooklyn with downtown Manhattan, and the longest is the **George Washington Bridge,** built in 1931 by O. H. Ammann and Cass Gilbert. The latter is a graceful suspension bridge with two stories and fourteen traffic lanes connecting Manhattan with northern New Jersey. The length of New York's tunnels ranges from 6,000 to 9,000 feet; in the **Lincoln Tunnel,** for instance, the border between New York and New Jersey is indicated in mosaic.

Manhattan's Landmarks

Manhattan developed from south to north primarily, although you will find the twin towers of the **World Trade Center** — New York's tallest landmark — in the south, while in the north a Dutch colonial farmhouse sits placidly among run-of-the-mill apartment houses (**Dyckman House**).

After the Dutch Colonial style in the seventeenth century and the Georgian style brought from England in the eighteenth (**St. Paul's Chapel** by Thomas McBean, 1764–1766; the **Morris-Jumel Mansion** in Harlem, ca. 1765; and the official residence of New York's mayor, **Gracie Mansion,** 1799–1801 are good examples), revivals became popular during the first half of the nineteenth century. At first these

were mostly public buildings resembling Greek temples, with Doric, Ionic, or Corinthian columns and pediments (a good example is **Federal Hall,** built in 1824–43 by Town and Davis). During the second half of the century, Gothic cathedrals were all the rage (for example, **Trinity Church** by Richard Upjohn, 1846; and John Renwick's **St. Patrick's Cathedral,** 1853, which on the outside resembles the cathedral at Cologne and on the inside English Gothic churches). The **Woolworth Building** by Cass Gilbert, 1913 — not without reason known as the "Cathedral of Commerce" — is another example.

At the end of the nineteenth and the beginning of the twentieth centuries, when America — and New York — were developing at a breakneck pace, buildings in a variety of styles sprang up at a dizzying rate as well. Along with the neo-Gothic you will find Renaissance palazzi (**Morgan Library,** 1906, and **Judson Memorial Church,** 1890, both by McKim, Mead, and White); Louis XVI palaces (**Frick Collection,** 1913–15, Carrère and Hastings); French Beaux-Arts (**Grand Central Terminal,** 1913, Whitney Warren and the engineers William I. Wilgus and Reed and Stem); and Byzantine churches (**St. Bartholomew's,** 1917–19, Bertram G. Goodhue, with a French Romanesque façade by McKim, Mead, and White).

New York's earliest skyscraper is D. H. Burnham's **Flatiron Building** with, for 1902, a daring height of twenty stories and unheard-of sleekness. The architects of the early twentieth century knew very well that Manhattan's solid bedrock would support any weight; moreover, there was no risk of earthquakes. Once they had steel and concrete at their disposal they built higher and higher, trying to outdo each other. In 1930, William van Alen erected the **Chrysler Building,** which only one year later was topped by the **Empire State Building** (Shreve, Lamb, and Harmon). The year 1940 saw the completion of the **RCA Building** in Rockefeller Center (Wallace K. Harrison and others). These three are good examples of Art Deco style.

The Newer Skyscrapers

You will meet the next generation of skyscrapers on Park Avenue. Good examples of the popular curtain-wall style (to be found not only in New York are the **Lever** and **Union Carbide buildings** (1952 and 1960, respectively, both Skidmore, Owings, and Merrill). The **Seagram Building** of 1958, by Mies van der Rohe and Philip Johnson, with its elegant brown-steel skeleton and gray-brown glass walls, is unquestionably the most beautiful modern building in New York. It is famous for its proportions and the security with which it occupies its small slice of land. Nearby, on Park Avenue, you will also find Frank Lloyd Wright's first New York work — the **Mercedes Showroom.** The **United Nations Headquarters** on the East River belongs to the above-mentioned group of trailblazing glass edifices; it was built in 1950 by a team of architects including Oscar Niemeyer, Le Corbusier, Max Abramovitz, and Wallace K. Harrison.

Harrison and Abramovitz were responsible to a large extent for New York's most ambitious architectural undertaking, **Lincoln Center for the Performing Arts.** Since the early sixties, when the idea of such a complex of buildings was first discussed, there had been much controversy about the viability of such a cultural colos-

Skyscraper at Rockefeller Center

Some secluded spots

sus. In any case, almost two hundred old houses were demolished in what was then a rather run-down part of town — where part of the film version of Leonard Bernstein's *West Side Story* was made — and a center for music and theater was built to the tune of $165 million. Different architects were in charge of the buildings. Among them, Philip Johnson's **New York State Theater** is by far the best. It has string of pearl curtains on the upstairs lobby balconies, which turn the intermission strollers into silhouettes, and two large, white marble sculptures by Elie Nadelman, generally known as the "yogurt ladies." The **Metropolitan Opera,** however, has been much criticized and mostly with good reason. When Harrison was asked during the opening ceremonies why he had not created a modern space comparable to the postwar houses of Europe, he replied that the present form had worn well and that it would have been madness to experiment with a house of this size (3,800 seats). The **fountain** in the center of the plaza, with its hundreds of sprays and complicated lighting arrangements, is also by Philip Johnson. The quiet pond behind **Avery Fisher Hall** (Abramovitz) reflects a large sculpture by Henry Moore.

One of the newer architectural statements in New York is the twin towers of the **World Trade Center** (Minoru Yamasaki & Associates and Emery Roth & Sons; 1,350 feet); with its 110 stories, it is the second largest building in the world (after Chicago's Sears Roebuck Building). Owing to an innovative design, the walls of the towers are reinforced so that the generous openness of the rooms is not spoiled by too many support columns. A highly developed elevator system has reduced shaft space and express elevators take you from one sky lobby to the next at a speed of 1,600 feet per minute.

New York's latest skyscraper is the **Citicorp Building,** a graceful giant with fifty-ne stories on stilts and a slanted roof like the mouthpiece of a saxophone. Hugh tubbins & Associates and Emery Roth & Sons built the aluminium-clad tower, hich proposes to end the era of the steel and glass boxes with its smooth — some ay slick — elegance. The metal is slightly reflecting and changes with the weather nd the time of day. The building is light gray on cloudy days, silvery in the scintil-ting noon heat, yellow in the setting sun, and blue at dusk.

Pressed into a corner of the Citicorp Building under the stilts is **St. Peter's hurch,** designed by the same architect as the tower itself. Inside there is a beautiful ooden organ by Johannes Klais and a chapel entirely designed by the well-known culptor Louise Nevelson. In another seven-story building nestled at an angle under e tower, Citicorp has created a shopping and restaurant complex on three floors hich is unsurpassed in New York. In the bright courtyard — with the tower rising bove a glass roof — you can sit under a tree, listen to music, drink coffee, or simply ad your paper. This is a public space that Citicorp had to make available in ex-hange for permission from the city to build higher than the usual number of stories. he result is much more than simply following the law. The atrium has become an asis, a popular meeting place in the most human of New York's skyscrapers.

Walking tours in knowledgeable company are arranged by several organizations in e city, depending upon their area of concern. You'll find a listing of such organiza-ons in the Key to the City, under **TOURS AND SIGHTSEEING.** For unaccompanied valks, the books listed there under **BOOKS ABOUT NEW YORK** should provide the asis for many days' adventures.

Brownstones and Other Townhouses

The major avenues of New York are lined with skyscrapers but the side streets have rows of **townhouses.** Most of these homes were built in the latter half of the nineteenth century with sandstone façades. Generally they are four stories high and the rooms are narrow and long, extending to the back where sometimes there are little gardens or courtyards. The brownstones remaining in Harlem are perhaps the most striking. On the Upper East Side, these streets are often shaded by lovely sycamore trees and there are plantings of flowers in window boxes. In other neighborhoods the townhouses have been broken up into apartments.

Townhouses are very much a part of New York's architecture, although very few of them qualify for landmark status or, for that matter, are of any real architectural importance at all. But here is where many New Yorkers live comfortably, avoiding the detachment that sometimes comes about when one lives in a high-rise. You get to know your neighbors, and you join with them to form block associations that work to upgrade the street. In some neighborhoods — for example, some run-down streets on the Lower East Side — a group of friends may form a cooperative. They'll buy a burned-out building, gut the inside, and then remodel it in innovative and individualistic ways. Most recently young couples with children have been discovering the roominess and charm of these old buildings in other areas of the city as well, and they have led the way to a Brownstone Renaissance.

Often there are house tours of townhouses, given usually by charities. They show what it means to rehabilitate a street, a block, or even an entire area. The theme may be New York's brownstones, and the tour will give you the opportunity to see interesting houses from the inside as well. Many of the tours are by invitation only, but some are actually advertised in the newspapers.

Where New Yorkers Live Un-New Yorklike

Up until a few years ago, people in New York continued inconsiderately to raze old buildings to make room for new ones. Consciousness of history, so it seemed, was possible only at the expense of history; and retaining the past was a luxury, it was felt, that could not be afforded. "Overturn, overturn, overturn" was the maxim of New York, Philip Horne, a former mayor of the city, wrote back in 1845. Not until 1965 was a law passed to protect some monuments, which led also to the preservation of many otherwise threatened buildings and districts.

Let us put the more obvious architectural sights aside for the moment and have a brief look at where some New Yorkers live in a manner unlike most of New York. If you travel down noisy Varick Street (the street runs parallel to the Hudson River), on which you are apt to feel oppressed by dirty, dreary factories, you can hardly imagine that three of the prettiest streets in New York are to be found here: **Charlton, King,** and **Van Dam streets.** The Federal and Greek revival (classicism) townhouses with small gardens in back were built around 1820 and are well preserved for the most part. They have been owned by the same families often for generations. The area all

Residences often maintain a quiet elegance

around them may be dilapidated, but the residents of these three streets protect their enclaves with grim determination.

An area with more greenery is **St. Luke's Place** in Greenwich Village. The vine covered, wrought-iron railings and the streetlights give this block a romantic, almost lovely appearance. Unfortunately, the view of an enclosed concrete playground immediately reminds one of New York realities. **Grove Court** strikes the viewer as almost aristocratic in its solitude; there are six houses that radiate an enviably peaceful atmosphere.

Patchin Place, at West 10th Street and Sixth Avenue, is too small and too narrow to be able to convey this attraction. It is, however, a little lane around which many legends from the twenties and thirties are centered, when Eugene O'Neill, John Masefield, and others lived here. Also located in Greenwich Village is the captivating **MacDougal Alley** (north of Washington Square), in which Jackson Pollock, among others, had a studio. Apartments on MacDougal Alley are the dream of any couple with children, for this alley forms a square with Sullivan and MacDougal streets; in the middle of it is a large park — neither visible nor accessible from the outside — which all residents enjoy together and which is a play paradise for children.

Stuyvesant Street in the East Village is an idyllic place and a refreshing discovery if you have developed sore feet from walking on Second Avenue or the once-chic (now run-down) St. Mark's Place. On the corner of 10th Street and Second Avenue is the entrance to the cemetery of **St. Mark's-in-the-Bowery,** one of Manhattan's oldest churches, now restored after a fire. In 1660, Peter Stuyvesant built a chapel which was rebuilt into the present church in 1799. His grave is in the cemetery.

Gramercy Park is not without good reason one of the best and most expensive addresses in New York. The square with the enclosed park in the center is open only to the residents, who have a key. It could just as well have been imported from London; the atmosphere is distinguished beyond all doubt.

Sniffen Court (152 East 36th, between Third and Lexington avenues) is very pretty. Have a look when you are in the area, but don't make an extra trip there. The same applies to **Henderson Place,** at 86th Street and the East River.

If you want to see an elegant and quiet residential street, go to **Beekman Place** (51st Street and the East River) or **Sutton Place** (51st to 54th Street and the East River). **Treadwell Farm** is also very beautiful. This is two blocks (61st and 62nd streets between Second and Third avenues) in which you can recover from a trip to Bloomingdale's, with a view of well-kept brownstones overshadowed by sycamore trees.

Also among the unexpectedly pleasant streets are **Striver's Row** (137th and 138th streets between Seventh and Eighth avenues) and **Jumel Terrace** in Harlem. Above all, the latter address, with a view of the Morris-Jumel Mansion in a lovely park, lets you forget for a moment where you are.

There are, naturally, other beautiful streets and places in New York. But scarcely one of the places mentioned is suitable for rest or a picnic; they are private streets and the residents there have a monopoly on the idyll.

Many older buildings have intriguing embellishments

House ornaments from the 1870s; the remains of this era are now energetically protected

Museums

Even if you don't normally spend your days in museums you should allocate a little time for that pastime while in New York, because here the museums really are worth a visit — especially in bad weather. New York abounds in such museums, whether they be concerned with art, history, science, or popular culture. There is a full listing of the major museums — and a few special minor ones — in the Key to the City, but here we'll describe a few.

Art in New York

The trend, started gradually in the beginning but now in full force, is to transform the dark, musty temples of art into popular community centers. This was brought about in large part by Thomas Hoving, the former director of the **Metropolitan Museum of Art.** By means of his much-criticized public relations sense (coupled with a sound art history background), the Metropolitan — the big mama among the New York art museums — acquired a new importance in the lives of many people. Most of the other museums adopted this form of publicity, and the result now is increasing and often unmanageable numbers of visitors everywhere, especially for the big exhibits.

In terms of its riches, the Metropolitan Museum can only be compared to the Louvre or the British Museum. Its policy is to establish the connection between the treasures of the ages and the present. In this respect, the period rooms are of great interest: furniture, pictures, objects, carpets, and curtains are assembled in a room, which reflects the taste of the time. All visitors are fascinated by the tiny rooms such as used by the first settlers, with low ceilings and simple, beautifully made furniture. Quite aside from their artistic interest, the rooms in the recently reopened and completely redesigned American Wing provide an insight into the social and economic climate of life in America.

The Metropolitan is noted for the special exhibits it holds throughout the year. Often these are traveling exhibits that either come from elsewhere or are headed, after their stay at the Met, to another major museum in another U.S. city. In the past, the Metropolitan has offered the Tutankhamen and Bronze Age of China shows; check their calendar of events to find out what is on special exhibit there during your visit.

Some of the other New York museums concentrate on one particular aspect of art, but however narrow or wide their scope, the quality of their holdings is almost always first class. The "robber barons," the captains of industry who amassed their fortunes during the last century, spent a great deal of their money on art, which they

View of the Cloisters from Fort Tryon Park

then donated to the museums. Their sons continued the tradition — often in order to lighten their tax burden. Once a large and famous collection had been assembled, its owner quickly built a palatial museum for it. Sometimes, as if there were nothing to it at all, the better part of a monastery was imported from Italy, France, or Spain.

John D. Rockefeller was one of these collectors. During the thirties he installed his **Cloisters** on a hill in the north of Manhattan Island. It is made up of bits from four different European monasteries. At the same time he bought a large undeveloped stretch of the Palisades — New Jersey's steep coastline across the Hudson River — so that the view would not be spoiled. Today the Cloisters — owned by the Metropolitan Museum of Art — is among the pleasantest oases in the city. You can walk around courtyards and well-planted gardens, listening to medieval music and enjoying the view across the river.

Some of the great magnates of the last century built palaces to live in as well as to house their collections. One of them, Henry Clay Frick, became a millionaire at the age of thirty. In 1913 he built himself a Louis XVI palace in New York in order to preserve his treasures from the sooty air of Pittsburgh. His house and collection are a marvelous example of how the very rich lived in New York at the beginning of the century. At the **Frick Collection** your steps are muffled by thick carpets as you walk through room after room full of masterpieces and fresh flower arrangements; clocks tick away quietly, correct to the minute.

Frick Collection, with furniture, paintings, sculpture

Even the **Museum of Modern Art** (MOMA), undoubtedly the largest and most important collection of modern art in the world, owes its inception to the children of nineteenth-century industrialists. The building itself is modern and quite functional, and will probably be crowned with an apartment tower to produce much-needed revenues for the museum. To wander around the sculpture garden or to watch people from the outdoor restaurant is one of the great pleasures New York has to offer.

The **Solomon R. Guggenheim Museum** and the **Whitney Museum of American Art** are monuments erected by their donors for themselves. At the same time and with good reason they are monuments for their architects. In 1943 Guggenheim asked Frank Lloyd Wright to build him a "Museum of Non-Objective Art," but not until 1959 could he move his collection into it. The New York Department of Buildings had held up the construction of a New York City landmark for so long! Even if you are not interested in the things on the walls, the building resembling the shell of a snail is interesting in itself, and you should take the elevator to the top and stroll down the spiral ramp.

Marcel Breuer used the narrow space on very expensive land on Madison Avenue so intelligently that his Whitney Museum — made of granite and concrete and resembling an upside-down pyramid — deceptively has as many as five stories and seven irregularly placed windows. All told, there are 30,000 square feet of exhibition space.

Museum of Modern Art exhibits often puzzle visitors

The **Cooper-Hewitt Museum,** which is part of the Smithsonian Institution, is the former Andrew Carnegie Mansion. It houses one of the most important collections of design and decorative arts in the United States. Here you will see excellent examples of wallpapers, textiles, ceramics, and other elements of the decorative arts — all in a relaxed, uncrowded setting of old-time opulence.

In Brooklyn, you will find some other leading museums — most especially the **Brooklyn Museum.** With a broad collection encompassing Egyptian, Classical, Oriental, European, and American Art, this institution offers an unusually varied cultural experience outside of Manhattan. In addition, behind the museum there is a strange, rather sad sculpture garden. It is not really a garden, and the sculptures you see there are not necessarily of great artistic merit. Rather, they are decorative elements saved just in time from destruction when the Brooklyn houses they adorned were torn down.

Some special-interest museums include the elegant and sedate **Morgan Library.** When J. Pierpont Morgan's mania for collecting assumed such proportions that his house, which was not exactly small, could no longer contain all his rare books and manuscripts, he had a neo-Renaissance palazzo built for them. Today the Morgan Library counts among its treasures a Gutenberg Bible, the Book of Hours of Catharine of Cleves, manuscripts by Balzac, and scores by Mozart.

Exterior of the Guggenheim reveals its structure

The **Asia House Gallery** and the **Japan House Gallery** offer specialized looks at these non-Western art forms, while the **Museum of American Folk Art,** the **Jewish Museum,** and the **American Craft Museum** concentrate on their subjects. In the case of all museums, it is worthwhile to check the particular museum's exhibition calendar, because the shows are often pertinent and unusual.

New York also has over 400 galleries, most of them concentrated in three areas: on upper Madison Avenue, around 57th Street, and in SoHo. They will show everything from the works of established masters to the avant-garde. You may find that in some of the very elegant uptown galleries you are treated with a touch of coolness if you are not known, but you should not let it worry you. Admission is usually free or only a nominal amount.

Gallery-hopping in SoHo is the best fun, but you had better do so on weekdays — on weekends you can hardly get into the large industrial elevators that take you from one loft gallery to another. Information on what the galleries have to offer appears in the *New York Times* on Fridays and Sundays, in various magazines, and especially in the *Gallery Guide,* a useful monthly listing available free of charge at many galleries and some museums.

Officially, the season runs from October to June, but not all galleries can afford such extended summer holidays. Galleries are usually open on Saturdays, and closed

A diorama at the American Museum of Natural History

on Mondays, but it is an arrangement that varies. About fifty New York galleries are members of the Art Dealers Association of America. Admittance to this rather exclusive organization is gained by means of "experience, a sense of responsibility, knowledge, and tangible contribution to the cultural well-being of the community." Some of the leading galleries in New York include **Hirschl & Adler, Knoedler & Company, Kennedy Galleries,** and **Wildenstein & Company.**

History in Museums

Although there are many museums of art in New York, the city does not lack others dealing with the past. There are elements of New York's history throughout the city, but these elements are all linked together in the **Museum of the City of New York.** The **New-York Historical Society** has the oldest museum in New York State and is the permanent home for folk art, primitive paintings, and period rooms. The **Museum of the American Indian** is a rare source of information for those interested in the ethnology and archeology of North American Indians.

At the base of the Statue of Liberty is the **American Museum of Immigration,** with its large collection of photographs reflecting the various waves of immigrants that have come to New York. Across the harbor, in lower Manhattan, is the **South Street Seaport Museum.** This cluster of restored buildings and ships gives the visitor a picture of what New York looked like as a busy nineteenth-century seaport. There is much to see and do here, including boarding the ships and visiting old-fashioned shops selling nautical goods.

Science Highlights

No description of museums in New York City would be complete without mention of the massive structure on Central Park West and 79th Street. This is the **American Museum of Natural History,** and alongside it is the museum's **Hayden Planetarium.** Perhaps the most wonderful part of this museum are the almost endless halls of dioramas showing animals and plants in their native habitats. Also there is the huge model of the blue whale, the world's largest mammal; or the numerous reconstructed dinosaur skeletons; or the spectacular gem collection; or. . . . The list could be endlesss, so rich is this museum and also such fun for children.

Next door, the Hayden Planetarium offers sky shows daily in its seventy-five-foot dome theater. These shows have always been a hit with New York City's children, but they are intriguing for adults as well.

Popular Culture

Not to be outdone by all the cultural sites in New York, some special exhibits have been started that show other aspects of life, including what we generally refer to as popular culture, or our daily existence. One place that tourists rarely hear about is the **Museum of Broadcasting,** which houses archives of the radio and television broadcasting industry. Here you can see old television comedies from the fifties or listen to old-time radio broadcasts.

The **Police Academy Museum** has the world's largest collection of police memorabilia, while the **Firefighting Museum** concentrates on that aspect of public service. The **Songwriters Hall of Fame** offers everything you would want to know about popular songs.

For those intrigued with the New York subways, a trip to the **New York City Transit Exhibition** is crucial. This exhibit occupies the mezzanine and platform areas of the IND Court Street Station, a station never actually put into use. It has been cleaned up and made to look as it would have in the late 1930s and early 40s. There are displays of old subway signals and turnstiles, old photographs and subway maps, colorful mosaics from the first subway stations, and old trolley cars. Pick up the **Nostalgia Special** at 57th Street and take it to this exhibit in Brooklyn; you'll be riding vintage subway cars with rattan seats and paddle fans.

A guide to museums in New York mentions over eighty of them. You should, of course, consider visiting the big ones, but if your time allows it, don't bypass some of the very small, specialized museums.

Color Photographs

DEPOSIT
LITTER IN
BASKETS

41

42

43

55

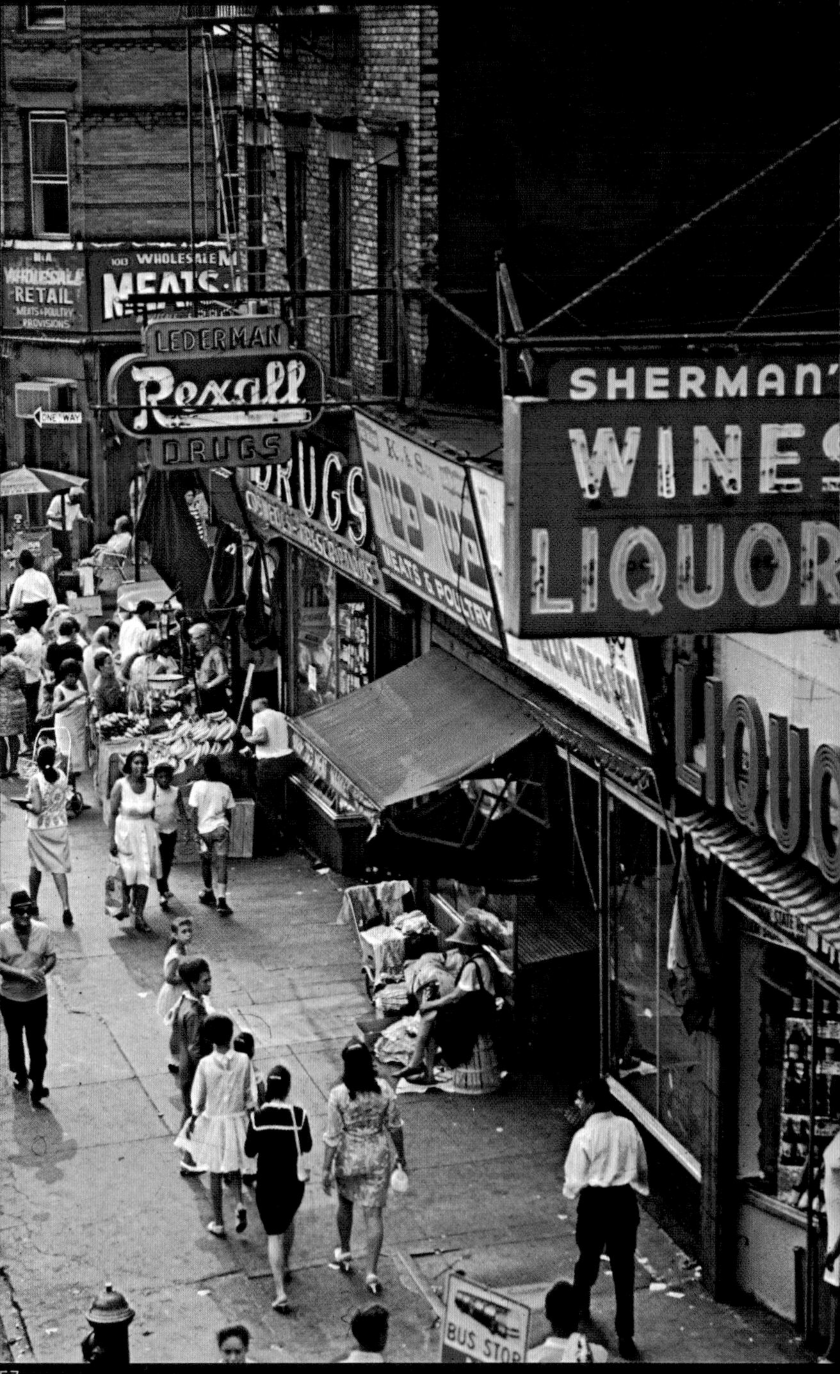
WHOLESALE
RETAIL
MEATS & POULTRY
PROVISIONS
103 WHOLESALE M
MEATS
LEDERMAN
Rexall
DRUGS
ONE WAY
RUGS
K. & S.
MEATS & POULTRY
SHERMAN'
WINE
LIQUOR
BUS STOP

New York in Figures

New York has everything, of course, but especially it has
more than one of everything. Here are some statistics to give
you a picture of the immensity of this grand city:

Population: 7,071,030
Size: 303 square miles, with 5 boroughs

New York also has 71 colleges, universities, and technical schools;
4,000 churches, synagogues, and other houses of worship; 2 million
apartments; 600 antique shops; 39 radio stations; 12 television
stations; 189 public libraries; 417 cinemas; 400 galleries;
83 theaters; and 120 museums.

In New York, there are 4 million people with a profession; 300,000
municipal employees; and 26 companies whose capital is larger
than 1 billion.

There are 6,400 miles of streets; 18 miles of beaches; 65 miles
of bicycle paths; and 1,100 parks and playgrounds.

New York gets 17 million visitors a year; at Kennedy Airport,
40 million travelers are processed each year.

"The New York dawn has
  four columns of mud
  and a hurricane of black doves
  that paddle in putrescent waters."

> Federico Garcia Lorca, *The Poet in New York*

"In Boston they ask, How much does he know?
  In New York, How much is he worth? In
  Philadelphia, Who were his parents?"

> Mark Twain, *What Paul Bourget Thinks of Us*

"The only credential the city asked was the boldness to
  dream. For those who did, it unlocked its gates and its
  treasures, not caring who they were or where they came from."

> Moss Hart, *Act One*

"The present in New York is so powerful that the past is lost."

> John Jay Chapman, Letter, March 26, 1898

Music and Dance

Concerts

People who ought to know have been saying for quite some time that New York has left London way behind as the music capital of the world. Quite aside from the New York Philharmonic, which is among the best orchestras in the world, Brooklyn boasts two symphony orchestras, the Bronx has one, and there are a few more in Queens and Manhattan. Chamber music ensembles are countless, among them such famous ones as the Guarneri or the Juilliard. You will find Chinese opera, Jewish choirs, balaleika and black orchestras, a bagpipe combo, and more. Moreover, there are countless amateur orchestras, some of them made up of neighborhood musicians, others of doctors, students, city employees, and other citizens.

The New York Philharmonic gives its concerts in **Avery Fisher** (formerly Philharmonic) **Hall** when it is not on tour somewhere. After Leonard Bernstein handed the baton to Pierre Boulez, a number of changes took place — not necessarily for the worse — among them the orchestra's sound and especially the programming. Under Boulez, the orchestra played a lot of electronic music, so much so that a wag was heard to wonder about the electrical supply. When Boulez stepped down, Zubin Mehta took over as music director and observers of the scene were breathlessly awaiting the tempestuous duels between conductor and critics that Mehta had fought during his term in Los Angeles (so far in vain, however).

Visiting orchestras of international repute, famous singers, pianists, and violin virtuosos usually give their concerts in **Carnegie Hall,** but sometimes in Avery Fisher Hall as well, especially since the latter (through the generosity of Mr. Fisher) has been remodeled for the third time in its short life and now has acoustics that work. Most of New York's music fans are convinced, however, that music in Carnegie Hall is unsurpassed, because even in the last row of the gallery a singer's most delicate *pianissimo* can be heard. Several times during its tumultuous life Carnegie Hall just barely escaped demolition. Now it belongs to the city and fills its cash register with revenues from sold-out superstar concerts.

Alice Tully Hall is a smaller house, used mostly for small ensembles and solo performances. It is a more modest building, but the visibility is very good and the acoustics are fine. Here also is where the New York Film Festival holds its premier showings each fall. Likewise, the **Carnegie Recital Hall** is used similarly for guest recitals and small ensemble performances.

Above: Foyer of the Metropolitan Opera House. Opposite: The fountain and plaza at Lincoln Center

Opera

Many New Yorkers lament the demise of their old Metropolitan Opera House. It stood on the corner of Broadway and 39th Street and was paid for in 1883 by the "nouveaux riches" (the Morgans, Goulds, Whitneys, and Rockefellers), because old New York Society would not have them in their Academy of Music. After a guided tour behind the scenes of the new **Met,** you'll find it easy to understand why musicians, stagehands, tailors, singers, and conductors all breathed a sigh of relief when they could move into their new house. The Met tends to spend a lot of money on productions and not always on a good singing team — except of course for one or two stars. It is often reproached for being cliquish, not only because of its expensive seats but also because of the hereditary subscription system; the best seats invariably go back to the oldest subscribers. If, however, you would like to hear perfectly good opera at a very low starting price, all you do is go across the plaza at Lincoln Center to the **New York State Theater,** where the New York City Opera is in residence from the end of August to the middle of November and from the middle of February to the end of April. Here you will find good teamwork, although not always of inter-

ational caliber. From the City Opera's ranks rose Beverly Sills, New York's much-
oved bel canto coloratura from Brooklyn, who is now its director. The New York
City Opera saves money by not going completely overboard with sets and costumes.
n addition, it offers a number of operas in English translation.

Music is not only made in concert halls, of course, but a great deal in churches (**St.
Thomas's,** for instance, has a good boys' choir), in the museums (**Metropolitan,
Frick, City of New York**), in the parks (**Central** and **Prospect**) during the summer
months, on the steps of the **Public Library,** and on street corners. At Christmastime,
for example, you might come across a quartet of students playing carols beautifully,
despite their blue fingers.

It is impossible here to tell you who can be heard where and when, because the
schedules vary a great deal and because they often are sold out almost before
tickets go on sale. Many performances have large subscription sales, so the tickets
that remain are often scarce; perhaps you might even have to stand in line for hours
for some special performances. In the Key to the City are some spots where
music is made more or less regularly. Newspapers and magazines (the *New York
Times,* especially on Fridays and Sundays, *New York* magazine, the *Village Voice,*
and the *New Yorker*) will give dates, times, and addresses of the various performances. Students and people over sixty-five can get tickets at half price for most performances. Many times standing room tickets are made available as well.

And if you can't get tickets for the big performance you had hoped for, try going
instead to one of the chamber music groups or an organ concert in one of the
churches. You'll be surprised at the high quality of performance, as well as the lower
cost of tickets.

Dance

New York City is referred to as the dance capital of the world. On almost any day, a variety of performances are offered, ranging from major classical ballet to dance-filled Broadway musicals, to the most esoteric premieres by young soloists in SoHo lofts. The **New York City Ballet,** founded in 1948, is the local company, in residence for long seasons at the New York State Theater at Lincoln Center. This company primarily presents works of George Balanchine, but occasionally shows the work of Jerome Robbins. The company is a tourist attraction of the first order.

The most renowned U.S. ballet company is the **American Ballet Theater,** founded in 1940. It has the most important repertoire of classic and contemporary ballet, including among many others the works of Agnes de Mille. The company includes great international stars.

Also to be recommended is the **Robert Joffrey Ballet.** It is smaller and, although it has a distinguished international repertoire, it is more typically American in feeling. Likewise, the **Eliot Feld Company** and **Dennis Wayne's Dancers** are other important ballet companies performing in New York.

On East 63rd Street is the **Martha Graham School of Contemporary Dance.** Martha Graham is one of the most important figures in the history of American dance, and her talents and achievements as dancer, actor, choreographer, scenarist, costume designer, theoretician, and teacher are singular. She has created a completely new dance vocabulary and form which, by now, has been adopted throughout the world. She choreographed her first work in 1926 and is still active, giving regular performances in New York.

Other important figures in modern American dance, such as Merce Cunningham, Paul Taylor, and Alwin Nikolais, studied and worked with Graham before going on to establish their own unique companies. **Merce Cunningham** is best known for his experimental works which involve "chance" and which are created without reference to the sound which accompanies the performances. In contrast to these non-narrative pieces, **Paul Taylor's** work tells stories, which are often full of delicious humor. **Alwin Nikolais**'s dance theater is remarkable for his fantastic lighting, used as decor, and for his electronic music and costumes, in which the human figure totally vanishes and the dancers become moving forms. These, and other groups, are the foundation on which contemporary dance in New York continues to develop and expand.

Important names you may find listed among current performances include dancer/choreographers such as **Kenneth King, Laura Dean, Douglas Dunn, Louis Falco, Viola Farber, Rosalind Newman, Twyla Tharp,** and **Dan Wagoner.** Their work is difficult to categorize. Nearly every form of performance is essayed, from circus-like feats of physical virtuosity to the most banal everyday movements.

Arthur Mitchell formed the **Dance Theater of Harlem,** a company which employs only black dancers for its classical ballet repertoire. On the other hand, **Alvin Ailey** is a black choreographer with a lively, cosmopolitan company, which dances eclectically composed programs of great theatricality.

Dance is alive and well in New York

Dance is performed at the Metropolitan Opera House and New York State Theater and at the City Center; in Brooklyn, there are performances at the Brooklyn Academy of Music. In addition, performances of less conventional forms of dance are given in school auditoriums, in galleries, in museums, in lofts and garages, and on the piers lining the New York waterfront. Balletomanes new in town should visit the **New York Public Library at Lincoln Center,** with its great dance collection and also its book shop in the main foyer, which stocks many dance periodicals that can give the visitor up-to-date information about the great and varied dance scene in New York City.

World-famous Rockettes are still kicking for crowds of tourists

TO
42 ST.
THE WORLDS' GREATEST
MOVIE
CENTER
VICTORY
FIRST TIME ON 42ND STREET
THE MIRACLE OF LOVE
ALSO
THE TAMING
SEVEN WOMEN
SAVE
FREE
TV!

Theater and Film

Broadway — The Great White Way

Broadway and Times Square definitely are among the most popular sights in New York. Hardly any visitor knows that Broadway is one of the longest streets in the world, extending from downtown Manhattan, all the way to Albany; Broadway to most people is not so much a street but rather a place name — and a collective term at that. "**On Broadway**" are the theaters which are located in the theater district around Times Square (roughly from 40th to 56th streets between Sixth and Eighth avenues); for example, 247 West 45th Street is also a Broadway address for a theater.

Like all districts with nightlife, Broadway is shabby during the day; as a matter of fact, it is even very plain-looking and disappointing. Times Square, which got its name from the *New York Times*, which in 1905 temporarily moved into the narrow building on the southern end of what used to be Longacre Square, today is the very essence of the seamy side of New York. Prostitutes, junkies, muggers, and bums here have found their choice field of activity. On every corner, vulgar pamphlets are being distributed, massage parlors invite people for a relaxing visit, while peep shows and adult bookstores lure in others with exaggerated claims. Knickknack and souvenir shops offer expensive junk, while street vendors often sell materials that likely have been stolen. A real fear of the area causes many suburbanites to shun the theater district; a visit to Broadway is a big risk in their eyes.

But in spite of everything, Broadway has not lost its fascination and magic. It is still the "Great White Way," the terminal for those with yearnings for stardom. In 1972, the city government began to realize the significance of theater life for New York. It passed a law which allowed every builder to put in additional stories if in return he would include a theater in the complex. Since then, four new stages have sprung up in the Times Square section — and they survived. In the meantime, the city and theater people as well have been fighting to eliminate or at least curtail the amount of pornography available in the area. It is heartening to note that a number of former porno theaters have now been converted to legitimate stages. The Broadway theater in New York is booming today. What tickets aren't sold in advance of performances are sent off to the special half-price booth (**Tkts**) on 47th Street to be offered the day of performance.

The musicals have always attracted out-of-towners; they are consistently good entertainment, with top-notch dancing and spirited music. After the successful big names such as Richard Rodgers and Oscar Hammerstein, and Alan Jay Lerner and Frederick Loewe, musicals began to gain another image, perhaps a bit more serious

125

Scenes of the wilder side

nd more contemporary. Today's musicals include the blockbusters *Evita*, *Barnum*, nnie, and *42nd Street* or the longer-running ones such as *A Chorus Line* or a revival f a former favorite. What will be popular when you arrive? Check the newspapers and magazines for this information.

Just as the musicals have changed, so have the dramatic productions. Many shows e limited in scope and have short runs, while others do remain on the scene for ears. Some productions begin off-broadway and once the show receives good otices it moves uptown. It is even more likely that you can take advantage of the lf-price bargains for these plays, since they usually are not as popular as the musi- ls.

Above: Broadway's usual hectic pace slows down for a snow storm. Opposite: Experimental theater

Off- and Off-Off Broadway

Broadway shows are not necessarily representative of that which goes on in American theater, at least they are not representative of that which is very new. It is the small stages, **Off-Broadway** and **Off-Off Broadway,** which account for the creative element in New York theater. They sprang up first in Greenwich Village and you could hardly have expected them to do so otherwise; the Provincetown Play-house was one of the first.

Off-Broadway means that the theater has fewer than 300 seats. It also means that it is beyond the range of labor union authority. The result is that there is less pressure to meet union pay scales and productions can be done less expensively. In other words, there is a possibility for staging drama and not just for putting on a show. Besides, low ticket prices attract a new public, and going to the theater for them is a cultural experience, not a social event. Of course, the progressives and the drum-beaters came, but the Off-Broadway producers did not stick too strictly to their original ideals. Many Off-Broadway productions today are as commercial as those of Broadway.

Rehearsal at La Mama

After Off-Broadway came the Off-Off Broadway theater: as experimental theater, as showcase theater. It discovered and promoted talents and it functioned as a theater guiding efforts along new lines. The range of these stages today extends from the renowned La Mama Etc. of Ellen Stewart and Joseph Papp's New York Shakespeare Festival, all the way to the loft and basement theaters of small, as-yet-unknown troupes.

La Mama, actually the first Off-Off Broadway theater, began in 1966. "It was not my idea," maintains Ellen Stewart in her rather odd Chicago accent. "I have no ambition and no ideas; I only love to have people around me who are creative. I love fine artists." The playwright Peter Foster and her brother, she says, "pulled her" into this entire thing, although she was not exactly dissatisfied with her job as designer for Saks Fifth Avenue. Ellen Stewart quickly became the intellectual center of is new theater world. People would meet at her place; they would discuss ideas and make plans, until one day she was reported as a black whore who received white men. An understanding officer on the vice squad quickly realized the charge as nonsense and advised her to open a café. That is how **La Mama Etc.** came about, and it very quickly developed into New York's most vital theater. Why the name La Mama? Ellen Stewart shakes her head uncomprehendingly: "I *am* La Mama."

The atmosphere is entirely different in the case of Joseph Papp, the On, Off-, and Off-Off Broadway producer. His **Public Theater,** with its seven stages, has become one of the most important centers of New York theater. Papp's New York Shakespeare Festival, the general term for his far-flung organization, has a budget that is even bigger than that of the Metropolitan Opera. "The Festival," writes New York critic Helen Epstein, "is a hodge-podge of directors, playwrights, composers, actors, and technicians who have come from such diverse backgrounds as the Yale School of Drama, Hollywood, TV soap operas, and the avant-garde theaters of Off-Off Broadway."

Papp is today not only the most agile producer in New York but also the one with the broadest range and the biggest contrasts. "He makes me mad; he makes bad mistakes, and he makes me furious," writes a theater critic for the *New York Times,* "but he makes theater exciting." And supporters and opponents agree on that. Something is always happening with Papp — from Lee Breuer's Mabou Mines Troupe, whose Beckett productions are a strenuous and intensive experience, all the way to musical whimsy by Elizabeth Swados. In the meantime, Papp also regularly offers avant-garde jazz and important films that would not survive in commercial movie theaters.

The **Truck and Warehouse Theater** had a huge success a few years ago with Divine, the star from the porno movie *Pink Flamingo,* who played a sadistic female prison guard in Tom Eyen's *Women Behind Bars.* The mostly homosexual male audience was absolutely beside itself.

Now and then, the **WPA** comes up with some good productions. Very original and therefore also interesting, even though you may not agree with the interpretations, is the **Performance Group.** In this theater the audience is often urged to come running along because every scene takes place in a different corner. In a performance there of Brecht's *Mother Courage,* the last scene was played on the street; the audience — to the utter consternation of passers-by — blocked the sidewalk.

Also take a look at the program of the **Circle Repertory Company** and the **Circle in the Square Downtown.** The **Jean Cocteau Repertory** is also quite outstanding. And something relatively new here is the **Entermedia Theater,** which offers everything from Vonnegut musicals to black drama.

Other Off-Off Broadway theater can be found uptown — for example, in the **Manhattan Theater Club** or the **Equity Library Theater.** And most recently, around the corner from Broadway itself, five new Off-Off Broadway stages have sprung up.

You can also see very good performances at the **Theater of the Riverside Church,** in St. John the Divine or at the **Universalist Church** at 76th Street and Central Park West. Lastly, avant-garde theater is performed at the **Open Space in**

SoHo and **Synesthetics,** among many others.

The quality of Off-Broadway and Off-Off Broadway productions is hardly predictable. In the case of *My Fair Lady,* or plays by Strindberg or Noel Coward, you roughly know what to expect. In the case of everything else — you are in for surprises. You may experience your most exciting theater evenings here or you may leave disappointed after the first act; the fact is that you can never be sure. But give this theater a chance. You will be getting away from the mainstream of tourists and you may have fun. The newspapers with the best information on these theaters are the *SoHo News, Village Voice,* and to a certain extent also *New York* magazine.

Black Theater

Black musicals on Broadway have for several years now no longer been the exception, but rather the rule. In the eyes of many blacks this is not real black theater but only the black copy of a white form of entertainment — moreover, it is theater frequently produced by whites. Black Broadway is in fact anything but the extended arm of the civil rights movement of the sixties. But it is tremendously spirited and colorful; it is accomplished entertainment which is fun. Political messages are of no interest here, and the committed might well turn their noses up at the low-level music hall on the Great White Way. But these pleasing shows achieved that which black theater had never been able to in terms of coping with the past or as a current sociopolitical statement. They have activated a black mass public. "For too long we failed to realize," a veteran of the black theater admits, "that the black middle class also wants to be entertained." Somebody who himself had just escaped the slums does not want to be taken back there in the theater. And those who still live in poverty and misery do not go to the theater in order once again to have their situation illustrated to them in a different way.

In contrast, it is precisely this misery which, for example, the active black playwright Ed Bullins described in some of his plays with oppressive scrupulous exactitude. Ghetto, prison, aggression, and violence are also the main themes of the theatrical troupe that goes by the name of **The Family**: the mostly black and Puerto Rican former prison inmates often present dramatizations of autobiographical experiences. Their social reality is staged relentlessly, in the Theater for the New City.

The outstanding **Negro Ensemble Company** (called NEC for short) also presents very intensive and realistic theater, although on a different level. Here we are not so much concerned with violence or ghetto life but rather with the effects, the psychological stresses of interpersonal relationships; their performances are mostly at the St. Mark's Playhouse and at the Theater De Lys.

Black theater with mixed actors can be seen at the **AMAS Repertory Theater.** Here, angry theater is rejected with disarming frankness and, instead, nostalgic retrospect is staged in a snappy, saucy style.

One of the most original black experimental theaters is the **New Federal Theater** at the Henry Street Settlement on the Lower East Side. Under the direction of agile Woody King, this group wants to bring black theater to those who are involved and

Ed Bullins at the New Lafayette Theater in Harlem

concerned. King views his theater as a neighborhood place; everybody should be able to come — there is no admission charge — and everybody should feel that he or she has been addressed (this is why King now and then also presents white plays in order to appeal to the remaining Jews and middle Europeans in the neighborhood).

Anybody who has never experienced black theater and a black audience will perhaps be surprised or even astonished by the spontaneous interaction between the audience and the actors, especially in the small theaters. The committed and often loud participation of the public must be viewed as a contemporary reflection of black theater's religious origins. Anybody who wants to see entertaining shows should go to Broadway; anybody who wants to experience authentic black theater had better go to NEC or to Woody King. "Regardless of how good the plays are," writes a critic in the *New York Times*, "the public is guaranteed a hit."

Opposite: The avant-garde is Off-Off Broadway. Above: Half-price tickets are available at 47th Street and Broadway

The Cinema

New Yorkers love to go to the movies, and the possibilities for doing so are inexhaustible. Interest is high whenever the latest film opens and people eagerly wait on long lines to catch the movie very soon after it has been reviewed. Although you probably aren't coming to New York to go specifically to the movies, it is likely that you might want to take in a film while you are here. If you wish to avoid crowds or long lines, you will find the movie houses much less crowded during the day or very early in the evening; later on at night is when the lines begin to form.

There are two film festivals in New York every year: the **American Film Festival** in May, held in one of the large hotels, where you can watch as many documentaries as you like for a single admission; and the **New York Film Festival** in late September–early October, for which the tickets are often sold out weeks in advance. The latter's films are shown in Alice Tully Hall and include the latest from the leading European, Asian, and American filmmakers.

Several theaters in New York show films by young independent directors, and these movies will never reach the large houses or be distributed nationwide. Check the latest copy of the *New Yorker* magazine for a listing, as well as some brief and intelligent descriptions of the films.

There are a couple of revival houses that only show old movies. Two such places are the **Bleecker Street Cinema** and the **Thalia.** For a full listing of such movie theaters, see the Key to the City under MOVIE THEATERS.

You can also see films at the **Museum of Modern Art**; their archives are perhaps the most extensive in the country. And movies are also shown at the **Public Theater** and occasionally also at the **Whitney Museum.**

d Shops

v York is a food town. On every other corner, there is a stand selling hot dogs, ee shop serving hamburgers and cheeseburgers, or a sandwich shop offering lad and tuna lunches. At the same time, the streets are lined with gourmet rants of every ethnic variety, food shops with shelves of imported delicacies, orner vegetable stands with appetizing produce. Food is a much-discussed, ly practiced topic. There are heated arguments about whether it is better to buy **Zabar's** or at **Murray's Sturgeon Shop** — both excellent delicatessens on the West Side. In fact, Zabar's, where the sausages, cooking spoons, and tea- hang from the ceiling, is a Sunday morning meeting place for neighborhood . And at Murray's, the lox is so delicately sliced that, says an admirer, stian Barnard would become pale with envy.''

ireenwich Village, **Balducci's** is an unequaled shopper's paradise, also offering portunity to see a rock star or singer as one purchases fresh vegetables. Io, food has become an obsession, and the headquarters is **Dean & DeLuca,** ll but tightly packed store with gourmet specialties of all kinds. Quail, n, caviar, and morels share limited space with dried fruits, fresh vegetables, tchenry. This is the finest of New York's food emporiums, and if you like g at such places or shopping for these things, this spot is a must-stop. In only years, the owners of this store have made it one of the truly famous. Farther n, **Macy's Cellar** is probably the largest gourmet section in the city's depart- stores, with the entire area devoted to coffee beans and teas, cheeses, pastries, getables, as well as cookware and gadgets. The new **Citicorp Building** on 3rd Street is virtually a palace for food. Shops and eateries of all sorts line the two floors of this building, offering an assortment of imported goods, fresh- pastries, and snacks of a more exotic nature. Upstairs is **Conran's,** a house- store devoted heavily to kitchen-related items.

many New Yorkers do their shopping at the city's **greenmarkets** — farmer's set up in certain neighborhoods on certain days. Fresh, in-season vegetables ld here, much as in the style of Europe's street markets. The prices are gen- lower than in the stores, since it is the farmer himself who trucks the produce n the outlying areas and sells it directly to the consumer. One of the largest narkets is at Union Square, held on Saturdays.

v York is famous for its bakeries, where calorie-laden cakes and pies tempt the sby. The best strudel, it is claimed, can be bought at **Lichtman,** while the best

137

torten is at **Dumas.** In fact, of the city's French pastry shops, **Dumas, Delices La Cote Basque,** and **Bonte** are the city's finest; many New Yorkers feel Parisian shops can offer no better.

New Yorkers swear by their cheesecake; they consume 10,000 such heavy delights every day, which amounts to about 60 million calories. They intensively follow *New York* magazine's search for the champion cheesecake. For sure, never did the *Playboy* Playmate of the Month attract so much attention, and so lustfully, as did the centerfold of *New York,* when they pictured the winner (from Junior's, in Brooklyn).

There are other types of food specialties in the city. For example, for those eager to acquire hard-to-find kitchen equipment, **Bridge Kitchenware** is tops. For others interested in unusual ingredients from all over the world, **H. Roth** carries a wide assortment of spices; they also sell prune and apricot butters (lekvar) "by the barrel." Nearby, **Paprikas Weiss** is best for varying strengths of paprika, strudel dough, and special honey, noodles, and flour. If you love pâtés and terrines, then go downtown to a very small store, **Les Trois Petits Cochons,** for their latest sampling. Exotic vinegars, tantalizing jams and preserves, and old-fashioned quality cakes and breads are the treasures at the **Silver Palate** on Columbus Avenue.

Manganaro's, the Italian grocery on Ninth Avenue, sells olive oil, mozzarella, and salami, but also stocks more than 500 different kinds of pasta, made on the premises. Also along the street are Italian and Spanish food shops: meat markets, vegetable stores, imported cheese shops, and more.

Places to Eat

As a visitor to New York, you will be seeking meals in all parts of the city. Quick meals are easy to find, from coffee shops and street vendors. You can eat well for very little money, especially if you are prepared to stand at a counter or find a resting spot in a park.

Coffee shops vary from good to awful, and offer the usual fare — mostly hamburgers. New York also has some chains, like Burger King, McDonald's, Steak and Brew, Zum Zum, and Chock Full O'Nuts; these have predictable food. But New York has lots of exciting and unusual food as well. The much-cited melting pot offers an unsurpassed choice of culinary treats.

Try the Italian pizza, pasta, or calzone; the Greek shish kebab, souvlaki, or felafel; Japanese sushi; Jewish bagels or knishes; Chinese dim sum, bean sprouts, tofu, or Sichuan dishes; or Cuban lomitos. Even the street offerings — traditionally limited to hot dogs, ice cream, and pretzels — have become more varied in recent years. Carts everywhere offer fresh orange juice — pressed right before your eyes; and there are nuts and raisins, and even homemade cookies, sold from small, bright red electric carts. On Sixth Avenue, around the midtown area, a black cook fries Chinese food in two huge woks, while a taco competitor is often posted in front of the Museum of Modern Art.

The Greek sandwiches — pastry pockets with shish kebab, highly seasoned rice, lamb, or spinach with feta cheese — are best when they come crispy from the pan. Bagels, hard round rolls with a hole in the middle, are Jewish breakfast specialties

Top: The famous Automat. Bottom: Sharing food in the park

Fast food chains have come here too

that are often spread with cream cheese and filled with smoked salmon. Bagels come in numerous variations — with onions, caraway, poppy, or sesame seeds — and are made best at the bagel bakeries in the Jewish neighborhoods like the Upper West Side.

Delicatessens pack a lot of pastrami or corned beef between two slices of rye bread, for a taste treat that is typically New York. Try the combination sandwiches for a filling and exciting lunch.

Many of New York's restaurants are well known, even to people who have never before been to New York City. The truly elegant and very expensive ones include **Lutece, La Caravelle, La Cote Basque, Le Cygne, La Grenouille,** the **Four Seasons,** and the **Cellar in the Sky,** a very limited-seating restaurant at the top of the World Trade Center which emphasizes fine wines. Also part of this list is the **Palace,** probably New York's most expensive eating place, where dinner can cost upwards of $100 per person. All of these spots feature only the best in cuisine and have fine wine cellars.

But if these prices scare you, you'll find a great deal of very good food in New York in the more average-priced restaurants. These places come and go with fashion, and today the most popular ones tend to stress lighter foods — fish and chicken dishes — with airy, natural decor and furnishings. Prices for meals range anywhere from $15 per person with tip and tax, to $35 or $40, excluding liquor.

Chinatown has some of the city's best restaurants

Some restaurants are innovative and offer exciting new combinations, while others never change their menus, preferring to keep to what they know best. Many of New York's most exciting eating places are those with ethnic food, whether it be Czechoslovak, Italian, Chinese, or Indian. For these types of restaurants, you are best following the leading restaurant guides to New York. One of the nicest is Milton Glaser and Jerome Snyder's *Underground Gourmet*. Also popular, and usually on-the-mark with recommendations is *The Restaurants of New York* by Seymour Britchky. We list a few key spots in the Key to the City, but for a more intensive eating session, consult these guides. Some of the smaller places have the characteristic of being short-lived, so it is always advisable to call the particular restaurant before you start out. In addition, for the popular ones, reservations are often required.

Of course, should you be in Greenwich Village or Chinatown, or Little Italy, you will never be in a fix. These areas have hundreds of restaurants; if one of those listed in a guidebook has closed, then you can almost certainly find the next only a few blocks away. In Greenwich Village, New York's student and artist quarter, the pubs and restaurants are open until late at night. The **Horn of Plenty** offers good southern cooking, an interesting atmosphere, and a markedly beautiful garden. Quieter and less expensive is **Mary's,** a small Italian cellar restaurant. But the list of restaurants is inexhaustible for the Village. To name just a few, there are **Trattoria da Alfredo,**

Il Ponte Vecchio, the **Coach House** (elegant and expensive), **Ye Waverly Inn, Chumley's, Starthrower Café,** or **O. Henry's Steakhouse.**

One is just as well provided for in Chinatown, where there are many of New York's 1,000 Chinese restaurants. Sweet-sour crab or pork with snow peas and walnuts can be eaten as part of a meal or packed into small cartons for take-out. Here you'll find **Bobo, 456, Phoenix Garden,** or **Oh-Ho-So,** along with many others. For those who wish to try dim sum, a Chinese-style brunch consisting of many small portions of very exotic dishes, try the **Silver Palace.** You might not always know what you are eating, but it usually tastes excellent.

In Little Italy, you can dine equally well at **Benito's, Angelo's,** or **Puglia's. Il Cortile** is the work of a modern decorator: white walls, large windows, marble floors, wood tables, Thonet chairs, and green plants everywhere. **Vincent's Clam Bar** and **Umberto's Clam House** offer cheap, dependable seafood.

If Ethnic food is something that tickles your palate, you will find the best versions of each in their respective neighborhoods. *A Complete Guide to Ethnic New York,* a new book, gives a very detailed listing of such areas. Be sure to consider trying the city's Hungarian and Czechoslovak dishes or the different kinds of South American foods, or the East and West Indian specialties. . . .

If you are combining dinner with the theater, you'll find over nineteen restaurants along 46th Street between Eighth and Ninth avenues. This is restaurant row, and along here you have a selection of **Joe Allen, Crepe Suzette, El Tenampa, Café de France,** or **Barbetta's.** Most of these places realize that the customers are headed for 7:30 or 8 PM curtains, and they gear their service accordingly.

New York also has omelette places and creperies, such as **Elephant & Castle** in the Village or the **Magic Pan** (a chain with branches midtown); soup and salad spots such as the **Front Porch** and **La Bonne Soupe;** and steak house like the **Cattleman, Palm Restaurant, Peter Luger's** (Brooklyn), or **Hoexter's Market.** Cafés where you can have cappuccino or espresso, perhaps along with a tasty pastry, include **Caffe Reggio,** the **Peacock,** or **La Fortuna.**

Two other famous spots, although quite dissimilar, are the **Grand Central Oyster Bar,** where you can swallow oysters at the counter for only a small price for each, or the **Automat,** where you make your selections and obtain your food through coin-operated wall units. Only one Automat is left in New York, so go to see it before it disappears too.

New Yorkers eat at all times of the day, so you will find an assortment of places that stay open twenty-four hours. One of the best of these is the **Brasserie,** where you can have good French food or a lovely breakfast. But for the most part, New Yorkers prefer to eat dinner between 7 and 9 PM, and most·restaurants begin serving the evening meal no earlier than 6. Some occasional restaurants offer a special early dinner price, assuming that you place your order before 6 PM. Many restaurants open for both lunch and dinner and a number close on Mondays or Sundays. In the Key to the City, we give particulars on these matters for the establishment listed. Bon Appetit!

Top: Streets are lined with inexpensive coffee shops. Bottom: Many restaurants feature bars as well

American
IMPORTS
DOMESTIC
SPECIALTIES
GREEK & SPANISH GROCERY
563
BIG SALE

*Ethnic foods are best
from neighborhood grocers*

Nightlife

Regardless of crime statistics, New York remains very much a twenty-four-hour town. Nightlife is strong here, with a limitless supply of cabarets, nightclubs, and bars. The subways and buses run all night, and the taxis never stop cruising the streets; in the early morning hours, especially on weekends, the sidewalks can be almost as crowded as during the day.

What is your interest? Whatever you like, there is a spot where you'll find it. New York offers top entertainment, whether it be comedy, jazz, or disco.

Nightclubs, Cabarets, and Dancing

For those seeking an elegant evening, many people find their way to the **Edwardian Room** of the Plaza Hotel, the **Rainbow Room** at Rockefeller Center, **Café Pierre,** or the **Stork Club** for candlelit dining and dancing. Others stop at **La Chansonnette,** which features French food and song.

Whereas the music at these dining and dancing spots is usually a trio, the big band sound can be heard and danced to at **Roseland,** that New York institution, or at the Lounge of the **Copacabana. Red Blazer Too** alternates big bands with small groups, and you can dance there also.

A wide range of performers appear nightly at the city's cafés and clubs. Good places to try for comedians or vocalists include **Top of the Gate** or the **Valentine Room** at Once Upon a Stove. Some cabarets serve only drinks, while others offer a fairly extensive menu. In addition, at a place such as **Applause,** the waiters are also the performers. Other spots, like **Catch a Rising Star** or **Improvisation,** are showcase clubs; that is, new performers get to "try out" their acts on the customers. You may have a chance to see someone before they make it big, or suffer through others who you will never again hear of. It's chancy, but fun.

Among New York's late-night spots are the nightclubs, most of which offer a flavor of the exotic. For example, the **Balalaika** has a Russian-style atmosphere, while **Club Ibis** is Middle Eastern and **Dionysos,** Greek. The comedian Rodney Dangerfield performs at his own club which is another standard spot for people to go.

Jazz in the Big Apple

Besides the big band sound, other types of jazz can be heard in New York. In fact, New York is today the only city in the United States where you can hear all variations, from dixieland and bop, all the way to electronic. There is jazz to be heard in concert halls and in hundreds of clubs, basements, and lofts in this town noted for its historic link with jazz.

Louis Armstrong came to New York in 1924, where he joined Fletcher Henderson's band playing at Roseland. During the following years, such legendary jazz musicians as Earl Hines, Charlie Parker, Dizzy Gillespie, Count Basie, and Duke Ellington made Harlem's Cotton Club their home base and thus one of the most famous nightclubs anywhere in the world. During the forties, Manhattan's 52nd Street became Swing Street. Even during the sixties, when many people declared jazz to be dead in New York, it could be heard in Greenwich Village.

Today the Village still is an important jazz center. Mary Lou Williams or Alberta Hunter appear regularly at the **Cookery,** bop can be heard at **Boomers,** and crossover jazz-rock is at the **Village Vanguard. Bradley's** is just as popular a place as **Sweet Basil.**

Jazz is elsewhere in New York also. On the Upper West Side, dixieland is played at **Jimmy Ryan's,** while nearby at **Eddie Condon's** the sound is more traditional blues. On the East Side, **Michael's Pub** steadily offers early ragtime and Chicago jazz; on Monday nights, Woody Allen joins in on the clarinet.

In protest against the established jazz restaurants and their nightclub atmosphere — where food and drink often play just as important a role as the music — the jazz lofts sprang up. In an unpretentious environment, they offer little except music (now and then there's wine, soft drinks, more rarely sandwiches). Jazz lofts in the meantime are playing an ever more important role. In contrast to the clubs, a more direct and intensive relationship is possible between the audience and the musicians; the feedback is undisturbed and there are none of the usual distractions.

Well-known jazz musicians have been performing in these lofts; for example, Philip Wilson at **Environ** or Dakota Station and Eddie Jefferson in the **Ladies' Fort. Jazzmania,** the most comfortable of the lofts, with its fireplace and sofas, reminds one of a huge living room. Again and again people are invited to jam sessions. Meanwhile, **Studio RivBea** is considered to be a choice spot for talent scouts.

Since 1972, the **Newport Jazz Festival** has been held in New York. For fourteen days, it turns Carnegie Hall, Washington Square Park, Avery Fisher Hall, and countless other squares, parks, and halls into a mecca for jazz fans, with names such as Eubie Blake, Dizzy Gillespie, Earl Hines, or Art Blakey.

Lastly, two other jazz-related ideas: a good jazz restaurant is the **Knickerbocker Saloon;** and every Sunday afternoon at 5 PM there is a jazz vesper at **St. Peter's Church,** the little church in the spectacular Citicorp Center.

Folk, Blues, and Country

New York's folk music scene is flourishing just as it did in the turbulent sixties. This is especially noticeable in downtown Manhattan, in Greenwich Village. All the clubs in which the legendary folk music movement had its start in the past are still here today. Gerde's **Folk City** (where Bob Dylan and Simon & Garfunkel began) is still there, as is the **Other End** (formerly the Bitter End). The other popular spot is **Kenny's Castaways.**

The legendary, now defunct, Fillmore East

Although it is hard for some New Yorkers to believe, country music is also popular now in the city, and the **Lone Star Cafe** is the place to hear it. There are top performers here — people who previously couldn't get a foot inside the city limits of this sophisticated metropolis. Roy Orbison only recently appeared here following his heart surgery.

Blues lovers can find their music at **Tramps,** with the sound of Lightning Hopkins, Buddy Guy, or Junior Wells.

Rock and Punk Rock

Rock music in New York is year in and year out a permanent pop festival, non-stop twelve months long. Hardly a day goes by without an important (large) concert being held in one or another of its numerous rock areas — be it in the gigantic **Madison Square Garden,** the largest arena in town, or in the smaller **Palladium** playground especially of the Heavy Metal rockers, or even in the **Beacon Theater** which — like Carnegie Hall and Avery Fisher Hall — specializes more in the subdued soft rock, jazz-rock, and other styles related to rock.

All the great rock stars have already performed on these stages, from the Beach Boys and the Eagles to Peter Frampton, Elton John, and the Rolling Stones. Actually the New Yorker misses very little; everyone comes through New York.

If you want to listen to rock music, then the old favorite, the **Bottom Line,** is the place to go. Somewhat more of an establishment, and thus more commercial than other places, the Bottom Line has become a platform for the record industry. This

*Rock music in the city:
musicians perform on the street;
fans wait in line for a concert;
a performance in a club*

I CAME TO NEW YORK WHEN
I WAS NINETEEN

i was in a word an immigrant from
another planet called new jersey.
there was no room for art in new
jersey. only cows and swamps.

new york
home of mutants niggers art prowlers
violent 78 speed

the ones with most stamina and
heart survive.

the illuminated hustlers.

the empire state building is the
perfect symbol of my city.

the great hypodermic. the towering
needle.

this needle sucks and drains the blood
of the people it shoots up on it.
god vomits a sweet pollution over
the heads of his subjects.

in new york we are subjected to the
violins of the great symphony halls
the violence and passion of pusher
streets and rock clubs and this
precious vomit . . .

Patti Smith

new in scene has also been publicized in several magazines. *Punk Magazine* and the *New York Rocker* carry detailed accounts of current events. Not a few careers of the newer superstars have been launched here: Bruce Springsteen, Phoebe Snow, South side Johnny and the Asbury Jukes. The Bottom Line is run by two clever, young managers who seem to know exactly what will be popular tomorrow and what will happen in the future of pop music. The Bottom Line — with about 400 seats – offers a continuous music program seven days a week, with two shows per evening, the last generally starting only toward midnight. The atmosphere is decent and cozy and the audience goes wild over each performance.

The socalled punks have become a steady part of the New York pop music scene, and punk rock is now an established thing. One of their domiciles is **CBGB's** long, tubelike club that seats about 250 people. Located on the Bowery, the street of the derelicts, CBGB's presents pure rock every evening such as has not been heard since the legendary days of Lou Reed and his famous Velvet Underground band. This music is loud, hard, and metallic — an acoustic decal of this metropolis that is nearly suffocating from noise in itself.

CBGB's, which opened at the end of 1974, has contributed decidedly to the New York underground scene that is flourishing again; it is almost like the time of Bill Graham and his legendary Fillmore East which, half dilapidated, is only a few steps away from this club. The term *underground* in this connection may seem somewhat strange and slightly anachronistic. On the other hand, it really concerns such phenomenon, at least in the original sense. Almost all groups that perform at CBGB's are for the most part not considered commercial bands; they have only very little to do with what counts above ground. Most of the groups play, as the Tuff Darts, one of the most famous New York punk rock groups, put it, "out of sheer love for rock 'n' roll" — a statement very seldom heard from the mouth of today's rock superstars. Moreover, figures like Patti Smith, Blondie, and Mink de Ville have given punk rock poetic qualities.

Following the success of CBGB's, New York's most famous underground spot – **Max's Kansas City** — has also awakened to new life again. After the departure of Andy Warhol and his superstar clique, who had frequented this well-known bar and restaurant, Max's was threatened by closure several times. However, this (reno vated) club is now "in" again.

Disco and Roller Disco

Although Studio 54 has closed, there are many other spots to visit. They range from places that combine pounding disco music with "dance rock"; for this type of sound, try **Zenon,** the **Electric Circus,** or **Bond International Casino.** For a more concentrated rock sound, the new **Ritz** is the place to go. There is an Art Deco decor and a large video screen; in addition live acts are interspersed with recorded music and recently Fats Domino was appearing. **Hurrah, New York, New York,** and **Le Mouches** have their individual atmospheres, with some of the most extravagant decors in the world. Almost all of these discos were conceived by well-known po signers, and their interiors include laser lights, fog machines, mirrors, pinball achines, and ultraviolet lamps.

The **Mudd Club** has only recently come out into the open, being a place that preously catered exclusively to a small, elite following. Many of the decorating emes you'll see at the Ritz were first used here. Uptown, the **Lorelei** used to be an d German beer joint, but now books underground rock bands.

For roller disco, try **Empire Roller Disco** or the **Village Disco Roller Rink;** you n rent skates if you haven't brought them with you.

p-to-Date Information

To find out what is going on where, check the local newspapers and the agazines that list such events. These include the *Village Voice* for items in their AFÉS, CLUBS AND COFFEEHOUSES section, or *New York* magazine or the *New Yorker* r details on the established clubs and cabarets. Fans of salsa music, reggae, and ack soul should check magazines like *Latin, N.Y., Carribeat,* and the *Amsterdam ews,* respectively. (Note that these clubs change their location and names very ften.) In addition, information on rock concerts is usually given on many of New ork's rock music radio stations; WNEW-FM (102.7) is known as the most proessive and WBLS (108) is all-black.

Special Interests

Sports and Recreation

Depending upon when you come to New York, you have a choice of catching some pretty exciting action. The New York Knicks play basketball at **Madison Square Garden,** while there is baseball (New York Mets and Yankees, respectively) at **Shea Stadium** and **Yankee Stadium.** Football action from the New York Giants and the New York Jets can also be seen either at **Giant Stadium** in New Jersey or at Shea Stadium in Queens. The New York Rangers play some tough ice hockey at Madison Square Garden, and boxing is steady at the **Felt Forum,** also a part of Madison Square Garden. Tennis, including the U.S. Open, is at the **USTA National Tennis Center** in Flushing, Queens. Lastly, there is horseracing at **Aqueduct** in Queens, at **Belmont Park** and **Roosevelt Raceway** in nearby Nassau County, and at **Yonkers** (Westchester) and the **Meadowlands** in New Jersey.

If you prefer participating, then you'll quickly feel at home in New York. Central Park, Riverside Park, and along the East River are chief **running** spots. You can rent a **bicycle** or a pair of **roller skates** for an excursion in Central Park, or rent a rowboat and really enjoy this lovely and peaceful spot away from the city's noise and congestion. In winter, many people like to rent skates and get out on the ice, either at the Rockefeller Center pond or at Wollman Rink in Central Park. **Horseback riding** is likewise a possibility, again in Central Park. And **tennis** enthusiasts will find a number of public courts and private clubs that will allow visitors to use the facilities.

If you have gotten a stiff neck from staring at the tops of too many tall buildings, you can work out the kinks at the **Kounovsky Physical Fitness Center,** with exercise and a sauna for $7.50 an hour. You can also go to one of the many health spas (check the yellow pages of the telephone book) and perhaps even find a swimming pool there. You can definitely swim at one of the **YMCA**'s branches (again, these are listed in the telephone book yellow pages).

Sightseeing with Children

Those who come to New York with children may soon find that their sightseeing expectations do not match those of their offspring. However, there are excursions that will be fun for both you and your youngsters.

One of the nicest and least expensive is a ride on the **Staten Island Ferry.** And a visit to the **Statue of Liberty** generally arouses great enthusiasm too. First, it in-

157

Central Park is fun for kids

volves a ride on a ferry and, second, the idea of climbing the copper lady to the crown stimulates the imagination of most children tremendously. Lastly, in the way of rides, there is the **Roosevelt Island Tramway** that takes you across the East River alongside the Queensborough Bridge.

During a bicycle ride through **Central Park,** you and your son or daughter could visit the Hans Christian Andersen statue or the one of Alice in Wonderland. There is also a merry-go-round in the park. And the **Children's Zoo** offers the opportunity to tickle the belly of a mammoth papier-mache whale or play on a pirate ship. Elephants, polar bears, and penguins are right nearby.

More peaceful, but also farther away, is the **Staten Island Zoo** in Barrett Park, which is especially known for its reptiles and has a nice children's zoo with sheep, chickens, pigs, and other animals. But the king of zoos is the largest one in the United States — the **Bronx Zoo** — offering everything from camel rides to feeding the pelicans, to cable-car trips to a children's zoo.

Let us stick to animals, but now to the stuffed kind in the **American Museum of Natural History.** This museum is both gigantic and exciting, and you and your children will feel as if you have been transported to another world, in the thirty-six dioramas depicting life in a variety of habitats. And don't forget to see the **Hayden Planetarium** nearby, which with its Zeiss projector in the domelike vault is bound to be a hit with any stargazer.

Those for whom a visit to the giant blue whale in the museum is not enough have to go to Coney Island to the **Aquarium.** And in Brooklyn is the biggest hit among children, the **Brooklyn Children's Museum.** This modern building, mostly underground, smoothly integrates an old-fashioned kiosk into its structure as the entrance and a corn silo as a fire exit. It is full of surprises; there is a stream of water — covered by a vault of steel, corrugated iron, and colored neon tubes — which flows behind a long walkway and which children can manipulate by dams and waterwheels. But the most obvious and greatest attraction of all is the climbing labyrinth of transparent, three-dimensional shapes that connect the different levels of the museum. There are also a greenhouse, musical instruments from all over the world, and dolls from all ages and cultures.

A children's museum opened recently in Manhattan too: the **Manhattan Laboratory Museum.** Much smaller in scope, nevertheless this museum describes various biological, anthropological, and optic facts to young people and is worth a visit.

Also amusing for children as well as adults is a visit to the **Burlington Mill** or the **Museum of Holography.** Three-dimensional photography, which is not photography in the traditional sense and which changes with the viewing angle, can fascinate and keep children busy. There is another diversion to be found on weekends by taking the **Nostalgia Special** to the **New York City Transit Exhibition.** Or a visit to the **New York Experience,** a multisensory show in the McGraw-Hill Building, can be exciting.

There are several children's theaters offering concerts, plays, and puppet shows. Check out the **Henry Street Settlement House,** the **Courtyard Playhouse, Big Apple Circus,** and the **Town Hall Theater for Children.** In addition, puppet shows are given at **F.A.O. Schwarz,** at the **Barnes & Noble Sales Annex,** and at the **Museum of the City of New York.** The **New York Public Library** has story hours at the Donnell Branch on 53rd Street. There are even children's discos.

If you are in New York during Christmastime, you have to see the large tree in Rockefeller Center, as well as the one at the Metropolitan Museum. And in any case you should not miss a performance by the New York City Ballet of Tchaikovsky's *Nutcracker Suite.*

There are babysitting services (see DAYCARE) available as well, but be certain to interview a prospective sitter or visit the daycare center first.

New Yorkers frequently consult one of the guidebooks to children's events in the city. If your stay will be a long one, we suggest obtaining a copy of the *New York Times Guide to Children's Entertainment in New York, New Jersey, and Connecticut.* In addition, the New York Convention and Visitor's Bureau publishes a quarterly calendar of events with features for children and the *New York Times* also lists events for children.

Women's Interests

Although the women's movement has a strong following in New York, the interests of its followers are so diverse that you will have difficulty identifying any strong networks, such as exist in many other cities. New York has two women's book-

Left: A ride on the Staten Island Fe
Above and below: Park scenes

tores — **Womanbooks** (located uptown) and **Djuna Books** (in Greenwich Village). It is at these two stores that you will find the largest selection of woman-oriented reading materials, as well as records, postcards, buttons, and the like. These stores also have a number of postings describing the current concerts, poetry readings, discussion groups, and other events taking place.

Some women's events are open only to women, and often daycare is provided for children. Concerts tend to be very popular, especially when a well-known singer such as Holly Near or Meg Christian is performing. Readings also are usually well attended. For additional information, consult *Ms.* magazine or call the National Organization for Women (NOW). Information on the art scene by and for women can be more or less reliably obtained at the **Women's Interart Center.** There are several women's galleries; for example, **Womanart** and **A.I.R. Women Make Movies,** a film distributor, is in Chelsea. For additional information of concern to women, check the women's guidebook, the *New York Woman's Directory,* which covers everything from abortion to consciousness raising to women-centered medical help.

Women executives are increasing throughout the country and in New York as well you will find women in high-paying, executive-level positions. There are many women-owned businesses, including the First Woman's Bank on the corner of Park Avenue and 57th Street. There are women chefs at many of the leading restaurants, and many of the shops in the city are owned by women. The **Allerton House for Women** and the **Barbizon for Women** are two hotels that offer secure and comfortable lodgings in the city.

Many women traveling alone are still afraid to go out for the evening meal. They feel that not only will they be forced to sit at an uncomfortable corner table and be served inattentively, but also that the men there will stare and talk about them. To quickly remise that, New York is no small town; nobody whispers when you identify yourself as single or alone. A woman is considered a good customer and given service equal to that of any other customer. Single diners are so common a sight in this business-oriented city, that the sex is hardly of concern.

As for dress in the city, daytime usually is casual or businesslike depending upon the nature of your visit. In the evening, it again depends on which restaurant you pick for your meal.

The Singles Scene

Those who want to really be "in" have successfully hustled their way through the established disco scene and now swear by the roller discos. This roller disco wave is a good example of a typical New York fashion phenomenon, and if you are curious you might take a look at one.

You will find the average singles bars along First and Second avenues in the sixties, seventies, and eighties, where bars and pubs and discotheques live cheek by jowl. Inside them, you will find just about every kind of decor imaginable: slightly moth-eaten Victorian, black-lacquer–and–mirrored elegance, half-heartedly revitalized dance hall mustiness, designer-look shacks, and every so often something that is really stylish. And the different decors will attract different customers. Some of these places are clubs, but by forking out a generous admission fee, you are likely to be let in even if you are not a member.

Those who prefer a quieter bar atmosphere and feel that contact is more easily established there might try **Friday's** or the perennially popular **Maxwell's Plum. Elaine's,** famous not just since Jackie Onassis broke bread there with bodybuilder Arnold Schwarzenegger, is very much "in" but not necessarily that much fun. The most popular downtown disco is the **Mudd Club,** but even there you may have to stand in line.

In a city such as New York the singles scene may play an even greater role than in some other places. Friendships are often hard to come by and meeting the right people with whom you are comfortable can be very difficult. This restless search for partners dominates the atmosphere in many singles bars and discos and has even persuaded a number of them to relegate singles to the bar and to allow only couples in their dining rooms and on their dance floors.

In addition to the bars, good pick-up places in New York are said to be museums and galleries when there are openings. Another good place is the lines that form in front of theater and concert hall box offices, where the common interest is an easy start for a conversation. Those who are not out to pick up or be picked up and who just want to be entertained should stick around Columbia University. **Marvin Gardens,** the **West End Café,** or the **Library** are cozy, easy-going, and unpretentious. A favorite student hang-out is the **Green Tree Hungarian Restaurant** on Amsterdam Avenue.

For Barflies

For some visitors, the best way to get to know the people who live in a city is through its bars and pubs. For the sports-conscious, **Gallagher's** and **Mike Manuche's** are two circular bars, around which gather the top players and journalists, as well as fans. It is a chance to enjoy some well-prepared drinks while mingling with others who gladly share opinions and stories.

Most people who come to New York have heard of the **21 Club,** and it is no secret that big deals take place here, whether they be concerned with publishing, television, or motion pictures. **Rose,** another decent watering hole, is easy-going and usually a hit with tired businessmen. But if you are seeking the famous, then **Sardi's** is the spot for theater people, **Costello's** is good for literary figures, and **Elaine's** famous for socialites. A nice pub-style spot is **P.J. Clarke's,** although it is almost always so crowded with singles. There is a duplicate of this famous bar in Macy's Cellar, but it just isn't the same.

The leading hotels have good bars as well, and the top ones seem to be that in the **Algonquin,** the **Oak Bar** in the Plaza, or **Bemelman's** in the Carlyle. Restaurants often also have bars that become local gathering spots. For these you'll have to follow your sense, although **Maxwell's Plum** is by far the most outstanding. Ask any New Yorker about a favorite bar and you'll get some enthusiastic advice.

The Gay Scene

Except for San Francisco, there is probably no other city in the United States with such a visible gay population. New York is one of the places gays come to find relief from oppression and to discover friends with whom they can share an important interest. Greenwich Village by far has the greatest concentration of gay bars, restaurants, and gathering places, but there are some popular spots located uptown as well. The gay scene in New York is not exclusively bars, although for many this form of social interaction remains a very important part. The **Oscar Wilde Memorial Bookshop** is a good place to start, since it is here that both men and women can find journals, newspapers, and postings of current events. Here you can also pick up a copy of the *Gayellow Pages,* a listing of goods and services for the gay community. You can also call the **National Gay Task Force** or the **Lesbian** or **Gay Switchboards** for additional information.

There are many more men's bars than women's, but the bars in New York are rarely mixed. Men's bars differ quite a bit, ranging from the very quiet to those for leather, to the sex bars. A typical Village spot is **Ty's,** a western spot. On the Upper East Side is **Chap's,** while on the Upper West Side, **Wildwood** is popular.

Women's bars tend to be less colorful. The atmosphere is friendly and out-of-towners usually receive a warm welcome. In the Village, the **Duchess** caters to a young crowd, while **Paula's** and the **Club** have older customers. Uptown, on the East Side, is **Peeches,** where the clientele is well-dressed business women. An alternative to the bars, the **Gay Women's Alternative** meets Thursday evenings at the Universalist Church at 76th Street and Central Park West.

Many restaurants in the Village cater primarily to gay customers, although the doors are open to anyone who walks in. **Bonnie's,** however, with its shabby façade, protects itself from unwanted patrons. Downstairs is a rugged bar, but one flight up is a lovely wood-paneled dining room. Only insiders find their way here and hardly ever does anyone come walking in by chance.

The New York gay community is exactly that — a community. They band together for the annual Christopher Street Parade, marking the time when gays began to protest the raids of bars that police used to hold. By and large, gays in New York are the pace-setters. They were dancing in discos long before such entertainment appeared for straights. Their fashions are picked up by the city's designers. And their decorating tastes and shopping fads are copied for huge success by others. Many gay men and women are open about their being gay, for this is a city that accepts and appreciates this aspect of human existence.

Shopping

From the exclusive shops like Cartier and Gucci, Tiffany and Ted Lapidus, Yves St. Laurent and Harry Winston; to the Caviarteria, which offers twelve different types of caviar; to a specialty store for trimmings and feathers, there is nothing that New York does not have. After all, this city is famous for that.

Sales and Bargains

There is always some sale going on in New York. On the Labor or Memorial Day holidays, and on Washington's or Lincoln's birthdays, the prices at the department stores slip to the cellar. And if there are no specials in the large department stores, then just travel to the Lower East Side or to Loehmann's in the Bronx, where there are permanent sales and where you get quality wares at reduced prices. The hunt for the chance bargain is more of a sport than an economy measure. *New York* magazine runs a special feature on "Best Bets" in each issue, and tips are also spread in offices, in restaurants, and on the streets.

Orchard Street is an address that has emotional meaning to fashion-conscious New York women. A surging, motley crowd surveys the cooking pots, jeans, books, and costume jewelry that flood the sidewalk. Honking horns and blaring music bombard people with children on their shoulders, backs, or stomachs, as they visit one shabby store after another. But behind the dull façades and poorly decorated shop windows, there are designs by Cacharel, Furstenberg, Hechter, and Halston that sell for up to 40 percent off the price usually charged by department stores. This almost totally Jewish street really hums on Sundays. Because of the large crowds, some stores have liberated themselves from the sabbatical laws and open their doors on Saturdays too.

You'll have to stand in line forty or fifty minutes to get into stores renowned for their choices and prices: **Altman** and **Friedlich** for suits, blouses, dresses; **Lace-Up Shoe Shop** for women's shoes; **Sam Popper Inc.** for men's sportswear; and **Bernard Krieger & Son** for hats, caps, and the like. However, don't expect to always make the find of your life here. Word gets around fast about newly arrived shipments and they are sold out in a jiffy.

When the door is finally opened to the promising shopper's paradise, your first impression may be a great letdown. The store is a backyard, a tubelike salesroom the size of a subway car, into which you must worm your way. The supply may be large, but the rush is still larger. Suits are hung so high and dresses so close, and the grabbing arms are so numerous, that only experienced customers can choose cooly

Tiffany's, on Fifth Avenue at 57th Street

and prudently. There are no dressing rooms. Looking, trying on, and buying all are done in the same spot. The novice is held spellbound in this chaos by the panic of shrieking and pushing customers, grumpy saleswomen, and masses of clothing. Your own blouse turns up carefully folded on the shelf, and the one you just tried on is already being buttoned up by the next woman. You leave the store with a whirling head and with empty hands or an empty purse. Credit, and that means having your check accepted, is only for those deemed worthy. Every sale is final; returns or exchanges are not permitted.

New York career women who dress stylishly but conservatively find themselves next to settled-in middle-aged mothers and aged grandmothers looking for jersey pantsuits, feather boas, and little black numbers at **Loehmann's,** one of America's most famous discount department stores. The firm has stores in all parts of New York except Manhattan; it is a store rich in tradition.

In 1921, Frieda Loehmann started out in a former automobile showroom in Brooklyn. She fitted it out with golden lusters, marble lion's heads, gilded angels, and black columns à la chinoise; and she stuffed it full of dresses, often remainders of the season, that she obtained for little money and resold cheaply. Frieda Loehmann became a legend and her store without dressing rooms became an attraction. She had an infallible instinct for style and publicity. She made her scouting trips on New York's Fashion Avenue in a hearse, polished as bright as a mirror, in which she transported her cheaply obtained goods, neatly piled, to Brooklyn. After Frieda's

168

Inside Tiffany's, where counters reveal some of the world's most famous jewelry

death in 1962, the plush temple was closed. Today the Loehmann stores resemble cheap department stores; the floors are covered with durable linoleum and the walls are painted with a plain, practical green. There are always at least twenty customers in the large dressing room where, under the supervision of a saleswoman, they undress, button up, and advise one another. A babble of English, Spanish, and Yiddish voices fills the room. If the purchase has to be something really fine, you go into the expensive back room, separated from the rest of the salesroom by a wine-red velvet curtain.

Department Stores

Whoever wants to see a caricature of real New York elegance goes to **Bloomingdale's,** New York's most famous department store. Here you'll find everything from the bargains in the basement to the Sonie Rykiel boutique on the third floor; from the gourmet food section to the continental men's styles, all the way to an Italian bedroom. When England's Queen Elizabeth II visited New York during the Bicentennial, Bloomingdale's was one of her only two stops. And during Christmastime, you can see in the model rooms how well-known actors, designers, or writers have furnished, are furnishing, or would like to furnish their rooms.

Those who wish to glimpse a portrait of the stylish should position themselves in front of Bloomingdale's on Saturday morning. Women in jeans or *haute couture*

St. Laurent Rive Gauche, Madison Avenue at 70th Street

enter and leave the same door, as do others with grayish blue tinted hair in tailored suits and silk blouses. The calorie conscious generally eat cottage cheese with fruit in Bloomingdale's 40 Carrots, while others visit the new Le Train Bleu, Bloomingdale's version of an old European dining car. Now Bloomingdale's has practically tailored their entire store to show the new goods from China. These items, ranging from housewares to clothing, were Asian-inspired American designs that the store commissioned to be manufactured in China and then sold here.

Perhaps the most expensive department store is **Saks Fifth Avenue,** which has a more homogeneous, more established, and — on the average — older clientele than Bloomies (as New Yorkers refer to it). Another landmark is **Lord & Taylor,** known for its elegantly tailored sportswear.

Anyone furnishing or redecorating a home and who needs sheets and bath towels has to include in his or her trip the sixth floor of **Macy's,** the world's largest department store. Hand and bath towels in all colors and patterns, permanent press sheets and pillow cases in indeterminable amounts and designs, can be bought here, especially during a white sale. Macy's is very close to the Empire State Building; a tourist here once almost missed his tour of the skyscraper because he got so caught up in the sheets and towels.

Macy's has five other floors, plus an enormous basement featuring food and food-related items. The selection of fabrics is also quite good, as are the many counters on the ground floor selling cosmetics and perfumes.

Boutiques and Specialty Stores

Whether you like to purchase or just window shop, a stroll along Lexington or Madison avenues and down the streets between 57th and 79th are in both cases a must. This is where the elegant and trendy boutiques are centered. By the way, many shops have — for security reasons — locked their doors and open them only when you ring a bell. The more you conform to the Madison Avenue look, the faster the entry is accorded.

Hundreds of boutiques and shops here offer practically everything from the bread-dough brooch from Ecuador, to the nineteenth-century English dollhouse (**Mini Mundus**), Italian suits and French ties (**DeNoyer, Inc.**), Mexican lace blouses and embroidered dresses (**Fred Leighton**) through coats of the finest leather (**Antarex**), stylish maternity wear (**Lady Madonna**) and unusual designs (**Rubicon Boutique**), to prepared butterflies and rare shells (**Collector's Cabinet**).

A walk on 57th Street is also recommended. Shops are there like **Ann Taylor** and **Henri Bendel's,** one of New York's most elegant but not always most expensive stores. China and glass lovers can find **Baccarat** and **Steuben** here. Also located along this street are **Tiffany, Buccellati, Ginori, Bulgari, Ferragamo, Salvatore** and — not too far away — **Eve's Garden,** a "sexual boutique created by women for women." **Honey Bee,** one of the few good-value boutiques in this area, is near the Museum of Modern Art.

To support New York's reputation that there is nothing this city does not have, a few more quick examples are in order: cat lovers can find little presents for their darlings in the **Cat Cottage,** and you can get natural creams, healing oils, salves, and soaps in one of the city's oldest drugstores, **Kiehl Pharmacy.** Scrapped army and navy surplus — parkas, camouflage shirts, raincoats, or pea jackets — can be bought at **Kaufman Surplus** or **Richard's Authentics.** Rare silk jackets with emblems embroidered on the back are at **Bogie's Antique Furs and Clothing.** Lefthanders buy their scissors and kitchen utensils at the **Left Hand,** and whoever is still enthusiastic about Mickey Mouse can find Disney memorabilia at **Old Friends.**

The war historian discovers a military history bookstore at the **Military Bookman,** and the criminal fan is in good hands for the entire afternoon at **Murder Ink®**, a bookstore specializing in detective fiction. The occultist goes to the **Warlock Shop** to buy books on ceremonial magic or Eastern religions, or to look over the huge selection of tarot cards. And the magician can find complete boxes of tricks at **Louis Tannen, Inc.**

Elegant Rizzoli Bookstore on Fifth Avenue

For a Good Cause

It is often worthwhile to make a detour to Third Avenue and shop for good values in one of the city's many thrift shops. These stores are a good source of clothing, old family silver, and discarded frying pans. Often they are a gold mine for second-hand books, for knick-knacks, or even for accessories that have become fashionable again. The profits go to the responsible charitable organization, whether it be for cancer research, assistance to the poor, or help for those with blood diseases.

Museum gift shops lately have come into their own, offering a wide array of items. Excellent reproductions of antiques (including jewelry, glass, silver, vases, and candlesticks) are sold by the **Metropolitan Museum of Art,** whose new three-story shop offers the biggest selection in town. The **Museum of Modern Art** shop is good for amusing toys, designed by famous artists, as well as puzzles, plexiglass building blocks, and piggy banks. The **American Museum of Natural History** has an extensive collection of nature books, plus a good showcase of reproductions from all cultures. Other museums offer the museum-goer and shopper postcards and books, as well as other small trinkets.

Bargain-hunting is a New York pastime

Downtown Shopping

Most but not all of the stores mentioned so far are located midtown. For the more unconventional and often more original (but also sometimes more trashy), go to the southern end of Manhattan. In Greenwich Village, the area is teeming with boutiques, antique and junk shops, second-hand stores, and modern jewelry shops. You can buy curios of all sorts at **Patina Antiques,** while good modern jewelry is sold at **Gallery 10. Second Childhood** is a charming toy store with miniatures and antique tin soldiers from the nineteenth century. Unfortunately, along 8th Street, between Fifth and Sixth avenues, the shops have become heavily commercialized and the entire block is a bit seedy.

Before Canal Street reaches Chinatown and its telephone booths become richly decorated pagodas, the section is a mecca for New York's hobby tinkerers, who go there to get electric saws, wrenches, used drive belts, car batteries, and the like. Yet tourists will find a Sunday morning stroll here amusing too. The atmosphere has nothing of the accentuated Madison Avenue elegance or the bustling Village casualness. This is where the bargain hunters come to rummage and deal. A gold mine for

F.A.O. Schwarz, famous toy shop

old clothes, books, records, or funny chit-chat is the **SoHo Canal Flea Market.** Good and cheap jeans, purses, or shirts are sold at **Canal Jeans.**

Take-Home Trinkets

Inexpensive and cheerful small presents can often be found at **Azuma,** with seven locations. Games, gags, posters, embroidered Chinese slippers, straw handbags, and baskets, as well as African statues, Mao jackets, bamboo birdcages, and cotton cloth in all patterns are offered here.

Whoever wants practical gadgets designed for leisure should go to **Hammacher –Schlemmer.** There they have items that are uniquely intended to solve a special problem. There are plastic thermal glasses that keep your drink cold for hours, electric porcelain tureens that keep your soup warm, battery-operated eyebrow pluckers,

St. Patrick's Cathedral steps are resting place for weary shoppers

and ballpoint pens with built-in electric lights.

The gadgets at **Tiffany's** cost a pretty penny: a silver baby rattle, a gold tooth-pick, a champagne twirler, or a silver ice pick are among the modest gifts under $100. The windows at Christmastime are striking.

For those interested in more expensive presents, there is the Elsa Peretti bra. You can get it for $4,000 and — the saleswoman assured us — it is definitely comfortable to wear. Another hit for New York's Christmas business a few years ago was Petropolis, an oil-industry version of Monopoly. Supplied with electronic calculators, the players buy oil-producing lands and search for sources of oil in their gilded supertankers and jets. The price of the game, which was all the rage at the time was $790. Jordan's King Hussein ordered twenty right away. And for those with "particular taste," **Van Cleef & Arpels** came out with the game in solid gold — for only $20,000.

Parks and Zoos

Vest-Pocket Parks

A good place to recover from an overdose of skyscrapers is one of the many small oases dotted about the city, which often have waterfalls or fountains but always have trees or shrubs. They are what grateful New Yorkers like to call vest-pocket parks. **Paley Park,** on 53rd Street between Fifth and Madison avenues, has a whole wall of waterfalls. You can sit under trees and even buy a sandwich, a Coca Cola, or an ice cream from a vending cart.

Greenacre Park, on 51st Street between Third and Second avenues, has water-falls thirty feet high, which cascade around very pretty seats arranged on three levels. **Exxon Park,** behind the Exxon Building on Sixth Avenue between 49th and 50th streets, has a waterfall that is twenty-one feet high and fifty-five feet wide (the pump manages something like 2,500 gallons of water a minute). In the summer at lunchtime there are sometimes small entertainments like concerts.

The **Seagram Building,** on Park Avenue between 52nd and 53rd streets, is New York's most beautiful skyscraper. At its feet are fountains in large pools, trees, and green marble seats — a generous gesture considering the narrow site it is built on. The **Burlington Mill Park,** behind the Mill's building on Sixth Avenue between 54th and 55th streets, is a small park with bits of greenery and benches.

The garden of the **Museum of Modern Art** offers you, for the price of admission, the opportunity to sit in the company of Picasso's lively bits-and-pieces goat or Rodin's *Balzac*; a pleasant interlude after too much sightseeing and street noise. In the summer, admission to the museum is free on some evenings, and young dancers, musicians, or mimes provide entertainment. Bring a cushion if you can, because there are never enough chairs.

Channel Gardens, at Rockefeller Center, are called that because they run be-tween the British Building and La Maison Française. The wide stone edges of the flower beds — filled with different and imaginative mixtures of plants according to the season — are good places for a rest. The small fountains provide a welcome change from the traffic and noise on Fifth Avenue. On some afternoons during the week there is entertainment of various kinds. And at the bottom, in front of Paul Manship's golden *Prometheus*, there is an open-air café in summer and an ice skating rink in winter.

The **Ford Foundation,** on east 42nd Street between First and Second avenues, has a building with offices in the shape of an L, surrounded by a ten-story atrium

Sailing a toy boat in idyllic Central Park

planted with tropical trees and shrubs around a small pond. **Tudor City,** from 40th to 43rd streets between First and Second avenues, has a park that belongs to this little Tudor-style enclave. It is popular with the people from the United Nations across the street. **Beekman Place,** between 50th and 52nd streets, between First Avenue and Beekman Place, is a neighborhood of very pretty, very well kept houses. The little park at the end of 51st Street gets its breeze from the East River.

Central Park — New York's Green Lung

New York's desert of stone can breathe because an 865-acre green rectangle in the heart of Manhattan produces "fresh air" — as fresh as possible in so polluted a city. **Central Park** is a place to take a break; it is a recreation ground, an athletic field, a picnic ground, an outdoor stage, a lover's lane, or a promenade for millions of New Yorkers who consider it their front yard, their stomping ground. With twenty-seven playgrounds it is a paradise for children. With a lake for rowing, rocks for climbing, athletic fields, bridle paths, and bicycle paths it is the dream of every fitness disciple, even though its dreamlike nature of course only too often is hidden under old beer cans, newspapers, crumpled cigarette packs, yogurt cups, plastic containers, sandwich remnants, and Coca-Cola bottles. Still, a tour on a rented bicycle or a boat trip on the lake (bicycles and boats can be rented at the 72nd-Street Boat

The Model Boat Pond

house), a walk, or a ride in one of the horse-drawn carriages (for hire at the Plaza Hotel, 59th Street and Fifth Avenue) through Central Park is a delight especially in spring. There is no auto traffic on the Park Drive from sunrise to sunset. Carrying picnic baskets, radios, and children, everybody crowds into the park from all sides. Magnificent magnolia trees draw your gaze upward and do not allow you to notice the dirt; something which in the late summer becomes a dusty gray is in spring a fresh green lawn. After a long, cold New York winter, people are grateful for every blooming cherry tree branch, every narcissus, every green bush in bud.

At Eastertime, the flowered hats for the next fashion season are shown here; black and Puerto Rican youth dance around Bethesda Fountain, listening to countless transistor radios; the heavy, sweetish odor of marijuana is in the air. But even on such a day you can still find an unoccupied rock, you can get away from the crowd at the Fountain or on the Mall, and you can have your own picnic without any blaring radios.

At the end of the nineteenth century, Central Park was as "in" as some discos are today. People would strut along the paths, magnificent coaches were driven on the well-maintained gravel roads, romantic evenings were experienced in red- and green-lit gondolas, and some people would bathe in the mineral waters of the Mineral Springs Pavilion. The park serves a different purpose today.

In 1858, Frederick Law Olmsted and the Englishman Calvert Vaux submitted a plan which was approved by the city and which called for a public park that would

Cathedral Parkway — W.110.St.

Block

Harlem Lake

W.106.St. — E.106.St.

Garden

The Pool

The Loch

W.100.St.

West

W.96.St. — E.96.St.

South Meadow Tennis Courts

Reservoir

Central

Park

Fifth

W.86.St. — E.86.St.

The Great Lawn

Obelisk

Belvedere Castle

Metropolitan Museum of Art

Shakespeare Garden

New Lake

E.79.St.

Alice in Wonderland Statue

Hans Christian Andersen Statue

The Lake

West

Conservatory Pond

W.72.St. — E.72.St.

Bowling on the Green

The Mall

Park

The Sheep Meadow

Fifth Avenue

Central

Wollman Rink

Childrens Zoo

The Pond

E.60.St.

Central Park South

181

Central Park Zoo

be welcomed, admired, and visited by both the "ordinary folk" and the "elite." In the tradition of English garden architecture, the plan stressed the retention of the natural terrain; the park was to become a work of art but not an artificial park.

For about $5 million, the city bought the land; drove out the squatters, bums, counterfeiters, and other crooks; and got rid of entire herds of sheep, chickens, and hogs. The first of 100,000 trees was planted symbolically in 1858, before Olmsted and Vaux — along with no less than 3,000 workers — got down to business. In 1965, Central Park and its buildings were declared a nature preserve and landmark.

Today the park is not only the center for those hungering for fresh air, but it also is the home of the Central Park Zoo, skating rinks, tennis courts, and athletic fields. Here also you have the Friedsam Memorial Carousel and the Alice in Wonderland and Hans Christian Andersen statues. There are five miles of bridle paths and many miles of bicycling routes. Belvedere Castle is an imitation medieval castle, while Cleopatra's Needle is a pink granite Egyptian obelisk over 3,000 years old.

In the summer, Central Park is still a place to go in the evening when there are performances by the Metropolitan Opera or the New York Philharmonic. Pop and rock music can be heard in the Wollman Memorial Rink (reached from 59th Street and Fifth Avenue), and classical quintets play on the Mall. Bands, mimes, belly-dancers, or magicians can always be found somewhere in the park on weekends.

When there are no shows or events underway, walking in darkness through the park should be absolutely taboo; but during the day, you are protected by police and volunteers on horseback, bicycles, or foot. Be careful not to fall for false propaganda that brands the park as dangerous terrain even in daytime. A frightened Japanese couple at one time in broad daylight asked whether they could walk to the Guggenheim Museum because after all it was supposed to be right at Central Park. At such moments a New Yorker realizes again and again how difficult it is to give tourists the mixture of caution and adventure which would be correct for New York. It is a mixture without which they cannot grasp the stimulating many-sidedness of this city, and without which they could hardly become familiar with its charms.

184

Other Parks

Central Park is not the only park in Manhattan. There are **Battery Park,** at the southern tip of the island; **Bowling Green,** at the bottom of Broadway; **Bryant Park,** adjacent to the New York Public Library at 42nd Street; **Carl Schurz Park,** alongside Gracie Mansion; **Gramercy Park,** which is private; **Riverside Park,** which runs along the Hudson River from 72nd to 159th streets; **Union Square,** at the crossroads of 14th Street and Broadway; and **Washington Square Park,** at the foot of Fifth Avenue. In addition, there are more uptown, including **Fort Tryon Park, Highbridge Park, Inwood Hill Park, Morningside Park,** and more. And there are also the parks in the other boroughs as well. For all its glass and concrete, New York is also a rather green city. All told, there are about 38,000 acres of parks in New York City. Some parks remain quiet retreats from the pressures of the urban scene, but others are spots for entertainment. For information on what is going on in any of the parks, call 472-1003 or 755-4100.

Gardens

By far well worth a visit, especially if you are also going to the Bronx Zoo, would be a visit to the **New York Botanical Garden.** The Conservatory was recently restored and is a crystal palace of exotic plants. The grounds are also lovely, with an extensive rose garden, a magnolia dell, and other specialties.

Brooklyn also has an excellent **botanical garden,** with a very large variety of trees and shrubs, including Japanese Cherry trees and bonsai. The **Queens Botanical Garden** is smaller and since all the exhibits are outside, the museum is seasonal.

Zoos

We've already described some zoos in the section on sightseeing with children (pages 157-159). But for adults and children alike, the **Bronx Zoo** is a winner, with the **Central Park Zoo, Prospect Park Zoo,** and the **Staten Island Zoological Park** also worth seeing. The **Queens Zoo** and **Children's Farm** are smaller in scope and fun, but not worth a separate trip.

Other Spots of Green

Even many New Yorkers think that the only wildlife there is consists of pigeons and muggers. However this city is alive with many species of birds and plantlife. To get a glimpse of this world, visit **Jamaica Bay Wildlife Refuge.** It is best for bird-watching, since it is a stopover for migrating land and water birds as they pass along the Atlantic Flyway. **High Rock Park Conservation Center** on Staten Island and **Pell Wildlife Refuge** in the Bronx are two other solid birding spots.

The **Davis Wildlife Refuge** in Staten Island and the **Hunter Island Marine Zoology and Geology Sanctuary** are two popular sites for hiking and picnicking. New York is rich in geological history, and another spot to see evidence of glacial action is the **Staten Island Greenbelt,** a circular trail about fourteen miles long.

Brooklyn Bridge and the East River, set against the New York Skyline

George Washington Bridge

Ramp to the Verrazano-Narrows Bridge   Brooklyn Bridge

Three bridges to lower Manhattan: Brooklyn, Manhattan, Williamsburg

Spotlight on the City

Every tourist coming to New York has heard about the various districts where special kinds of business take place. There is the theater district, the Wall Street area, Madison Avenue's advertising section, Rockefeller Center, the garment district, and so on. You'll encounter these areas on the walking tours or in the course of following up other suggestions in this book. We especially recommend that you take the Heritage Trail walking tour, since that excursion takes you through the cavernous streets of lower Manhattan, to where the stock exchanges are, and where the leading banks have their corporate headquarters, to the City Hall area where the affairs of the city are settled.

New York is also a conglomeration of residential neighborhoods, with some names that will be familiar to any out-of-towner: Greenwich Village, Little Italy, Chinatown, Harlem, and so on. Other sections have achieved more fame only recently, like SoHo or Tribeca, because these have only started becoming residential. The neighborhoods of New York are especially colorful, with shops and restaurants that reflect the ethnic backgrounds of their residents.

In this chapter, we highlight for you some areas that have received less attention elsewhere. We put the spotlight on two business districts and three residential areas.

The Garment District: Dress Carts and Yard Goods

First New York replaced London as the swinging city, and now it is well on its way to dethrone Paris as the fashion metropolis. That at least is the feeling of some enthusiastic observers of the New York fashion scene. The comparison, however, is not quite correct: Americans reject the principle of *haute couture,* which predominates in Europe, and prefer the phrase ''ready to wear.'' The attitude toward fashion, it seems, is different here. Grace Mirabella, editor-in-chief of *Vogue,* emphasized that American fashions are ''practical, individual, sexy and at the same time quite normal.'' The important thing is not to slip into a prestige wardrobe but rather to dress so that one's personal touch is preserved.

Of course there are fashion authorities here too, including Oscar de la Renta, Halston, Ralph Lauren, Geoffrey Beene, Calvin Klein, Scott Barrie, or Mary McFadden. Anybody who wants to touch, admire, try on, or perhaps even buy their products will find them in the big department stores. But if you want to see where these desirable garments of tulle, chiffon, and silk — or perhaps also where Macy's dresses from the rack — are being made, go not to an elegant street with exclusive fashion studios but rather to the noisy, colorful, shabby, bustling, and witty

Garment District (Seventh Avenue and Broadway between 35th and 41st streets). On Seventh Avenue, here renamed Fashion Avenue, you can see large carts with bolts of material and huge, oversized clothing racks with expensive items enveloped in plastic; or you'll spot simple factory-made merchandise being rolled, pushed, and guided across the streets. Behind a shabby façade is where Diana von Furstenberg, a former jet-set princess who now holds a top position in the American fashion industry, designs her smooth-fitting jersey dresses. This is also where Ralph Lauren dictates his casual Western line for the next season.

The garment industry, formerly the preserve of Jewish immigrants who often moved from sweatshop to sweatshop with their sewing machines on their backs, today is among the most important production centers in New York. About a quarter of a million people are employed here. Huge trucks squeeze through the narrow, dark streets; drivers and handymen whistle at the seamstresses and showroom mannequins who populate the sidewalks during the lunch break.

Walk around a little bit in the district, and look, smell, and listen; in short, come not just to observe but to sharpen your sensory organs. Observe a bit of the hard-working hustle and bustle that takes place here. For fashion-conscious but economical women looking for accessories, this part of town is pure joy. The selection of straw, fabric, felt, and leather hats; of flowers and ribbons; of velvet cloth; of glittering, arabesque or Art Nouveau braiding; of little pearls for embroidering or wooden balls for threading; of porcelain hearts on straps; or of satin loops, buttons, and feather boas is inexhaustible. Go first to the expensive fashion jewelry shops to get some ideas, then purchase the cheapest ingredients here for homemade versions. On 38th Street between Fifth and Sixth avenues, in a rather grayish block, you'll find one rummaging emporium after another.

A diamond merchant; a delivery man
Garment District, with its hand carts and delivery trucks

A Street of Diamonds

After you have had your fill of buttons, bows, and baubles, walk north a couple of blocks and catch the dazzle of genuine glitter — millions upon millions of diamonds. On 47th Street, between Fifth and Sixth avenues, is **Diamond Row,** the biggest and probably most famous diamond exchange in the world. At first sight you'll hardly imagine that these brilliant (and often ugly) stones are all really genuine, but 80 percent of the world's diamond trade is handled here. This is where the Orthodox Jews, the Hassidim, rule.

Some women, wearing cloth wigs, stand behind the counters and cash registers; men with forelocks and yarmulkes sit at desks piled high with papers. Here everything takes place in one room: merchandise is displayed in front, negotiation and grinding takes place in the rear. Now and then these big rooms are also topped by luncheonettes (for example, at 2-8 West 47th Street) on raised galleries. While you eat your sandwich, you can calmly observe the checking and examining, the weighing, and the trading. But trading also goes on out in the street, in front of the doors of the Diamond Exchange. Here bearded Hassidim, in their long, black coats and black hats, stand in small groups speaking with other merchants and dealers wearing regular street clothes. A handshake is considered a contract, a gentlemen's agreement is binding.

On Saturday (Sabbath) and on Jewish holy days, this area is deserted. Then only the Gotham Book Mart, which stands here quite unexpectedly among this tumult of jewels, invites the visitor to browse, read, and buy books — with its motto, "Wise Men Fish Here."

Greenwich Village: Still Bohemian?

Greenwich Village, roughly speaking the area west of Broadway, south of 14th Street, and north of Houston Street, is everything New York is not: quiet, peaceful, romantic, unconventional, and unpretentious. It is full of corners and narrow alleys — certainly not laid out with a ruler, but growing naturally; not standardized but quite original; not stereotyped but rather individual. This area (mostly the West Village) has a heart of its own, a character of its own; it is cozy, or — as people here say with pride — it is almost European, a neighborhood with traditions.

In Greenwich Village, people do not just live. Here they live life to the fullest before they settle uptown. Addresses in New York are more than just the designation of a place where you live; they reflect your ideology. And if you live in Greenwich Village, but you are a banker and over thirty-five, you do not at all fit in with the idea that most Villagers have about themselves. This purported neighborhood of artists and Bohemians nurtures its own anti-establishment character.

The Village lives on its reputation as the gathering place for nonconformists. At the beginning of this century, Greenwich Village indeed was everything that it still would like to be: it was the center of a spontaneous and vital intellectual group of writers and journalists, of artists and anarchists. All of them came to the Village with the conviction of being able to change the world. It has been said that this was the time of naïve egotism, of newly discovered libido and cheap dives. Cubism, sex, anarchism, yellow journalism, and Freud were the main topics of passionate discussion. And uptowners were the quintessence of middle-class convention, with narrow-minded attitudes toward literature, art, politics, and morality. John Reed, Carl Sandburg, Bertrand Russell, and Maxim Gorky wrote for the socialist monthly *The Masses;* Mabel Dodge maintained a salon in her apartment on Fifth Avenue, where Walter Lippman, Gertrude Stein, and Isadora Duncan came to visit.

Eugene O'Neill and Louise Bryant (Reed's wife) founded the **Provincetown Playhouse,** which for a long time was the center of avant-garde theater in America and which is still one of the most interesting Off-Off Broadway stages. Dylan Thomas drank himself to death in the **White Horse Tavern,** still at the corner of Hudson and 11th streets. But New York's wealthy liberals soon discovered the Village and settled in the expensive apartments in newly built high-rises. Many musicians, painters, poets, and actors moved south, to SoHo or to the East Village, which in the meantime began to compete for Greenwich Village fame. Several of the most exciting and stimulating theater and blues or rock stages — and some of the most original restaurants — established themselves here. In the West Village remained students who were no longer as young as they used to be and no longer quite as stormy; also remaining were some fiery avant-garde journalists, choreographers, writers, curators, producers, models, and liberal politicans. Here now live Lauren Hutton and Ramsey Clark. Bette Midler resides on Barrow Street, while the battling Democratic politican Bella Abzug is on Bank Street — just a few houses away from Merce Cunningham, the grand old dad of modern dance in America. Even Mayor Koch prefers his apartment in the Village to Gracie Mansion.

Washington Arch, gateway to the Village

Still offbeat: Village styles of socializing

In the Village you'll see more homosexual and racially mixed couples than in any other neighborhood. In effect, the Village is different from the rest of New York, but then again, it is typically New York — a miniature edition of the city. It is just this mixture that makes up the charm of the Village. You can find squeezed together everything that you would otherwise have to criss-cross Manhattan for. You can eat Italian, French, American, Armenian, or Greek cuisine all in one region. A butcher warbles Italian arias while he deftly bones a chicken breast; the Puerto Rican street vendor touts, with rolling accent, his peaches and nectarines at the subway exit.

The street cafés are overcrowded in summer and people drink Gin and Tonics, Spritzers (white wine with soda), or Perriers with lime. The true Villager lives in a brownstone or on a mews; in other words, they prefer houses that are beautiful copies of London houses, on quiet green streets. The Village is where you can ride your bicycle to pick up fresh bread from the Italian baker, then consume it in your own little garden behind the house, while the birds sing. But the Village is also commercial, with honking cars and loud music, the decor of the pizza joints and hamburger places. On one block you will find a relaxed atmosphere while in another you will see hectic activity. Both these places are only two minutes away from one another.

A less fashionable part of the Village

In the Village you naturally dress differently from when you travel up to the Upper East Side. The casual Village style follows a pattern just as much as anything else and can be recognized from far away, like any other fashion which is supposed to express a philosophy of life. Informal, comfortable, and patched together are the key words — and the results range from worldly chic to hasty sloppiness. ''We are self-sufficient here anyway,'' said an actress, and ''everything and everybody is here anyway.''

SoHo — Today's Avant-Garde

The essence of **SoHo** (derived from ''South of Houston Street'') is something that you can best observe where West Broadway intersects Spring Street. On the south west side of the intersection, a trendy restaurant offers the latest in nouvelle cuisine on the northeast corner, in the house at 157 Spring Street, four galleries with four

196

Warmer weather brings out the crowds

different programs provide competition in art for each other. In the house next door, there is still a place where they sharpen scissors. And on the northwest corner — at 167 Spring Street — the Dutchman Jaap Rietman has a roomy art book store for himself. Here you can get information about everything that is being published in the field of art — in books, art magazines, or reproductions. The now-expensive art of SoHo can be purchased at a more reasonable price as an art book from Rietman.

Diagonally across, in the **Spring Street Bar,** you can down a whiskey, beer, or glass of wine and, in the process, easily start up a conversation with a well-known artist. Sometimes Dennis Oppenheim or Richard Serra will be sitting at the bar; at the table you might see John Baldessari, who recently moved here from California and who has shown his latest works in the Sonnabend Gallery. If you no longer have any desire for ancient Bob Dylan records, which are played regularly in the Spring Street Bar, and if you are getting hungry, then you can get a good salad or hamburger, with a French touch, in one of the three back rooms.

Residents fight to keep their apartments

SoHo has been in existence as the "city block of the avant-garde," as German art dealer Rene Block described it, only for the past fifteen years. Before that, the area between Houston Street on the north, Canal Street on the south, Thompson Street on the west, and Crosby Street on the east was part of a larger section that city planners had forgotten. This area was considered underdeveloped. It was simply called "the Valley," and during the late nineteenth century, it was occupied and dominated by small-scale industry. But even before it became an industrial section, during the 1850s this part of town was the navel of elegant New York. On West Broadway, at the corner of Spring Street, stood one of the largest and most luxurious hotels at that time (the first one with central heating!) — the St. Nicholas Hotel. It was torn down and replaced with five-story or six-story factories, in whose lofts artists today have comfortable apartments and roomy studios. But those buildings were not comfortable back then. Immigrants from Eastern Europe, Ireland, or the Palatinate were exploited as they toiled under the scandalous and unhygienic working conditions of the late nineteenth century. These factories, frequently erected with cast iron and with Corinthian-column decorations, were supposed to symbolize the ideals of the factory owners who felt that such copies of Greek architecture were noble. At the same time, these buildings were symbolic of the pragmatic thinking of American business, which appreciated prefabricated parts and practical construction. Just a few years ago, landmarks such as the **E.V. Haughwout Building,** at the intersection of Broadway and Broome Street, were considered worthless remnants of a sweat-shop era which was better forgotten. Today these cast-iron buildings are protected from further destruction, due in large part to the efforts of the resident artists.

Many SoHo warehouses are now studios or apartments

When it was still illegal to live in the lofts, when the artist-pioneers secretly moved into SoHo via Houston Street to the south, many lofts were empty. The small-scale manufacturers were suffering in the wake of more effective sales and production methods used by large industry, and they were forced to move out of New York or close down. For the first inhabitants of SoHo, the streets were deserted at night. There was no street lighting; industrial waste was piled up daily in front of the doorways. Only **Fanelli's** old worker bar on Prince Street — which has retained its original furnishings to this very day (and which has become one of the most popular bars for artists) — provided a little bit of life in the evening. The few day-time restaurants — **Joe & Mike's** on Spring Street and the tiny coffee shop opposite the present-day **Gallery Shop** at 420 West Broadway — with their night-time emergency lights and shabby furnishings created the impression of torpid and dust-covered restaurants of a ghost town. In 1967, there were neither supermarkets nor galleries, neither drug stores nor groceries, neither newsstands nor trees; in summer, the place stank. But more and more artists moved in to the area because this was where they could find something that was not available anywhere else: lots of room and low rents. Art became the essential activity in SoHo, an activity which blended well with the remaining industrial work because artist and worker shared a respect for craft.

By 1968, so many artists were living on Wooster Street, on Green Street, or on Mercer Street that the authorities had to approve their right to live in the lofts. SoHo had become a big studio for a new generation of artists, and where artists are, art dealers are not far away. Paula Cooper established her first gallery on Prince Street

Left: Cast-iron façades in Soho.
Above: A loft gallery.
Opposite: Avant-garde art

above Fanelli's. She was followed by many others, including the already established art dealers from uptown, such as Castelli or Emmerich. They were soon joined by Ileana Sonnabend as the first European woman and John Weber in the present-day meeting place of the international avant-garde. The first women's galleries sprang up in SoHo; for example, there is **A.I.R.** or **Women in the Arts.** Also to appear soon were the jazz lofts and the loft ''performing spaces.'' Poetry readings and modern dance performances could be seen in the **Ward-Nasse Gallery** while avant-garde music, dance, and video could be found at the **Kitchen.** The *SoHo News* quickly replaced the *Village Voice* as a progressive sheet, and as the public kept crowding in, the streets increasingly turned into boulevards for people who wanted to see and be seen. Comfortable buses now bring ladies clubs from the rich New York suburbs. And just about every week, a new boutique, restaurant, gallery, or antique shop opens up.

Today more than twenty galleries of different qualities and art directions compete for the public's favor within a half-mile stretch of West Broadway. Twice as many have settled in the side streets. The style — including the style of the few galleries oriented toward the avant-garde — is guided by the cool and minimal facilities of **Castelli, Sonnabend,** and **Weber.**

On weekdays you can still saunter through old SoHo. Trucks parked sideways block part of the streets; row upon row, they push their opened rear-ends against the

high loading ramps so that bolts of fabric, barrels, crates, cartons, or paper can be unloaded. In the evening and on weekends, SoHo becomes a New York-style neighborhood. Anybody who wants to get a whiff of Bohemia will promenade on West Broadway, will sit in the bars, and will find out where the most exciting and craziest loft parties are going on. The Rolls-Royce of a well-known rock band stops in front of the Spring Street Bar. A black limousine with chauffeur discharges a smartly dressed gentleman in front of the **Oh-Ho-So.** This restaurant, operated by art dealer Ivan Karp, characterizes the new commercial spirit of present-day SoHo; here customers must wear neckties. Not much is left of the old SoHo here.

Why New York? An Artist At Home

Why New York? Because it is the only city in the whole world that is crazy enough for me. Nobody bothers me here when I go through the streets in my sometimes very strange outfits. That is just my style and I have little desire to conform. People have sometimes looked around at me, and the taxi drivers who eat in the tavern below do still whistle — but nobody is really shocked. Don't get me wrong, I don't think everything far out, crazy, and extraordinary is always good, but I want to be left alone even if I do look so odd.

My friends are meanwhile surprised when they see me in a tee-shirt and jeans; that is sensational for them. What I mean by that is that the people here have become used to me. They know my eccentricity and accept it.

But when I was in Europe recently, I felt somewhat like a little exotic animal. It was nice that I had two exhibitions and the artists I met therefore thought they could fit me in, but the people on the street looked somewhat indignant.

I believe my way of dressing — antique Russian dresses, bodices, stylish high-heeled ankle boots, flowers, hatpins, etc. — is as much a response to our world today as is my art, and that means above all a response to New York too. How should I say it? New York is the here and now.

Even as a child I was always building my own world, dressing up and withdrawing from others. And actually, I'm still doing the same: I'm creating my own oasis — and New York has quite a considerable influence there. It's true the energy here, the stress, the people, the speed, and rush are stimulating, but also pretty exhausting. One can use this energy creatively, or be overwhelmed by it and crack up. I want to keep control over this energy and control over myself, and for that I need a place where I feel at home and natural. Therefore my home looks just like my environments — the hollows of parachute silk are the womb into which I withdraw to recover.

Many people think my rooms are a fantasy, my escape when New York goes to my head. But that is not true. They are my reality. I don't go there to bouy myself up with castles in the air; I go there to recover my senses. Many people who visit my home or look at my objects do not grasp this dimension. They think the dirty streets below and the cold light of day are real and that my environment is both an illusion and a stronghold of defiance. Well, what is true and real for some is simply illusion for others. To me, this way of living right here in New York is less a play fantasy than rather a simple necessity.

An exhibit at the Cooper-Hewitt

I find my work, for example, also not as romantic as many describe it, although I believe without reservation in feelings and emotions, especially when one lives as hectically and in the final analysis anonymously as in New York. Our world is controlled by the mind; I find that false. That excludes romance and craziness, and we need the balance.

If we make all our decisions with our head alone, we make a tremendous number of mistakes. We need romance as compensation. That doesn't mean being sentimental; New York would hardly give one even the time and room for that, then one would be finished here. This city forces you to use your head and it allows you to develop your feelings fully. Under these cir-cumstances, how could I live anywhere else?

Harlem: It's More than a Slum

During the twenties and early thirties, it was considered chic to go to Harlem. The famous nightclubs, such as the Cotton Club or the Apollo, were meeting places for whites in search of amusement. They applauded the black entertainers and danced the night away to the music of black jazz bands. Of course, black people never got into these clubs as patrons. In the years that followed, most clubs closed. The **Apollo,** which for many years existed only as a sleazy movie house, now again offers live entertainment and hopes for a rebirth. Even the **Cotton Club** has reopened.

Geographically, Harlem extends from 110th to 155th streets, from the East River and Harlem River to Morningside Avenue and St. Nicholas Avenue. Dutch settlers named the original Indian village *Nieuw Haarlem* in 1658 and built their country estates and farms there. Not until the end of the nineteenth century did the Village of Harlem become a part of New York. After the construction of the Harlem Railroad, t was New York's first suburb. .

For a while it was chic to live north of Central Park. Luxurious single-family dwellings and apartment houses began replacing the stately mansions. But many apartments remained empty because of an excessive building boom. This was then a unique opportunity for the black real estate broker Philip Payton to purchase the empty buildings cheaply and rent them to blacks. Harlem was "lost" for the whites, who in panic left their increasingly black neighborhoods as the black-white proportion tipped away from their favor. During the Great Depression in the thirties, Harlem quickly became the black ghetto it is today.

And so it is that *Harlem* for many people has become synonymous with *slum.* Between 1950 and 1970, Harlem's population shrank by about one-fourth; today about 550,000 people live here. Approximately 50 percent of the apartments in this section of the city are substandard; the unemployment rate is estimated at 25 to 30 percent, and more than one quarter of all its families are welfare recipients.

Why come to Harlem? Because it is important to also see the other face of Harlem. A new administration building on 125th Street looks rather imposing for its surroundings, but it is symbolic of Harlem's upswing. Surrounding the building is the historical Harlem, with the **Morris-Jumel Mansion, Marcus Garvey Park, Hamilton Grange,** and the **Abyssinian Baptist Church.** It is the Harlem of tree-lined streets with two-family homes, the modern high-rise apartments with doormen (Lenox Terrace), the housing developments with condominiums and private security officers (Riverton, on 135th Street, east of Fifth Avenue). Here you will find a bourgeois ambiance in rich contrast to the slums only a few rows of houses away; this is where the black middle and upper class live. It will be a surprise to the person not otherwise familiar with Harlem.

The librarian who directs the biggest library (worth seeing!) for black history (**Schomburg Collection**) in a run-down block said, "I was born and educated in Harlem and I never got the idea of being anything other than middle class." And a black woman journalist who grew up in Harlem protests against being stereotyped. "My father never beat my mother and is no alcoholic either; I have never seen a rat,

A Harlem street

Above: Blacks and Hispanics find companionship in a fight against oppression.
Opposite top: Famous Apollo Theater; below: Harlem children

nor was I raped for the first time at the age of twelve and I was not sent out into the streets at the age of fifteen, nor was I ever arrested for drug abuse.''

Lawyers, doctors, and judges live today on so-called **Striver's Row** (137th and 138th streets between Seventh and Eighth avenues), which are among New York's architecturally most beautiful streets. ''It could be something like Bath,'' enthused the English writer V. S. Pritchett about the sandstone houses built by the famous architect Stanford White. These have now been declared monuments, but the fourteen-room residences just a few years ago could be purchased for the ridiculous sum of $25,000. At that time no ''reasonable person'' would invest in Harlem to renovate the still-cheap brownstones on streets in the 130s and 140s, near Convent Avenue or on Sugar Hill (Edgecombe Avenue and 155th Street). Residents here now send their children to the best private schools in the city and have summer homes in the country.

Many Harlem inhabitants feel that information about Harlem is often distorted. Some feel white New York wanted to starve out Harlem in order then to be able to buy it up cheap and rebuild it. The results would be high prices and high rents which few blacks would be able to afford; the remaining residents would have to move out. This luckily did not happen.

Frequently, wrong ideas about Harlem are simply based on ignorance. People again and again hear about the drug trade going on by the black Mafia; about dangerous school conditions; about misery and murder. This information is usually projected against the entire black ghetto. But all of Harlem must not be equated with Central Harlem (99 percent of its inhabitants are black, and the unemployment rate

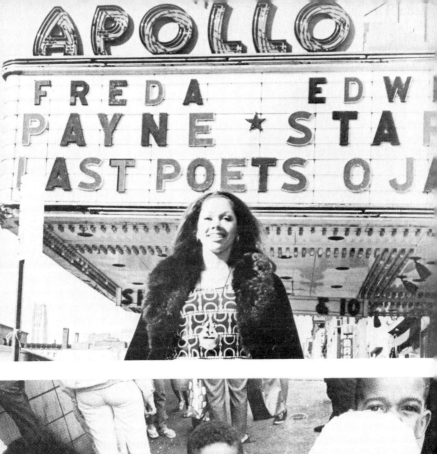

Harlem street scenes

*A street is closed
to allow children to play*

is more than 50 percent) or Spanish Harlem (severe slum conditions, where many
Hispanics live). Actually, conditions in Central Harlem easily surpass any notion
one might have had beforehand. Romanticism in the style of *West Side Story* is not
found here. Dirt, poverty, hopelessness, and aggression could hardly be manifested
more brutally than through the aimless loitering of hundreds of unemployed.

The other Harlem is right around the corner; for example, see the **Studio Museum
in Harlem** where a calm and neat atmosphere makes you forget only too easily that
you have just come in from noisy, blaring 125th Street. Here talented black artists
often display their works. Around the corner is the **Black Fashion Museum,** where
is shown the influence of black fashion designers — from unknown slave seamstresses to the present-day stars — on American clothing. You can go for lunch to
La Famille and eat Virginia ham with applesauce in a nice middle-class ambiance.

Anybody who wants to undertake a soul journey to truth should go to Barbara
Ann Teer's **National Black Theater,** a theatrical presentation with psychotherapeutic objectives. By involving the public through fraternization and even through

the union of audience and actors, "the eyes and the hearts are to be opened, the soul and thus the truth are to be discovered in oneself." But only the person who thinks that he or she can shed conventional ways of behavior should come here.

Regular theater is performed in the **New Heritage Repertory Theater** and good dance groups often perform at the **Harlem Performance Center.** If you are lucky, you can watch a public rehearsal of the Dance Theater of Harlem, the first permanent black classical ballet troupe in the United States. Founded in 1969 by Arthur Mitchell (a pupil of George Balanchine), the troupe at first encountered widespread prejudice. But it was this ballet that in a few years achieved something which others are still striving for after twenty years: successful runs on Broadway and ovations by critical Londoners in the Saddler Wells Theatre.

Perhaps the best introduction to Harlem would be a ride through the entire area for several hours with the **Penny Sightseeing Tour.** Then walk the streets that interest you, keeping some element of safety in mind. Harlem is much more than a slum and you will find the experience myth-shattering.

New York's Other Boroughs

Among the five boroughs of New York, only Manhattan and perhaps Brooklyn ave achieved worldwide reputation. The remaining areas are for many an amorhous mass. When most people talk about New York, they mean Manhattan.

The anger, envy, and disappointment that the residents of the Bronx, Queens, Brooklyn, and Staten Island feel toward the often haughty Manhattanites are often vident in city-wide elections when they demand of officials more attention to their eeds. Even in their dealings with other people, Queens or Staten Island residents end to reveal a slight inferiority complex; they know they have been categorized by Manhattanites as soon as they give their address and they find they are shunted aside r branded as less than real city-dwellers. This arrogant little island dominates the cene in the city and it does so very rigorously.

Actually, Brooklyn has 2.5 million inhabitants and the Bronx has 1.5 million. Queens is almost five times bigger than Manhattan and even Staten Island is twice as arge, although it only has about one-fifth of Manhattan's population. New York's tal population has been estimated at 8 million, but only 1.5 million live in Manhattan.

As a tourist, most of your activity will probably be centered in Manhattan as vell, although you should consider visiting the other boroughs if you have the time. They also are New York and your visit will not be complete without a visit to them.

The Bronx

The Bronx, the only borough of New York where the definite article is a part of e name (the Broncks, Danish immigrants, used to have a farm here called The roncks Farm, which obviously became "The Bronx"), is known primarily for its ronx Zoo and also its **New York Botanical Garden.** Only few sports fans realize at **Yankee Stadium** is in the Bronx; otherwise people really know little or only egative things about this part of town. Photos and reports on the desolate and urned-out South Bronx, which has become a symbol of urban decay, have made e rounds of the entire world. But it so happens that Edgar Allan Poe lived here etween 1846 and 1849 in **Poe Cottage;** the **Grand Concourse** — planned as the hamps-Elysées of the Bronx — used to be a very impressive place; and the Greek evival–style **Bartow-Pell Mansion** was built here in 1836–42.

Also in the Bronx is the **Van Cortlandt Mansion,** which dates back to 1758 and rved as headquarters for both American and British troops during the Revolution.

Brooklyn brownstone contrasts with a Bronx apartment complex

The **Valentine-Varian House** is a remarkably preserved fieldstone farmhouse buil in 1758, which shows the extent of colonial craftsmanship at that time. The **Hall o Fame for Great Americans** (a semicircular, open arcade), built by the frequentl mentioned architectural firm of McKim, Mead & White around 1900, contains th busts of almost 100 famous Americans. **Woodlawn Cemetery** is the final restin place for many statesmen, businessmen, and entertainers, including F. W. Wool worth, Bat Masterson, George M. Cohan, Duke Ellington, and Admiral Farragu The **Museum of Bronx History** offers guided tours of displays showing the contri butions of Bronx residents to all aspects of American life. Meanwhile, the **Bron Museum of the Arts** exhibits the works of contemporary painters, sculptors, an photographers, and the **City Island Historical Nautical Museum** displays memora bilia and artifacts dealing with nautical life on the island.

City Island itself is worth a visit as a sharp contrast to the rest of the city. Here it as if a bit of New England was moved to this spot, as shipyards, fishing boats, an nautical shops line the streets. The **Mott Haven Historic District** is a section tha dates back to the Civil War times. And **Riverdale,** an area of handsome homes an estates, is where the wealthy have lived for over a century.

The Bronx Heritage Trail is a little tour of this borough that can be accomplishe in about three and one-half hours, and allows you to visit the Museum of Bron History, the Valentine-Varian House, Edgar Allan Poe Cottage, and Van Cortlan Park and Mansion.

Queens

If you fly to New York, then you almost cannot avoid Queens. Both LaGuardia and John F. Kennedy airports are located in this borough. Queens, named for Catherine of Braganza, the wife of Charles II, is known for its **Shea Stadium** and **Forest Hills Tennis Club** (former site of the U.S. Open). But Queens has many other sites of interest as well.

Commonly referred to as the "bedroom borough," Queens is characterized by single-family dwellings and high-rise apartments more than with industry, although there are many small factories in Long Island City, just across the East River from midtown Manhattan. Much of Queens is middle class or lower middle class, but there are some pockets of poverty and other sections populated by the wealthy. Getting around the borough is a bit more difficult than in the Bronx, and the tourist may prefer to rent a car. If you are traveling to Queens by car, then a good way to come out from Brooklyn would be along the **Interborough Parkway.** This ride is often referred to as the "Cemetery Belt" because the parkway winds among several old cemeteries. It will also give you a view of some of Queens' parkland and some older residential areas.

Queens historical sites concentrated in the Flushing area include the **Bowne House** (seventeenth century) and the **Friends Meeting House** (1694). Also here is

215

John F. Kennedy Airport; Long Island Railroad Station in Jamaica; Coney Island boardwalk; Brooklyn dockside

the **Kingsland Homestead,** the second oldest house in Flushing. **Town Hall** dates back to the mid-nineteenth century and is a national landmark. When in Flushing, go to the **Queens Museum** and also see the **Weeping Beech Tree,** planted in 1849 by Samuel Parsons.

The **Hunters Point Historic District** has rowhouses dating back to about 1870 which are examples of Italian and French architecture. Nearby is **Project Studio One,** which used to be a school; in fact, this building is the oldest school building in the borough and today it is used as a center for experimental artists. By now, about fifty artists have set up their studios in the individual classrooms of this huge old brick building built in the neo-Romanesque style popular in 1890. Exhibits are changed constantly in the gallery rooms and avant-garde performances take place frequently in the large auditorium. And, for movie buffs, the **Astoria Studios** is a thirteen-building complex now open to the public. Once the filming site of such movie greats as W. C. Fields, Gloria Swanson, Rudolf Valentino, and the Marx Brothers, the Astoria Studios has most recently been used for modern-day productions including *The Wiz, The Warriors,* and *All That Jazz.*

Also in Queens is the **Hall of Science,** on the grounds of the 1964 World's Fair. This museum concentrates on space travel especially, with models of space vehicles. The **Storefront Museum/Paul Robeson Theater** in Jamaica is in an old auto warehouse, but now is a cultural center for black artists in this predominantly black area of the borough.

Because it is so far removed from the steel and glass of Manhattan, people forget that Queens has miles of beaches and other types of natural shoreline. And also far from the madding crowd is **Jamaica Bay Wildlife Refuge,** where the birdwatching is ideal especially in the early morning.

Brooklyn

Contrary to what some travelers think, Brooklyn is not all a black slum. There are indeed depressing sections here, as there are in the other boroughs. But Brooklyn is very much more than just that. Thomas Wolfe titled one of his stories, "Only the Dead Know Brooklyn," and when it comes to summing up this borough's sights, this indeed may be true. As a tourist you probably will not be able to take in all of Brooklyn, but an attempt is well worth your effort.

Brooklyn is three times as large as Manhattan and has almost twice as many inhabitants. In one section, such as Williamsburg, you find mostly Hassidic Jews, and in Bay Ridge, traditionally a Scandinavian section, the population now is largely Greek. By itself, Brooklyn would be the fourth largest city in the United States.

Mae West and Winston Churchill's mother, Jennie Jerome, were born in Brooklyn; and Lola Montez, Horace Greeley, Currier & Ives, and Boss Tweed are among the notables buried in beautiful **Greenwood Cemetery.** Other famous Brooklynites include Mary Tyler Moore, Beverly Sills, Harry Houdini, Barry Manilow, Arthur Miller, Margaret Sanger, W. C. Fields, Zero Mostel, Jackie Gleason, Barbra Streisand, Walt Whitman, Danny Kaye, Lena Horne, Susan Hayward, Floyd Patterson, Woody Allen, John Steinbeck, Clara Bow, Thomas Paine, Alan Arkin, Lauren Bacall, and Eubie Blake. Quite a history!

Tiffany used to have a studio here and Norman Mailer and Truman Capote lived in **Brooklyn Heights** for many years. Brooklyn Heights is also where the American poet Hart Crane spent part of his life. This is the most exclusive and most expensive residential section of Brooklyn. The view from the promenade on Brooklyn Heights toward downtown Manhattan is always impressive. The atmosphere here is friendly; people know one another and they nod as they pass on the street.

Apartments and stores along Coney Island's Surf Avenue

During the early nineteenth century, Brooklyn Heights was New York's fanciest suburb, where a fresh climate and a close proximity to Manhattan offered an ideal combination. When the Brooklyn Bridge was completed in 1883, and when Brooklyn became accessible to the masses, the neighborhood lost its exclusive character, although today it has regained it in part. **Borough Hall,** a Greek Revival palace, is only three blocks from **Grace Court Alley,** a mews which is one of the lovely streets in this section. Along **Henry Street,** to the left and right, you'll notice well-maintained brownstones that are among the most beautiful in the city. **Montague Street** is noted for its small boutiques and restaurants, while **Hicks Street** offers some peaceful seclusion. **Plymouth Church** was an underground railroad stop during the Civil War, and there is a statue of preacher Henry Ward Beecher in the courtyard. The **National Maritime Historical Museum** is a former fireboat station. If you have the time, come to Brooklyn during the day, and plan on returning to Manhattan on foot via the **Brooklyn Bridge** shortly before the start of dusk. This is an unforgettable and impressive experience.

Montague Street in Brooklyn Heights is, as mentioned, a trendy shopping street; but Brooklyn has other interesting shopping streets. Along **Fulton Street,** in the center of downtown Brooklyn, is a pedestrian mall and at the center of the mall is Abraham & Straus. Nearby, **Gage & Tollner** is a Victorian period restaurant, noted for its excellent seafood. **Atlantic Avenue** is one of the most amusing streets, along

The beach at Coney Island

which you will find good and cheap Near Eastern restaurants, bakeries, and magnificently smelling spice shops. There also are a few small galleries and some rather amusing trashy antique shops. Here you won't see much charm, but do get for yourself a Lebanese meal at **Son of the Sheik.** Stick your nose in and take a whiff of **Sahadi Import,** and buy yourself a sticky pastry at the **Damascus Bakery. Paté Vite** is a very small bistro with excellent food.

Seventh Avenue in Brooklyn, between Flatbush and Ninth Street in Park Slope has several good antique shops and fine gourmet food stores, including **One Smart Cookie.** In Bay Ridge and the surrounding blocks you'll find Norwegian sweaters at **Olivia of Norway,** delicious baked goods at **Olsen's** or **Leske's,** and garlicky sausages at **Fredricksen and Johannesen.** The **Borough Park** area's shops are largely Jewish, resembling the Lower East Side. **Kings Highway, Bushwick,** and **Red Hook** are other curious shopping stops.

Culture does not stop at Manhattan's borders, either. In Brooklyn is the very excellent **Brooklyn Museum,** whose Egyptian collection is one of the biggest and most important in the world. Designed in 1895 by the firm of McKim, Mead & White, this large edifice houses famous collections in African and pre-Columbian art, as well as twenty-eight period rooms for American architecture and design. And not at all least is the museum's gift shop, one of the best in the city.

Other museums in this borough include the **Brooklyn Children's Museum** (see

*Bicycling across the
Brooklyn Bridge from Manhattan*

page 159), the **Museum of the Long Island Historical Society** (yes, Brooklyn is part of Long Island), the **New Muse Community Museum of Brooklyn,** and the **New York City Transit Exhibition** (see page 95).

At the **Brooklyn Academy of Music,** on whose five stages such famous ensembles as Twyla Tharp's ballet troupe have danced, people can also see performances by the Royal Shakespeare Company, the Comédie Française, and Dublin's Abbey Players. Sarah Bernhardt played Camille and Edwin Booth was Hamlet at BAM also.

In Brooklyn there is a small but noteworthy **Botanical Garden,** which during almost any season of the year is a relief for urban-weary visitors or residents. **Prospect Park** was conceived by Frederick Law Olmsted and Calvert Vaux, and they considered it their masterpiece. It has a seventy-five-acre meadow, a sixty-acre lake, and miles of rambling drives. A ride around the park to Park Slope, Crown Heights, or Flatbush is rewarding and surprising. Eastern Parkway and some of the side streets, especially President and Union streets, create a bourgeois ambience of nice prosperity.

Coney Island is a name familiar to most who come to the Big Apple. America's first amusement park directly on the sea, this was where someone could alternate between the roller coaster and sun-bathing. Today it is, unfortunately, a run-down fairground for the masses. Peeling paint, rusty steel structures, and broken-down booths are less than attractive. Even **Nathan's,** famous for its hot dogs, can hardly make up for the miserable sight. You can still try most of the rides and stuff yourself with cotton candy, but you'll miss the splendor of the old days; after all, the Parachute Jump no longer operates.

Nearby Coney Island is **Gargiulo's,** considered by many to be the city's best Italian restaurant. And also close is the **New York Aquarium,** where all sorts of sea creatures can be viewed.

Brooklyn sights can be visited mostly by subway or bus, but you should also consider taking Lou Singer's knowledgeable tour.

Staten Island

According to the story, the Duke of York, a sports enthusiast, in 1664 decided to settle a dispute between what was then New York and New Jersey with the help of a sailboat race. Thanks to a favorable gust of wind, New York won the race at the last moment and got Staten Island as a reward. Around 1830, the island became an elegant bathing suburb for prominent New York families, who enjoyed the rural seclusion and ocean breeze. Today you can still find elements of a friendly village atmosphere in some parts of the island, although it is developing rapidly. When the Verrazano-Narrows Bridge was opened in 1964 and Staten Island was more accessible, many people came to live here, especially if getting to work only meant a ride on the ferry. Staten Island today is New York's fastest-growing borough.

Staten Island is famous above all for its **ferry,** said to be the best bargain in the city. But only a few people know that here also are rare examples of early American architecture. The **Billiou-Stillwell-Perine House,** built in 1662, is the oldest on the island, while **St. Andrew's Church** is from 1708 and was used as a headquarters for British troops during the Revolutionary War. **Voorleger's House,** the original "Little Red Schoolhouse," is the oldest elementary school in the United States. It was built in 1695, and is now part of the new **Richmondtown Restoration.** This restoration is an ambitious project involving the restoration of thirty buildings and illustrating the development of an American village from the seventeenth to the nineteenth centuries.

South Ferry terminal

Snug Harbor Cultural Center, formerly known as Sailor's Snug Harbor, has wonderful Greek Revival buildings on its eighty-acre site. Now a cultural center, it has an art gallery and offers performances by guest musicians and dance groups. The **Garibaldi/Meucci Museum** is an old farmhouse where Giuseppi Garibaldi took refuge after his defeat by Napoleon III. Antonio Meucci invented an early version of the telephone. Exhibits here commemorate both these men.

The **Fort Wadsworth and Military Museum** is at the Staten Island end of the Verrazano-Narrows Bridge. The fort is the oldest continually manned military installation in the United States, and it has always been important because of its position at the entrance to New York Harbor. The military museum has memorabilia of all the wars fought in the area.

*Ferry terminal in Staten Island,
looking across to Manhattan*

The **Conference House,** alternately known as the Billopp House, dates back to 1680. Here Benjamin Franklin, John Adams, and Edward Rutledge met with Lord Howe of the British forces, in an attempt to stave off the American Revolution.

For contrast, the **Jacques Marchais Center of Tibetan Art** is noteworthy not only because of its beautiful location on a hill, but also for its collection of Buddhist art. There is a large library as well.

Staten Island also has an **Institute of Arts and Sciences** with special exhibitions and displays of archeology; and some good nature preserves (**High Rock Park Conservation Center** and **William T. Davis Wildlife Refuge**).

Touring Staten Island is not easy for tourists, in that once you go beyond the ferry terminal, you have only limited transportation. Your best bet would be to rent a car.

Working New York: A Taxi Driver

I grew up in the Bronx and when I brought somebody to Manhattan the first time, he had to tell me how to get back — I didn't have the foggiest idea of where I was. But today I can manage quite well and prefer driving only in Manhattan. It is not as routine and not as dangerous as the Bronx; the people here are simply crazy and the women prettier.

The other day a guy read me his poems in a rolling accent the whole way to the airport; sentimental stuff, I thought. When he left he gave me a little book with his autograph. Naturally I thanked him, but to tell the truth, I really didn't look at it. One of my next fares did though, and he about hit the ceiling. Turns out this fellow was one of the most famous Russian poets, and a dope like me never once realized it. That can probably only happen in New York.

Yesterday I had a rather nervous type who kept sliding back and forth on the seat, and it really began to bother me. Suddenly he stuck his head through the window separating us and asked if I could close it, because he had to really let out a scream. And then that's what he did — and how! I was really afraid some pedestrians would call the police and sic them on me. It was unbelievable. I was sweating like a bull, but it evidently did him some good. He looked like a completely different man when he got out and disappeared into the crowd with a beaming smile — and he didn't even leave me a proper tip for my pain.

Some really crazy things have happened. Last year, for example, I drove a couple of jolly people twice in the same evening. When they got in the second time, they promptly invited me to come along and party too. So then we all had something to eat and just had a good time till 4 in the morning.

And then there are always the fares that are afraid of us — especially the newcomers and the tourists, who all think every New York taxi driver is a crook anyway. And also women. It's really a shame because you meet some real nice women who are often just as lonely as you are, but you don't have the courage to say, "O.K., let's have a cup of coffee together," or ask for her telephone number.

But a friend of mine was lucky. He actually found a wife for his son — and a decent and pretty one at that. Oh well, I haven't given up hope completely yet either.

Sometimes, by the way, we have to be a jack-of-all-trades. One time I was driving with a lady through her neighborhood a whole hour looking for her cat that ran away. Another time I had to drive around the same block over and over for a half hour until this young lady, who was crying the whole time I was driving, had settled down enough to go home to her husband. People are constantly baring their souls to us — just like to a bartender or a barber.

What really gripes me is that our good advice is free, while the phony psychologists make a lot of money doing this. Sometimes I think I should change jobs. If I had all my crazy fares as patients, I could get rich quick for sure. I don't know if I'd stay in New York then, though. Sometimes I dream about a house in the country.

Five Walking Tours

1 Madison Avenue

This tour will take you through a variety of neighborhoods and you will discover the diversity of this grand city. Allow almost a full day for your tour, so that you can enjoy all the stops. Begin downtown at Fifth Avenue and 23rd Street, where Madison Avenue springs into being on the eastern flank of **Madison Square.** This is a welcome green space where Broadway crosses Fifth Avenue at 23rd Street, and continues as a serious working street up to about 57th Street.

This area was not always the way it is now. At the corner of 25th Street, where today you see the New York Life Insurance Building (at the bottom neo-Renaissance in limestone, at the top wedding cake) there used to be the station for the New York and Harlem railway line — for trips to the country. In 1853, P. T. Barnum built his hippodrome on this spot, where for two exciting seasons spectators could observe, among other things, two hundred ladies who — on horseback, of course — were chasing a bunch of ostriches around the arena. Unfortunately this sort of enterprise precipitated his bankruptcy; his hippodrome was torn down and New York's favorite architect Stanford White (of McKim, Mead, and White) built the first Madison Square Garden on this site, complete with a copy of the Giralda in Sevilla on top, only to be shot dead a few years later on the roof of this extravaganza by the husband of his (former) mistress.

The avenue then climbs **Murray Hill.** At 29th Street you might turn left toward Fifth Avenue and visit the **Little Church Around the Corner** on the northern side of the street. It has been called this since 1870, when the pastor of a big church in the neighborhood refused to bury George Holland because he was an actor, and suggested having the last rites performed at the little church around the corner. It has ever since been the parish church of all theater people in New York.

Back on Madison Avenue and crossing 32nd Street, you may want to imagine that less than two hundred years ago there was a pond in this spot famous for its good fish. A few blocks to the north you will pass the back door of **B. Altman's** (34th Street), and if you have to buy something, you will find that it is much quieter here than at Bloomingdale's, that the sales people are very friendly, and the crowds bearable — but don't expect the very latest in everything, as you would find at Bloomies.

On the other side of the avenue, at 36th Street, you have reached the **Pierpont Morgan Library,** built in 1906 by McKim, Mead, and White of pink Tennessee marble in the neo-Renaissance style. Notable aside from the many changing exhibitions of drawings, prints, and rare manuscripts is Mr. Morgan's sumptuous private library, left unaltered after his death (see page 92).

General Motors Building; Parke-Bernet Auction Galleries

Many people think that Madison Avenue is synonymous with the advertising industry and indeed a number of agencies have their offices in the many blocks in the forties. A change of pace is provided by a number of shops, among them **Paul Stuart,** where very chic young men go shopping, and **Tripler** and **Brooks Brothers** (both sell rather conservative men's clothes). The latter is the oldest and until recently *the* bastion of male accoutrement. Now, however, they have been invaded by women executives and are willing to sell skirts and blouses as well. The **Victory Shirt Co.** (between 44th and 45th streets) will sell or make you very good shirts. On the other side of the street is the **Vogue Building,** where the models with their large portfolios full of photographs provide a welcome change from the many somber business suits as they run from one well-paid appointment to the next. At 50th Street you'll think for a moment that you are in Renaissance Italy. Behind a beautiful cast-iron gate three typical New York brownstone houses were joined and given wings. Known as the **Villard Houses,** they resemble a palazzo and that illusion would stay with you for a while if your eyes were not pulled upward by the 51-story hotel growing out of the roof.

With the **Fuller Building** in pure Art Deco style on the northeastern corner of 57th Street, Madison Avenue turns artsy. A number of galleries are to be found at this address, among them **Pierre Matisse** (modern European masters) and **Andre Emmerich** (contemporary painting, pre-Columbian sculpture). One block up and across the street you will come upon the black-and-white-striped **General Motors Building.** It is not especially beautiful, and in winter a particularly icy wind whistles around it, but it does have a small rock garden at its feet with benches for tired walkers.

Widely traveled New Yorkers say that from this point Madison Avenue could easily be mistaken for the Rue St. Honoré or the Via Veneto. And indeed you will find all the international boutiques, from **Rodier** to **St. Laurent,** from **Armani** to **Ambienti.** Only **Halston,** who has done so much to revolutionize American fashion and to get it worldwide attention, has kept a lonely outpost among all the immigrants.

On your walk up Madison Avenue you will pass large apartment houses, hotels (**Bemelman's Bar** in the Carlyle on 76th Street is a good place to rest), churches (there are lunchtime concerts in the **Madison Avenue Presbyterian Church** at 74th Street), but your overall impression will be of small shops, some of them on the second floor of small town houses. It is worth your while to look up and across the street (something New Yorkers never do) because otherwise you might miss the best addresses. For instance, there is **Krön,** where the best chocolate in New York (if not in the world) comes in rather original shapes and sizes.

You will see very quickly that Madison Avenue not only offers food for your eyes. A phenomenally successful chain of shops called **Pasta and Cheese** (with three branches on Madison Avenue alone: at 64th, 72nd, and 88th streets) will sell you fresh pasta in all possible variations, every kind of cheese you could possibly think of, and along with that the best bread in town from a bakery in Greenwich Village. The wine for your picnic can be chosen at **Surrey Liquor** (69th Street), for instance, and your dessert should come from **William Greenberg** (89th Street), who creates some of the best sweet things in town. In fact his brownies, a specialty, are so well known that fans come from far and wide for them.

Specialties, but not of the edible kind, abound on Madison Avenue. You might want to browse for difficult-to-find or esoteric (but not only) books at **Books & Co.,** a marvelous store with knowledgeable sales people (75th Street). Consider the purchase of a music box from **Rita Ford's** large and amusing selection (69th Street); or buy yourself a miniature army at the **Soldier Shop** (78th Street). A Paris-inspired haircut can be yours at **La Coupe,** a chic but not cheap hairdresser (63rd Street). And if your purse was damaged en route you can take it to **Artbag** (64th Street) and have it fixed.

If you have walked as far north as the **Guggenheim** or the **Cooper-Hewitt museums,** you might consider having lunch at **Summerhouse,** a pretty and not too expensive restaurant (91st Street), not far from them. But if you are overcome by hunger in the sixties, you can eat relatively expensively at **Woods** (64th Street), or relatively cheaply at the **Confetti Café** (68th Street). If there are lines at both places you might try the **Right Bank** (69th Street); it is not as new as the other two but popular with gallery people, and the hamburgers and quiches are fine.

With Marcel Breuer's **Whitney Museum of American Art,** which looks quite a lot like an upside-down staircase before you at 75th Street, you have reached one of New York's three art centers. Two blocks north and across the street is **Sotheby-Parke Bernet,** whose auctions invariably bring record prices. For the next ten blocks you will pass one gallery after another, and it is a good idea to turn into the side streets toward Fifth and Park avenues, because the entrances are often hidden around the bends. You might pay a visit to **Blum Helman** for their amusing and original exhibitions (13 East 75th Street); **Sabarsky** (77th Street) for German

Columbus Circle

Expressionism and Blauer Reiter; **Aberbach** (77th Street) for the Vienna School; **Gimpel and Weitzenhoffer** (79th Street) for modern European masters; **Saidenberg** (16 East 79th Street) for Picasso and the Cubists; and **Shepherd** (21 East 84th Street) for nineteenth-century art. **Lucien Goldschmidt** (83rd Street) has the most beautiful old books, bindings, engravings, and drawings. On your way to 96th Street, small shops and galleries crowd each other on both sides of the avenue, with a cinema, a few drugstores, and a supermarket or two thrown in for good measure. By the time you have reached the neo-medieval façade of the armory at 94th Street, behind which hides a public school, you are almost in Spanish Harlem, and the staccato sounds of Puerto Rican Spanish begin to mingle with the babble of tongues heard on your way up cosmopolitan Madison Avenue.

It should be pointed out that most of the galleries and a great number of shops on Madison Avenue are closed during July and August, so reserve this tour for other times.

The Upper West Side

The renaissance of Columbus Avenue, a New York journalist recently noted, is probably the most dramatic transformation of a section of this city that has come about without bulldozers or city planners. Some twenty years ago, there were rows upon rows of bleak façades here, with dingy *bodegas,* drab laundries, greasy coffee shops, and discount appliance stores. Peeling paint and worn-down steps determined the scene.

Used furniture shops — often pompously called antique shops — were the first ones to locate here. They attracted new customers: young people who had just moved into these large West Side apartments and wanted to furnish them cheaply. Then followed the real antique dealers who — reflecting the tastes of their customers — offered an original mixture of exalted odds and ends, second-hand furniture, dishes and clothing, as well as antiques in the true sense.

With the construction of **Lincoln Center for the Performing Arts** at 65th street came the restaurants and boutiques, elegant delicatessens, and renovated apartment buildings. The boom started around Lincoln Center, but has continued to grow northward every year until now it reaches past 86th Street and is moving westward to Amsterdam Avenue.

Prosperity is evident. Everywhere houses are being painted and apartment buildings upgraded. Everywhere also, the prices are going up accordingly and soon it will be hardly possible to rent more cheaply on Columbus Avenue than on the East Side. The large apartments, charming ethnic restaurants, and trendy shops are getting known, as the commercial aspects of the Upper West Side are being quietly concealed or moved out.

Take the IRT Broadway Local to 86th Street or the 8th Avenue line to 86th Street and Central Park West. Then go either two blocks east from Broadway or one block west from Central Park West to Columbus Avenue (in this region, the streets still retain some of their earlier shabbiness).

At **Johnny's** on the west side of Columbus, between 85th and 86th streets, you can get old records and magazines in addition to teenage love stories; right next to it on the corner of 85th Street, a dilapidated antique shop waits for the rare customer; while business seems to be good at the **Soul Den Record Shop** between 84th and 85th streets.

It gets chic already at the northeast corner of 83rd Street where folding Japanese mattresses are sold at **Shinera.** Right next door is the quite good restaurant **Oenophilia** and then comes the very elegant antique shop **Coming Too.** Between 81st and 82nd streets is the **Pure Food Market** offering sun-dried fruits, dates, figs, and pumpkin seeds in addition to natural shampoos. Diagonally across, on 81st Street, is a new gay bar, **Cahoots**: "A Place for Liaisons," frequented by men who probably bought their outfits at the nearby **Rough Rider.** Not only should you look into the stores and bars on Columbus, but also glance down the side streets for some often delightful examples of brownstones.

On 80th Street, on the west side, is **Sherman and Mixon** who offer a jumble of old and new; of kitsch and the tasteful; of glass, frames, jewelry, and gadgets. On

79th Street is the **Public House,** a restaurant in front of which is a sidewalk café in the summer. It's on a noisy corner, but in return you have a view of the pretty park an the Museum of Natural History. On 78th Street, there are several dealers together in a basement marked "Browsers Welcome," but unfortunately their prices have already climbed several stories. Between 77th and 78th streets is **Mythology,** one of the funniest stores here, where an amazingly real-looking lollypop turns out to be a ball-point pen, the pralines are magnets, and the spaghetti is soap. Then comes **Edith's Nostalgia,** specializing in old lamps and **As Time Goes By** for Art Deco pieces.

On the other side of the street and a block down, between 77th and 76th streets, **Gently Worn** has old things and gadgets, while **Putumayo,** between 76th and 75th streets, has fascinating South American clothing and nice Peruvian blankets. You can rent roller skates at **Sport Stripes,** between 75th and 74th streets, and swing to disco or simple skate for sport in nearby Central Park.

On 74th Street, a little east of Columbus Avenue, is the neatest flea market for old clothing and table linen; here you need not rummage to find bargains, for they hang starched and ironed on the racks. Also on 74th Street is **Anita's Chili Parlor** where you can get delicious chili; in summer, you can sit outside here too and let the chic Westsiders pass by you. Opposite are two stores with the same name, **Design Observation:** one sells fancy duds for men and women, and the other expensive and modish novelties, like a coke-bottle radio or a porcelain Miss Piggy pot.

On 73rd Street is **Only Hearts** — a shop for the shameless romantic where everything from underpants to umbrellas is shaped like a heart or imprinted with hearts.

On 72nd Street is **Jezebel,** surely one of the best shops in New York for old clothing. It is worthwhile going in and looking at the often delicate creations, even if you do not wish to buy anything.

Opposite are several gourmet shops: The **Silver Palate,** a take-out and catering spot, offers delicious salads and jams, breads, and pickles. In The **Natural Source,** you can buy health foods.

A little farther down, between 69th and 68th streets, there is once more something to eat, at **Maya Shaper: Cheese and Antiques,** where you buy the antique cheese plate and butter holder at the same time you get your Brie.

After this, if you are tired of window shopping, walk over to the **Lincoln Center** and, after a cup of coffee or hot cider, take the tour of backstage areas.

If you would like to see how Columbus Avenue looked before its hip time, wander back on Amsterdam Avenue. Turn right, then continue up Amsterdam on to 68th Street. Turn right to cross to Broadway and stay on it to 72nd Street. **Street and Co.,** between 69th and 70th streets, is for Broadway an unusually chic and expensive boutique. Turn onto 70th Street briefly once to the right and look at one of New York's more unusual buildings, unfortunately now slowly decaying. But the Buddhas on the capitals and the spouting lions high above on the merlon are still a delight for the eyes that is worth the detour.

Back on Broadway and from 72nd Street to Amsterdam Avenue, you'll pass the **Phone Center Store.** Betwen 74th and 75th streets, you can get slightly funky men's

Whitney Museum

clothes at **The Loft** and oriental food at **Tanaka and Co.** next door. The **Golden Ass,** between 75th and 76th streets, may sound pornographic, but it is actually a cozy coffeehouse. Then come antique shops that still have a storeroom character; the **Way Back When, Born Yesterday,** or **Better Times Antiques** entice you with their nostalgic names. These will surely also soon be tidied up and made to fit the clean look of Columbus Avenue. But in addition in between is the **Istanbul** on 75th Street, a tiny Turkish restaurant where you can eat well and cheaply on plastic tablecloths and with the wine that you bring yourself, or the **Salsa Record Shop** between 81st and 82nd streets. Next is the **Botanica La Fe,** selling religious articles and madonnas.

The atmosphere here is unpretentious and neighborhoodlike, but also still more dilapidated and neglected than on Columbus Avenue. Sloppy figures rather than modish trendsetters walk around here, yet only a block separates these streets. Each street is interesting by itself but the constrast, so typical for New York, is fascinating and illuminating for the visitor.

3 Greenwich Village

Greenwich Village is probably one of New York's most famous neighborhoods. Before beginning your tour, however, we suggest that you read the descriptive material on pages 191-194.

In planning a trip to the Village, do not go there at 9 or 10 o'clock in the morning. Boutiques and shops mostly do not open before 11 or 12 o'clock and hardly anybody saunters through the streets here in the typical Village style at that time. In addition, many of the narrow streets are blocked by trucks delivering new merchandise. The Village is most beautiful in the afternoon if, after long pavement-pounding and with tired feet, you down a glass a wine or cup of capuccino in one of the street cafés and later on go to eat. Depending on how you feel, you might also be able to drop in at one of the many good jazz bars.

Take the Broadway Local or the IRT Seventh Avenue Express to 14th Street, and come up through the exit leading to 12th Street. On the east side of Seventh Avenue stands **St. Vincent's Hospital,** which has become famous not least because of Woody Allen's film *Sleeper* as the hospital in which he was placed in deep freeze. Walk a couple of steps south on Seventh Avenue and then make a right turn onto Greenwich Avenue. At the **Starthrower Cafe** you should look to the left down **Bank Street,** which is one of the most beautiful and quietest streets in the Village. On the way to Abingdon Square, look in at **Aurora** to the west on 12th Street (235 West 12 Street), where you can often find nice kimonos. At Abingdon Square, turn left onto Eighth Avenue, briefly visit the **Science Fiction Shop** (56 Eighth Avenue), and continue on to the corner of Hudson and Bank streets. On the opposite side of the street, you will find one of the best-known and most expensive Italian restaurants around — **Trattoria da Alfredo.** Turn left onto **Bleecker Street,** the longest street running through the Village east to the Bowery. Here you will find fortune-tellers and boutiques, bars, theaters, and delicatessens, as well as expensive antique shops. At no. 394 is **House of Leather;** no. 390, **Early American Folk Art;** at no. 388, you can get vegetarian sandwiches; at no. 386, you can buy exquisite smoked salmon and herring; no. 382 promises tarot-card readings; nos. 353 and 309 are **Pierre Deux,** where expensive Provençal antiques are sold. Here there are many things to see but little chance to rummage around for.

At the corner of Charles Street, is the **Horn of Plenty** restaurant. No. 361, on the left side, has antiques, and no. 359 has fashionable gifts. Leather lovers should not fail to visit **Marquis de Suede** at 321 Bleecker. This area — Bleecker and Christopher streets — today is the focal point for the city's gay life. Individuals gather both at Marquis and at The **Leather Man** at 85 Christopher Street. Styles change and preferences for gathering spots shift, so most tips like these become dated rapidly. Keep your eyes and ears open.

Allow yourself to be swept along a little bit by the colorful hustle and bustle on Christopher Street. At **McNulty's** — no. 109 — there are all kinds of teas and coffees. Nuts, candy, herbs, and rather good chocolate are sold at **Lilac Chocolates,**

West 14 Street

0   300 m
          975 ft

N

Fifth Av.

University Place

West 12 St.

Greenwich

Eight Av.

Gansevoort St.

Washington St.

Greenwich St.

Hudson

Seventh

Abingdon Sq.

West 11 St.

Bleecker St.

Bank

Avenue

West 10 St.

Avenue

W. 8. St.   E. 8. St.

Mac Dougal Alley

Washington Mews

Sheridan Sq.

St.

Charles

Christopher St.

Grove St.

Av.

of

Washington Square Park

Bedford St.

Barrow

South

the

St.

Mac Dougal St.

West St.

Bleecker St.

W. Houston St.

W. Houston St.

King St.

Hudson St.

St.

St.

Charlton St.

Vandam

Varick St.

Americas (Sixth Ave)

Sullivan

Thompson St.

Broadway

Prince St.

Broadway

Spring St.

Wooster

Greene

Mercer

Spring St.

Broome St.

Holland Tunnel

Watts St.

St.

Grand St.

Canal

Street

Hudson River

Ericsson Pl.

235

a couple of houses down at 120 Christopher Street. Opposite The Leather Man at no. 111, we have **Richard Utilla** at no. 112, the best organized second-hand shop I know of. The **Erotic Baker** is at no. 117; it offers all parts of the body in marzipan and sugar molds.

Continue on Bleecker Street eastward to Grove Street, into which you turn to the right and continue to Grove Court (see page 84); do not miss no. 17, one of the most enchanting buildings. Turn left onto Hudson Street and then again turn left onto Barrow Street. The twin houses on the right side between Barrow and Commerce streets, with their Empire style and the Mansard roofs, stand in remarkable contrast to the Village brownstones.

At the corner of Bedford and Commerce streets we come to the **Isaacs-Hendricks House,** which was built in 1799. As you continue to the right and down along Bedford Street, you will see New York's narrowest house, **no. 75½.**

If you continue on to Bleecker Street, you cross Seventh Avenue on the right, and you then get to the block on which the Village gourmets purchase their ingredients. Italian butchers and Greek bakers are to be found here.

You should absolutely look in on no. 283, **Second Childhood,** where you can find tiny, hand-made dollhouse furniture and tiny plates with hot dogs, bagels, and hamburgers made of ceramics. At no. 239, The **Golden Disc,** you can find old and new records at frequently low prices.

On Sixth Avenue turn left onto MacDougal Street for a capuccino in the traditional **Caffe Reggio** (no. 119). If you want to visit the **Caffe Borgia** (no. 185), make a right turn. Walk around in a square pattern and look into Sullivan, Thompson, and West 3rd streets. Play chess at 240 Sullivan Street for an hour for 50 cents at the corner of West 3rd, or buy a nice-smelling essence or a special oil for your evening bath in the hotel at **The Bathhouse,** 215 Thompson Street.

Walk north after that, to Washington Square and take a look at the **Elmer Holmes Bobst Library** of New York University which was completed in 1973 by Philip Johnson. This huge, red sandstone building — rejected initially as being too monumental and too overwhelming by the people living all around — has an impressive interior whose geometric design is aimed at graphic effects rather than practical subdivision. It is really worth seeing.

The **Judson Memorial Church** (see page 79), likewise on the park's south side, was built probably in 1892 by Stanford White in the style of the Italian Renaissance. The marble **Washington Arch,** the triumphal showpiece of the park, was erected in memory of Washington's inauguration (1789) by White in 1892. The brownstones on the park's north side, called **The Row,** are among the most beautiful row houses in New York. No. 32 Washington Square Park West is worth seeing; it is decorated by small reliefs of George and Martha Washington above the door.

Fifth Avenue starts at the triumphal arch. At 1 Fifth Avenue you can eat a magnificent meal; at 2 Fifth Avenue you can watch the source of the by-now-underground **Minetta Brook** bubble in a glass column.

If you are not too tired, go to University Place, which will take you into the center of numerous auction houses and antique shops. Do not forget to look to the left into **Washington Mews** (or later on farther to the west into **MacDougal Alley**); the former stables are a rather unusual sight in the middle of Manhattan.

You can forget about the somewhat trashy 8th Street but do visit **Azuma** — open until 10 o'clock at night — or the **Brentano's** bookstore, which is open till midnight. Opposite you will find the **Cookery,** a good jazz spot.

Turn left onto 11th Street (39 West 11 Street is an imposing townhouse from the year 1842, and at the corner of Sixth Avenue there is an old Jewish Cemetery). After reaching Sixth Avenue, you can look at or purchase gourmet foods at **Balducci's** or — if there is too much of a crowd — diagonally across at the **Jefferson Market** where Greenwich crosses Sixth. On the west side of Sixth Avenue, at the corner of Patchin Place, stands the **Jefferson Market Courthouse** which was built as a women's prison in 1876 and whose preservation is due to citizens' efforts. This turreted little castle has now come to house a public library. Somewhat farther south is **Trude Heller,** a well-known night spot with live entertainment.

Go past the Jefferson Courthouse to Greenwich Avenue and from there through Charles Street to Seventh Avenue, into which you turn from the left and continue on to Sheridan Square. Have a drink at **Jimmy Day's** (186 West 4 Street) or around the corner at **Sandolino** (11 Barrow Steet) and try to decide whether you should eat in one of the many places in this area or take the Broadway local to the theater, to SoHo (see page 196), back to the hotel, or to the Upper West Side.

A Village restaurant

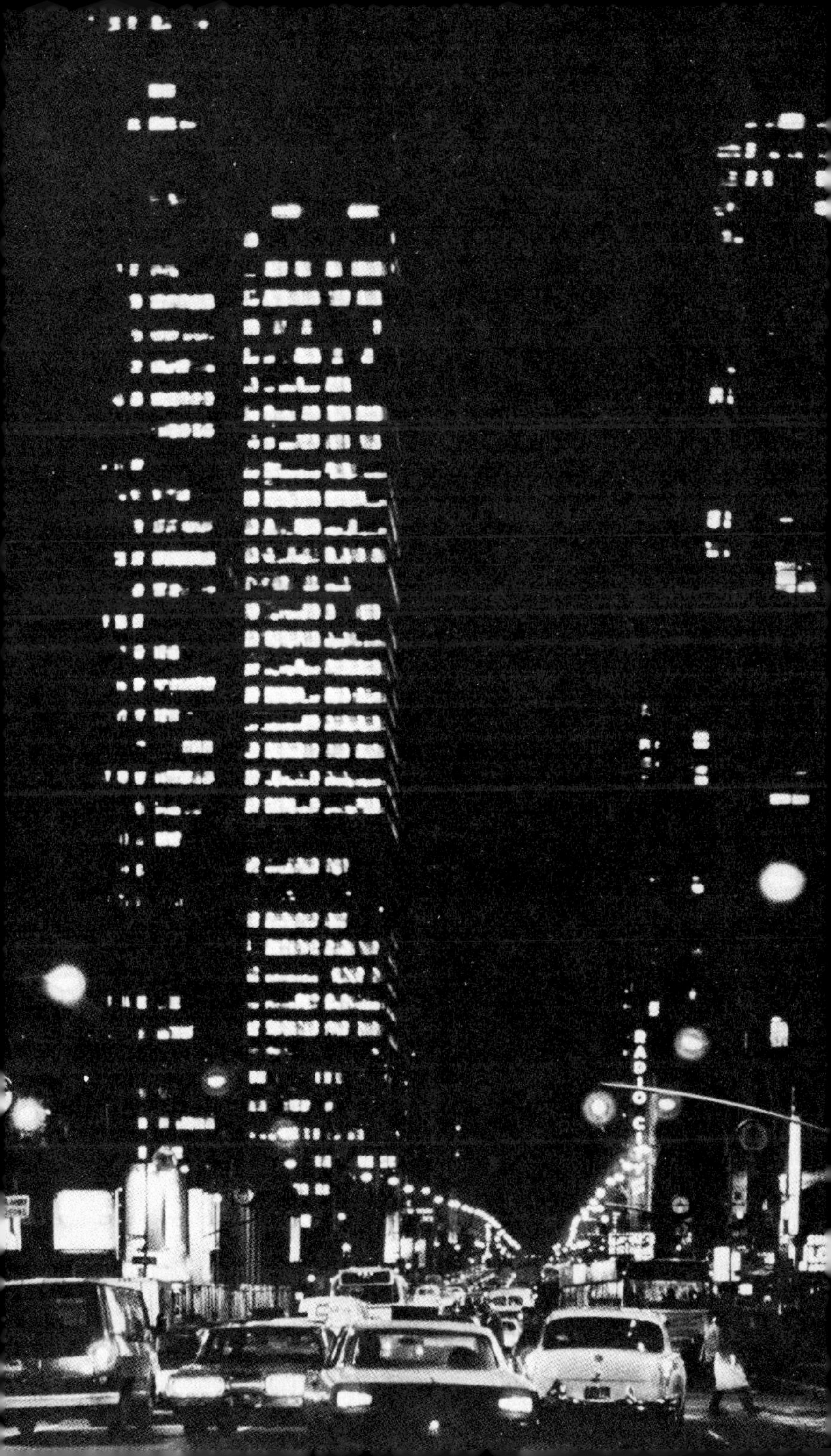

4 Lower East Side

It is best to visit the Lower East Side on a Sunday. It is true that you will then encounter swarms of tourists on some corners, but on any other day the somewhat more out-of-the-way streets are not as active and interesting.

Take the Lexington IRT local to **Canal Street** and then head east, toward the Manhattan Bridge. On Canal Street, you can anticipate Chinatown at no. 232, a Chinese grocery. Chinatown is no longer famous only for its restaurants, but also its gourmet shops. Nearly opposite, at no. 213, **Bak Lei Tat Inc.** offers kung fu and karate, uniforms and weapons.

On the south side of the street, nos. 212, 214, 216, and so on, are rows of vegetable and fish shops, one after another. This area is full of bustling activity on Sunday morning, and you can watch with amazement how the Chinese — talking and gesticulating incessantly — buy lotus roots, bitter melons, Chinese cabbage, duck eggs, sun-dried fish bellies, tree mushrooms, and shark fins. Nearby at the **Art Gallery,** no. 210, there are embroidered items and other needlework gifts. Past the jade jewelry on the street and the roast duck in the windows, you come to **Song Chong Co.** (corner of Canal and Mott streets), where you can buy souvenirs, kimonos, fans, and teapots.

Turn right onto Mott Street, Chinatown's main street. Some 25,000 Chinese now live in Chinatown (roughly the area between Canal and Worth streets, and between Baxter Street and the Bowery). This area has more than 200 restaurants, dozens of souvenir shops, several bookstores, and five daily newspapers. In recent years, the Chinese have not only been pressing out beyond Canal Street toward Little Italy, but at the same time they have been traveling the way from a peaceful, although in many respects neglected, enclave to American big-city reality. They have become a political force, but also have begun to find themselves confronted with a soaring crime rate. The youth have banded together into many gangs that fight bloody

Chinatown

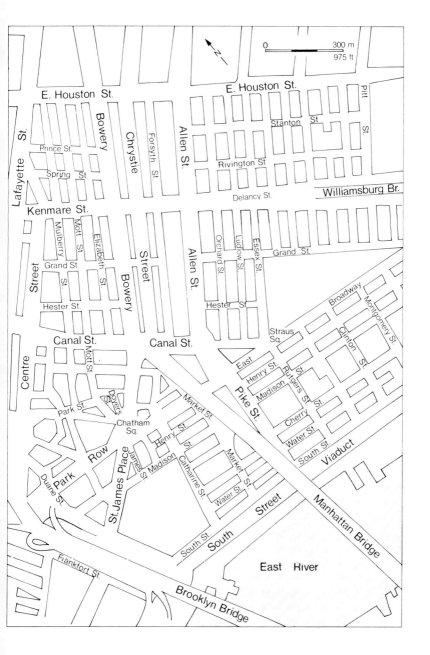

0   300 m
975 ft

E. Houston St.

E. Houston St.

Bowery

Chrystie

Forsyth St.

Allen St.

Lafayette St.

Prince St.

Spring St.

Stanton St.

Pitt St.

St.

Rivington St

Williamsburg Br.

Delancy St.

Kenmare St.

Mulberry

Mott St.

Elizabeth St.

Street

Allen St.

Orchard St.

Ludlow St.

Essex St.

Grand St.

Street

Grand St.

Bowery

St.

St.

Broadway

Montgomery St.

Hester St.

Hester St.

Straus Sq.

Centre

Canal St.

Canal St.

Clinton St.

Mott St.

East

Henry St.

Rutgers St.

Madison

St.

Dover St.

Park St.

Cherry

Chatham Sq.

Market St.

Pike St.

Water St.

Row

Henry St.

St.

South St.

Viaduct

Duane St.

Park

St. James Place

James St.

Madison

Catharine St.

Market St.

Water St.

South

South Street

Manhattan Bridge

Frankfort St.

East River

Brooklyn Bridge

241

struggles for power among themselves, and often subject the frightened residents to a regime of terror. Crimes in Chinatown are frequently personal acts of revenge, therefore you can continue your tour with an easy mind and naturally with the usual caution.

At no. 70A Mott Street, you could probably not decipher the Chinese books and pictorials; no. 68A is a mom-and-pop delicatessen, and then there are rows of souvenir shops, one after another, where you can get just about anything from Chinese lamps to Spanish dolls and few simple things, like Chinese birdcages. At the **Tai Heng Lee Company,** no. 60A, you can admire the ivory woman that recalls the days when physicians were not permitted to examine female patients themselves; they had to ask questions using such models and then make their diagnoses. Several stores here carry nicely embroidered Chinese satin slippers for children and pretty jade jewelry.

At no. 8 is the **Chinese Museum.** Downstairs is an amusement arcade, with humming and rattling gaming machines and a chicken looking somewhat plucked, "The Dancing Chicken," that dances for you for 25¢. The museum itself, tucked

away in a windowless backroom on the second floor, houses a couple of theater costumes, a China Quiz (by which one can find out that the Chinese, not the Italians, invented spaghetti), and in a gloomy corner, a papier-mache dragon. This heraldic animal of the Chinese lights up eerily and wags its head and tail. Meanwhile, if you are in the mood for dim su, the Chinese tea brunch, turn left at Chatham Square and go immediately left again to Doyers Street. At no. 13, in the **Nom Wah Tea Parlor,** trays with undefinable delicacies are carried around from noon from which one chooses items. **Hong Gung,** 30 Pell Street, is also known as one of the best dim sum places.

Go back to Chatham Square and cross it to view the city's oldest Jewish cemetery; look through the bars on the south end of St. James Street. Then go to Henry Street and take a rest from the bustle in **The Mariner's Temple Baptist Church.** This church, decorated completely in turquoise and white and with windows looking out onto green trees, is a wonderfully peaceful oasis.

Go left along Catherine Street or the next one, Market Street, to East Broadway where you turn right and go under the Manhattan Bridge. The first culture shock of this tour awaits you here. It will not only be very much quieter. The streets are more deserted, when all of a sudden you discover at the corner of East Broadway and Rutgers Street that you see hardly any more Chinese faces. You are surrounded by old Jewish people. In the entirely kosher **Garden Cafeteria** (which has no garden!), they drink Sunday afternoon coffee and eat blintzes. The nearby **Süsswein Bakery,** 181 East Broadway, has delicious cheesecake. Probably no other area in New York can show the transformation of a neighborhood clearer than this one, and the streetscape demonstrates the transition. Old people are white and mainly Jewish, while the young are black, Puerto Rican, and occasionally Chinese.

If you turn left at Strauss Square (the corner where the Garden Cafeteria is) to Essex Street, you are in the remaining little corner of the Lower East Side. This scene gives you an impression of how everything must have looked fifty or sixty years ago. At **no. 47,** the store for Jewish devotional articles, an orthodox Jew with high hat, ringlets of hair, and a black coat is at the window weaving Torah rolls and prayer shawls. Next door, **Emanuel Weisberg** sells Hebrew religious antiques.

At no. 35 and no. 27 Essex Street, delicious pickled cucumbers and tomatoes are available from huge barrels. Have a look on the left side of Hester Street; this street became famous again recently because of the film about Jewish immigrants who started out here. **Gus' Pickle Emporium,** so many claim, has the best pickles in the city.

Turn left from Essex Street onto Grand Street. On the corner of Grand and Allen streets, at **Ezra Cohen,** you can find the bed linen patterns that were sold out at Macy's. Wander up to Mulberry Street, the narrow north-south thoroughfare known as the pulsebeat of Little Italy.

Little Italy has been declared a special district by the city, which should lead to a social revitalization of the district and to its cultural independence. Building regulations have been tightened. New shops and restaurants have to fit the image architecturally and old ones are being renovated. Pedestrian zones will stimulate the original street life. Although a Chinese laundry has sprung up next to some pasta shops, and Chinese bean sprouts are being sold next to Italian artichokes, one speaks in Little Italy with some optimism of "resorgimento."

If you like Italian food, you can get Neapolitan, Milanese, or Florentine here. On the way to Mulberry Street, on the corner of Grand and Mott streets, you will get in the Italian mood at the sight of mozzarella, salami, and ricotta at **Di Palo's.** Pass by **Café Ferrara's** (195 Grand Street), whose wedding cake arrangements fill several shop windows; it's also famous for its espresso and capuccino. When you turn left onto Mulberry Street, you can eat in one of the oldest Italian places — **Paolucci's** (149 Mulberry), or also at **Angelo's** (146 Mulberry). There's also **Umberto's Clam House** (129 Mulberry), where a mafioso was shot several years ago while peacefully eating clams, or **Puglia's** (corner of Hester and Mulberry streets), or **Il Cortile** (125 Mulberry), the most beautiful modern restaurant here.

Italian books, records, and perfumes are sold at no. 130, and espresso machines at no. 127. At **La Bella Ferrara** (no. 108), you can still quickly buy yourself some home baked pastries for the return trip. Turn right onto Canal Street and go back to the starting point of our tour, the Lexington Avenue IRT subway station.

Little Italy

5 Lower Manhattan — Heritage Trail

Everybody knows that New York behaves just like a child with building blocks: it pulls everything down in order to build better, higher, but most important, to build differently. It is a habit that has covered many of the traces of its not exactly boring past, and New York aficionados are forever organizing "archaeological digs" with often fantastic results.

If you follow the plan for an interesting walk put together by the Downtown-Lower Manhattan Association, you will not only be taken into the here and now of the World Trade Center, to the colorful street markets on Chambers, Reade, and Duane streets, to Chinatown and Little Italy, but you will pass fifteen spots that are closely linked with New York's history. This walking tour is reprinted courtesy of the Friends of the Heritage Trail.

1. CIVIC CENTER — The Civic Center is composed of Foley Square, the New York County Courthouse, the United States Courthouse, the Municipal Building, the Surrogates Court, and the Tweed Courthouse. **Foley Square** is situated a few blocks north of City Hall, at the southern end of the former Collect, or Fresh Water Pond which served as a source of fresh water during colonial days. Fronting on Foley Square at 60 Centre Street lies the **New York County Courthouse** by Guy Lowell which was built in 1926. A low hexagon with a majestic Corinthian portico 100 feet wide, it is reached by a monumental flight of steps. Adjacent to the south, the **United States Courthouse** completes the eastern enclosure of Foley Square. Designed by Cass Gilbert (architect of the Woolworth Building and the Custom House on Bowling Green) and Cass Gilbert, Jr., in 1936, it is now a City Landmark. Standing on Centre Street, across from City Hall is the **Municipal Building** by McKim, Mead, and White which was completed in 1915 and houses city government offices. It is crowned by a gilded statue of "Civic Fame" by the sculptor Adolph Weinmann. Diagonally opposite to the northwest at 31 Chambers Street is the **Surrogate's Court.** It was designed as the Hall of Records for the City by John R. Thomas and was built during 1899–1907. Behind City Hall and fronting on Chambers Street is the **Tweed Courthouse.**

2. CITY HALL/CITY HALL PARK — **City Hall** is considered one of the City's finest architectural gems. It was built between 1803 and 1811. Its architects Joseph Mangin and John McComb, Jr., combined Georgian form with French Renaissance detail. The central domed space contains twin spiral marble staircases. Several state funerals were held here, including those of Presidents Grant (1885) and Lincoln (1865).

City Hall Park was originally a pasture and parade ground during the Dutch period. The Declaration of Independence was read here before George Washington and his troops on July 9, 1776.

3. WOOLWORTH BUILDING — This building was conceived by Frank Woolworth, founder of the Five-and-Ten Cent store chain, as a modern office tower of landmark character. This "Cathedral of Commerce" was executed in 1913 by Cass Gilbert (who also designed the Custom House at Bowling Green).

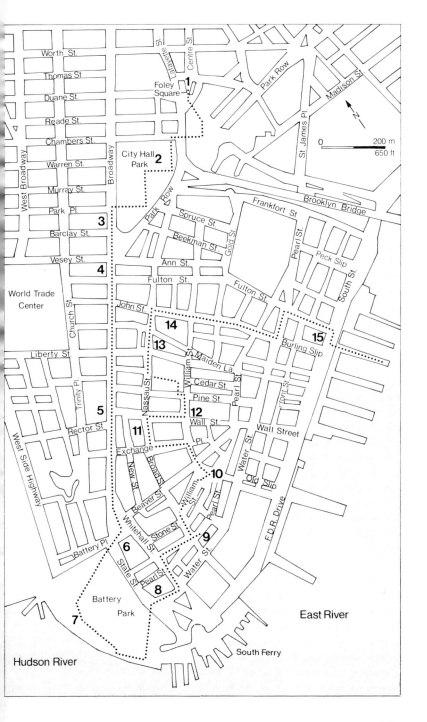

Worth St.
Thomas St.
Duane St.
Reade St.
Chambers St.
Warren St.
Murray St.
Park Pl.
Barclay St.
Vesey St.
West Broadway
Broadway
Lafayette St.
Centre St.
Park Row
Madison St.
St. James Pl.
Foley Square
1
City Hall Park
2
3
4
Brooklyn Bridge
Frankfort St.
Spruce St.
Beekman St.
Ann St.
Fulton St.
Gold St.
Pearl St.
Peck Slip
South St.
World Trade Center
Church St.
John St.
Fulton St.
14
15
Burling Slip
Liberty St.
Trinity Pl.
Nassau St.
William St.
Maiden La.
Cedar St.
Pine St.
Pearl St.
Front St.
13
5
Rector St.
11
Exchange Pl.
Wall St.
Wall Street
Water St.
12
New St.
Broad St.
10
William St.
Pearl St.
Old Slip
F.D.R. Drive
West Side Highway
Beaver St.
Whitehall St.
Stone St.
9
6
Battery Pl.
State St.
Pearl St.
Water St.
8
Battery Park
7
East River
South Ferry
Hudson River

0   200 m
650 ft
N

Magnificently detailed in an adaption of Gothic style it was, until 1930, the tallest building in the world.

4. ST. PAUL'S CHAPEL — The Chapel was built between 1764–1766. This Georgian structure is the oldest surviving church in Manhattan. The tower and steeple were added in 1796. George Washington worshipped here during his presidency.

5. TRINITY CHURCH — This is the third church to occupy this site. The design was executed in 1846 by Richard Upjohn. The City's oldest Episcopal parish, Trinity received a sizeable land grant from Queen Anne in 1705. Notable features include the Chapel of All Saints, the bronze doors by Richard Morris Hunt, and the pleasant church yard containing several gravestones of famous Americans, including Robert Fulton and Alexander Hamilton.

6. CUSTOM HOUSE/BOWLING GREEN — The **Custom House** is a Beaux-Arts style building designed by Cass Gilbert. Built in 1901–1907, the building incorporates a vast central rotunda with a flat dome on which murals of early New York harbor scenes were painted by Reginald Marsh. Four massive sculptures by Daniel Chester French (sculptor for the Lincoln Memorial in Washington) represent the continents of Asia, America, Europe, and Africa.

Bowling Green is the site of the legendary sale of Manhattan Island to Peter Minuit in 1626. It served as a cattle market, a parade ground and, for an annual fee of one peppercorn, was leased by its owner as a quasi-public bowling ground in 1732. The fence surrounding the park dates to 1771 and is a City Landmark. An equestrian statue of King George III was toppled from its base in the park by an angry mob of colonists during the Revolution following the reading of the Declaration of Independence in City Hall Park on July 9, 1776.

7. BATTERY PARK — The Park gets its name from a row of guns that were placed along the original shoreline (present State Street). It consists mainly of landfill that gradually increased its size to the present twenty-two acres. **Castle Clinton,** which now stands well inland, was constructed in 1807–1811, some 300 feet off the shore, as one of three forts in the defense network in the harbor during the War of 1812. The structure which now houses a museum served, at various times, as a fort, an immigration depot, a performing arts center, and the city's Aquarium. Visible from the Park's promenade are three islands situated in the Upper Bay of New York Harbor: Ellis Island, Liberty Island, and Governors Island. **Ellis Island,** originally used in the 1600s by the Mohegan Indians as an oyster fishery ground is most widely known as the ''gateway'' to the United States — over 12 million immigrants were passed through the island between 1892 and 1954. Formerly Bedloe Island (after the Bedloe family), **Liberty Island** was purchased by the state of New York in 1796 and was ceded to the federal government in 1800 for the construction of Ford Wood, part of the harbor defenses of 1811–1812. The star-shaped fort wall now forms the base for Auguste Bartholdi's Statue of Liberty which was dedicated by President Cleveland on October 28, 1886. In 1637, **Governors Island** was purchased by the Dutch colony of New Netherlands from the Manhattas Indians. The Island has served as a race track and summer resort, a prisoner of war prison and a troop embarcation point. Castle Williams, a massive masonry bastion stood sentry over New York Harbor during the War of 1812, assisting in the deterence of a possible attack by the British fleet.

8. STATE STREET ROW/EAST RIVER FERRIES — The building at no. 7 State Street is presently the Rectory for the Shrine of Saint Elizabeth Ann Seton, and is the only survivor of a once-elegant row of Federal-style mansions. Constructed in stages between 1793–1806, its graceful curved portico is set off by slender, free-standing Ionic columns.

At the southern end of State Street stand the two remaining ferry terminals that are still in operation in Manhattan. The earliest recorded ferry crossing in the region connected Hoboken, New Jersey, and New Amsterdam in 1661. Ferry operations on the East River began about 1695 when service between Brooklyn and Fly Market Slip was inaugurated.

9. FRAUNCES TAVERN/FRAUNCES TAVERN BLOCK — In his conjectural restoration of Fraunces Tavern in 1907, William Mersereau incorporated the few remaining structural elements of the Stephen DeLancey House which was built here in 1719. Samuel Fraunces, a West Indian, became the proprietor of a tavern there in 1763. Following the war in 1783, Washington bade farewell to his troops in the Long Room above the tavern. The Fraunces Tavern Museum complex lies at the end of one of the very few remaining complete blocks of eighteenth- and nineteenth-century buildings. Land for the block was produced from land-fill. Prior to 1700 the shoreline stretched along present-day Pearl Street.

10. INDIA HOUSE/HANOVER SQUARE — **India House** is an outstanding example of the Italianate style of architecture. Presently, it houses a private club and a maritime collection.

The adjoining park, known as **Hanover Square,** was the City's original printinghouse square where, nearby, William Bradford established the first printing press in the colonies in 1693. The square was almost completely destroyed in The Great Fire of 1835.

11. NEW YORK STOCK EXCHANGE/FEDERAL HALL — The **New York Stock Exchange,** dating to the signing of an agreement under a buttonwood (sycamore) tree on Wall Street in 1792, was formally constituted at the Tontine Coffee House on May 17, 1792. It grew out of a need to create a formal marketplace to handle $80 million of stock which was issued by the Congress of 1789–1790 to pay the Revolutionary War debts. The present building was completed in 1903 from designs by Trowbridge and Livingston.

Federal Hall is located on the site of the city's second City Hall, which was constructed in 1701 to replace the old Stadt-Huys on Pearl Street. It was in this City Hall that George Washington took his oath as first president in 1789. The present Doric-columned temple structure, by architects Town and Davis, features a striking interior rotunda and, on the Wall Street steps, a statue of Washington by John Q. A. Ward done in 1883.

12. BANK OF NEW YORK/CITIBANK — The **Bank of New York** is the oldest bank in New York City. The structure, built between 1927–1928, is the bank's third home on this site since 1798. The bank's founding in 1784 resulted from the need to establish a new financial institution to help rebuild the city. Alexander Hamilton drafted the bank's state charter which served as a precedent for future banking rules in the country. The present structure, designed by Benjamin Morris, contains an ornate banking room with eight wall murals that depict the commercial and industrial development of New York during the eighteenth and nineteenth centuries.

The **Citibank** building is actually a composite structure, the lower portion of 55 Wall Street was built in 1836–1842 from plans by Isaiah Rogers. In the early 1900s, an upper section was added based on designs by McKim, Mead, and White.

13. FEDERAL RESERVE BANK/CHAMBER OF COMMERCE — The **Federal Reserve Bank** is housed in a neo-Renaissance fortress of limestone and sandstone which is said to be modeled after the Palazzo Strozzi of the fifteenth-century Florentine banking family. The decorative treatment throughout the building utilizes iron (200 tons of it) gracefully wrought by Samuel Yellin. Designed by York and Sawyer, the New York Federal Reserve Bank was built in 1923–1924 and serves as one of twelve area banks that carry out the many functions of the "Fed," including regulation of credit and cash flow.

The **Chamber of Commerce** building is of the same family or style as the Custom House at Bowling Green and the Surrogate's Court on Chambers Street. This Beaux-Arts structure, housing the New York Chamber of Commerce which was founded in 1768, was built in 1901 from plans by James B. Baker. The dominant interior feature is the splendid Great Hall — a vast volume 90 feet by 60 feet with an elaborately decorated ceiling 38 feet above — in which is housed a highly valued portrait collection.

14. JOHN STREET METHODIST CHURCH — John Street Church, the oldest Methodist Society in continental America, is the mother church of American Methodism. Philip Embury, an ardent Irish Methodist, organized the Society in 1766 and conducted the first services on the upper story of "The Old Rigging Loft" on William Street between John and Fulton. The present church, the third at this location, was built in 1841. Many stout handhewn beams remain from an earlier chapel on the site that was demolished in 1817.

15. SOUTH STREET SEAPORT — Soon after its settlement by the Dutch as a trading post in the 1620s, New York became a thriving seaport. Through successive landfills, the original shoreline of Pearl Street gradually became present-day South Street. The several-block area of the Seaport still contains buildings dating from the early nineteenth century that once sheltered merchants, clerks, sailmakers, riggers, printers, and grocers.

From the end of Pier 16, at the foot of Fulton Street at the Seaport, a fine unobstructed view can be had of the **Brooklyn Bridge,** John A. and his son Washington Roebling's splendid engineering achievement of 1860–1883. The majestic Italian Renaissance-style granite bridge towers stand in sharp contrast to the open tapestry of its cables. During the period 1883–1903, it was the longest suspension bridge in the world.

Statue of Liberty towers above Liberty Island

The skyscraper city was spread out before me in the brilliance of the midday sun; its tallest buildings towered over my tall hotel. I recognized New York as the settlement of my era and it pleased me very much; it bewitched me and it fulfilled all of my expectations. Like turrets and castles made of steel, aluminum, concrete, and sparkling glass, the skyscrapers grew everywhere out of a jumble of other relatively and astonishingly low roofs, cut up in a rectangular pattern by the streets. The tall ones, which proudly reached to the heavens, seemed to greet each other over the tops of the little buildings.

Wolfgang Koeppen, *New York*

Key to the City

Manhattan Street Guide 258

nclusion of a particular store or service in this guide should not be construed as a ecommendation from the publisher. All noted sources and services subject to change; we uggest that you phone ahead.

Manhattan Street Guide

To determine the approximate cross street for addresses located along the avenues, ■ the following formula. Remember, however, that these are only approximations and th the actual location may be 1 or 2 blocks in either direction.

For most of the addresses, use the building number and eliminate the last digit, divide by 2, and then add or subtract the number given below.

First Avenue	+3
Second Avenue	+3
Third Avenue	+10
Fourth Avenue	+8

Fifth Avenue

to 200	+13
to 400	+16
to 600	+18
to 775	+20

from 775 to 1286, eliminate the last digit but do not divide by 2; instead, subtract 18

to 1500	+45
over 2000	+24

Sixth Avenue	−1
Seventh Avenue	+1
(but above 110th Street, +20)	
Eighth Avenue	+1
Ninth Avenue	+1
Tenth Avenue	+1
Amsterdam Avenue	+6
Broadway	−3
Columbus Avenue	+6
Lexington Avenue	+2
Madison Avenue	+2
Park Avenue	+3
West End Avenue	+6

Central Park West: Divide number by 1 and add 60

Riverside Drive: Divide number by 1 and add 72

Arrival in New York

By Air

All transatlantic and most transcontinental flights arrive at (and depart from) **John F. Kennedy Airport** (JFK for short) in the borough of Queens. A number of airlines have their own terminals with passport control and customs; other flights originate and/or terminate at the International Arrivals Building. When a number of planes arrive simultaneously at the Arrivals Building, it may take a while to get through immigration and customs, but don't despair.

If you are not a U.S. citizen, all you need is a valid visa in your passport and a clear conscience. You are not allowed to bring in animals, plants, or fresh foodstuffs. As a tourist you may however bring in one quart of liquor and two hundred cigarettes. Naturally the possession of marijuana and other drugs is prohibited, and the penalties are stiff.

Shorter-distance flights arrive at **LaGuardia Airport**, which is about half-way between JFK and Manhattan, or at **Newark Airport** in Newark, New Jersey. Both these airports are slightly smaller than JFK, although if you are not used to very large airports, they will also seem immense. It takes the usual amount of time to collect your baggage and pass through the gates to the street.

For your trip to the city from any of the airports you can take one of the yellow taxis (if there is a dispatcher, so much the better). Don't take taxis whose drivers offer their services outside their cab; they are supposed to stay inside except perhaps to help you put your luggage into the trunk. The fare however can easily be $25 plus tip. The airports are all a distance from the main part of New York, and the ride usually takes at least 30 minutes.

There is a bus which will take you from JFK to the East Side Air Terminal (38 Street and First Avenue; 632-0500). The fare is $4 and it runs every twenty minutes. You can use it to return to the airport too. Or you can take the JFK express — the Train to the Plane. Follow the sign with a white plane in a blue circle. At various stops a bus will pick you up and take you to a special (blue) subway car which will take you into town in about an hour for $3.50. There are several stops in Brooklyn and Manhattan — among them Borough Hall; downtown Manhattan; 34 and 42 streets; and 57 Street (Sixth Avenue).

There is now regularly scheduled helicopter service from JFK, LaGuardia, and Newark airports to the 34th Street Heliport (alongside the East River). The helicopters carry nine passengers and operate Monday through Friday, with more limited service on Saturday and Sunday. The present fare is $26.67 between LaGuardia and Manhattan; $31.90 from JFK; and $41.90 from Newark.

By Rail

Trains to New York arrive at either **Grand Central Station** or **Pennsylvania Station**. Grand Central is located at 42 Street and Lexington Avenue, convenient to Manhattan's East Side. From Grand Central you can take a taxi, bus or subway in a variety of directions. Pennsylvania Station is at Seventh Avenue and 32 Street, on Manhattan's West Side. Both buses and subways stop at Penn Station, and taxis cruise in front of the Seventh Avenue entrance almost constantly. Penn Station has been remodeled, but Grand Central is a remarkably interesting building that dates back to a more glorious era. You can take a tour of the station and see parts of it that are no longer in use.

By Bus

Buses from all parts of the country arrive in New York at the **Port Authority Bus Terminals**: one in midtown at Eighth Avenue and 41 Street, and another uptown at the George Washington Bridge and 178 Street. The Port Authority Bus Terminal is a less than desirable way to arrive in the city. The midtown station is noisy, dirty, and uncomfortable, yet safe. Buses and subway service the terminal, and again cabs are usually cruising by on the Eighth Avenue side. The immediate area around the terminal in midtown is not one of New York's finest, so move on quickly to where you are going.

By Car

First of all, arriving in New York by car is not recommended. Traffic moves fast in the city (requiring you to know in advance where you are going and how you plan to get there) or else it crawls along, constantly avoiding construction obstacles, stalled cars, or double-parked limousines. If you *are* driving to New York, you are also faced with the problem of storing your car. Parking in New York is expensive in the garages, but that is probably your only choice. Enter the city by way of one of the tunnels, bridges, or ferry, then locate your hotel and ask the doorman to direct you to a nearby garage. Even if you are lucky enough to find a legal parking spot on the street, it probably won't be legal the next day. (New York has alternate side-of-the-street parking.)

Antiques

see SHOPPING.

Art Galleries

Galleries in Manhattan are generally open Tuesday through Saturday, from 11 AM to 5 PM.

Madison Avenue

Aberbach Fine Art, 988 Madison Avenue (77 Street); 988-1100. Vienna school.

Acquavella, 18 East 79 Street; 734-6300. Impressionists and twentieth-century masters.

Cordier & Ekstrom, 980 Madison Avenue (76 Street); 988-8857. Modern painting and sculpture; imaginative exhibits.

Gimpel & Weitzenhoffer, 1040 Madison Avenue (79 Street); 628-1897. Modern art.

Hirschl & Adler, 21 East 70 Street; 535-8810. European and American art, mostly nineteenth and twentieth century.

Knoedler Contemporary Art, 19 East 70 Street; 628-0400.

Monique Knowlton, 19 East 71 Street; 794-9700. Modern art.

Lefebre, 47 East 77 Street; 744-3384. Modern French artists.

Perls, 1016 Madison Avenue (78 Street); 472-3200. Modern art. (Note the Calder sidewalk in front of the gallery.)

Ronald Feldman, 33 East 74 Street; 249-4050. Contemporary art.

Saidenberg, 1018 Madison Avenue (69 Street); 288-3387. Picasso and cubists.

Serge Sabarsky, 987 Madison Avenue (76 Street); 628-6281. German Expressionism, Grosz.

Shepherd, 21 East 84 Street; 821-4050. Nineteenth century.

Wildenstein, 19 East 64 Street;

879-0500. European and American masters.

Willard, 29 East 72 Street; 744-2925. Contemporary art.

Xavier Fourcade, 36 East 75 Street; 535-3980. Modern Art.

57 Street Area

AAA, 663 Fifth Avenue; 755-4211. The place for prints.

André Emmerich, 41 East 57 Street; 752-0124. Contemporary painting; pre-Columbian sculpture.

Allan Frumkin, 50 West 57 Street; 757-6655. Modern American art.

Betty Parsons, 24 West 57 Street; 247-7480. Abstract art.

Kennedy, 40 West 57 Street; 541-9600. Fine American painting and sculpture.

Light Gallery, 724 Fifth Avenue; 582-6552. Photography.

Marlborough, 40 West 57 Street; 541-4900.

Martha Jackson, 521 West 57 Street; 586-4200. Contemporary international painting and sculpture; prints.

Pace, 32 East 57 Street; 421-3292. Contemporary American art.

Pierre Matisse, 41 East 57 Street; 355-6269. Modern European masters.

Robert Miller, 724 Fifth Avenue; 246-1625. Contemporary art.

Rosa Esman, 29 West 57 Street; 421-9490. Twentieth-century American art.

Sidney Janis, 6 West 57 Street; 586-0110. From Cubism to Pop; Mondrian, Albers.

Womanart, 50 West 57 Street; 757-4644. Women's paintings and drawings.

Zabriskie, 29 West 57 Street; 832-9034. Classical modern art.

Downtown

A.I.R., 97 Wooster Street; 966-0799. Women's art.

Clocktower, 108 Leonard Street; 233-1096. Very avant-garde.

Holly Solomon, 392 West Broadway; 925-1900. Pattern painters and decorative art.

John Weber, 420 West Broadway; 966-6115. Modern Americans.

Leo Castelli, 420 West Broadway; 431-5160. Recent contemporary art in an old cast-iron warehouse.

O. K. Harris, 383 West Broadway; 431-3600.

Paula Cooper, 155 Wooster Street; 677-4390. A SoHo pioneer.

Phyllis Kind, 139 Spring Street; 925-1200. Chicago school.

Sonnabend, 420 West Broadway; 966-6160. Avant-garde.

Sperone Westwater Fischer, 142 Greene Street; 431-3685.

Ward-Nasse, 131 Prince Street; 475-9125.

Women in the Arts, 435 Broome Street; 966-5894.

Auctions

Art and Antiques

Christie's, 502 Park Avenue (59 Street); 826-2888. This is the American branch of the English auction house; handles only first-class things.

PB 84, 171 East 84 Street; 472-3583. Sotheby Parke Bernet's "little sister." Many New Yorker's have furnished their apartments with items from this less-expensive branch.

Sotheby Parke Bernet, Inc., 980 Madison Avenue (77 Street); 472-3400. The most exciting auctions take place at this address.

Other

General Post Office Auctions, Main Post Office, 33 Street & Eighth Avenue, Room 3021; 971-7731. Abandoned parcels could contain treasures; most often one finds small pieces of jewelry and the like.

Land Auction Agency, 888 Seventh Avenue (56 Street); 757-2525. If you like it here so much, you can buy some land.

Police Department Auctions. For information call 982-2190. These take place three times a year and usually include stolen or lost bicycles, other miscellaneous items left with the police.

Swann Galleries, 104 East 25 Street; 254-4710. Rare books.

Tepper Galleries, 3 West 61 Street; 246-1800. Furniture and rugs.

Bars and Pubs

Algonquin, in the Algonquin Hotel, 59 West 44 Street; 840-6800.

Barrymore's Pub, 267 West 45 Street; 541-4500.

Bel-Air East, in the Sherry Netherland Hotel, 781 Fifth Avenue (59 Street). For sighting Hollywood types.

Bemelman's Bar, in the Carlyle Hotel, 35 East 76 Street; 744-1600.

Charley O's, in the restaurant, 33 West 48 Street; 582-7141

Costello's, 225 East 44 Street; 599-9614.

Elaine's, 1703 Second Avenue (88 Street); 534-8103. Swarms with prominent people.

Fanelli's, 94 Prince Street; 226-9412 Sawdust on the floor.

Flanagan's, 1215 First Avenue (66 Street); 472-0300. Irish.

Friday's, 1152 First Avenue; 832-8512.

Gallagher's, 150 West 52 Street 582-5483. Sports fans.

Garvin's, in the restaurant, 19 Waverly Place; 473-5261. Very cozy.

King Cole Bar, in the Hotel St. Regis Fifth Avenue and 55 Street; 753-4500 Marvelous Art Deco interior.

Lion's Head, 59 Christopher Street 929-0670. Literary.

Martell's, 1469 Third Avenue (83 Street); 861-6110. Sidewalk cafe.

Maxwell's Plum, in the restaurant, First Avenue and 64 Street; 628-2100.

McSorley's Old Ale House, 15 East 7 Street; 730-9044. Originally not fo women.

Mike Manuche's, 150 West 52 Street 582-5483. Circular sports bar.

Oak Bar, in the Plaza Hotel, Fifth Avenue and 58 Street; 759-3000.

P.J. Clarke's, 915 Third Avenue (55 Street); 759-1650. A bit of old New York

Rose, 41 West 52 Street; 974-9004.

Sardi's, 234 West 44 Street; 221-8440.

Spring Street Bar, 401 West Broadway 431-7637.

Toots Shor, One Penn Plaza; 279-8150 A New York institution.

21 Club, 21 West 52 Street; 582-7200.

United Nations Plaza Bar, First Avenue and 44 Street; 355-3400.

White Horse Tavern, 567 Hudson Street; 243-9360. A favorite hangout o Dylan Thomas, now frequented by poets and artists.

Windows on the World, World Trade Center; 938-1111. The view is worth your last penny.

Babysitters

see DAYCARE.

Beauty Salons

The good and/or famous ones are very expensive, and are generally located in the vicinity of 57 Street and Fifth Avenue. Here are some for your convenience.

Elizabeth Arden, 691 Fifth Avenue (54 Street); 486-7929.

Georgette Klinger, 501 Madison Avenue (52 Street); 838-3200.

Michel Kazan, 16 East 55 Street; 688-1400.

Kenneth, 19 East 54 Street; 752-1800.

Pierre and Fred, 131 East 70 Street; 535-4002. In Tiffany's townhouse.

Vidal Sassoon, 115 East 57 Street; 751-7721.

Banks

see MONEY.

Bicycle Rentals

see RENTALS.

Books About New York

Burgess, Anthony. *New York*. New York: Time-Life, 1977. An impressive picture book with an intelligent text; gives a sensitive portrait of the city.

Edmiston, Susan, and Cirino, Linda. *Literary New York*. Boston: Houghton Mifflin, 1976. Literary sites in all the boroughs.

Flaste, Richard. *New York Times Guide to Children's Entertainment in New York, New Jersey, and Connecticut*. New York: Quadrangle, 1976.

Glaser, Milton and Snyder, Jerome. *The Underground Gourmet*. New York: Simon & Schuster, 1975 (paperback).

Green, Frances, ed. *Gayellow Pages: N.Y./N.J. Edition* 13. New York: Renaissance House, 1980. Source book covering all types of businesses.

McDarrah, Fred. *Museums in New York*. New York: Quick Fox, 1978 (paperback). Describes all the museums in New York.

Michelin Touring Services. *New York City*. Lake Success, New York: Michelin Tire Corporation, 1979 (paperback). Very useful for the bird's-eye views of the important sections of New York.

Stern, Zelda. *The Complete Guide to Ethnic New York*. New York: St. Martin's Press, 1980 (paperback). A guide to all of New York's ethnic neighborhoods, festivals, restaurants, and shops.

White, Norval and Willensky, Elliot, eds. *AIA Guide to New York City*. New York: The Macmillan Company, 1978. Put together by the American Institute of Architects; historical, geographic, and generally informative.

Bookstores

see SHOPPING.

Boutiques

see SHOPPING.

Buses

see PUBLIC TRANSPORTATION and ARRIVAL IN NEW YORK, by bus.

Calendar of Events

January
There are a number of shows and conventions in New York in January, from the Automobile Show to the National Needlework Convention, but the most important event is the Winter Antiques Show in the Seventh Regiment Armory on Park Avenue and 67th Street (end of the month), attracting visitors from all over the world.

February
The first new moon between January 21 and February 19 brings the Chinese New Year to Chinatown (for exact dates each year and other information call the Chinese Community Center, 247-5780). Thousands of ear-splitting firecrackers accompany processions of colorful lions and dragons snaking their many-forked tails through the narrow streets.

On or near his birthday, February 22, George Washington is given a parade on Fifth Avenue around noon.

March
March 17 is the birthday of St. Patrick, the patron saint of Ireland, and in his honor there is a parade. Not only the Irish participate (they started all this in 1779 when a major in the British army tried to enlist them and they — brand-new Americans — chased him along the streets shouting), but along with black bands, Puerto-Rican school children, and delegates from Chinatown, many other ethnic groups are represented. They all wear something green in honor of St. Pat; carnations tinted green are very popular and sold at every street corner, mostly by enterprising young boys. Naturally orange, the color of the protestant Irish, had better not be seen on anyone.

The Greeks celebrate their independence on March 25, and hold their parade on a convenient Saturday or Sunday near that date. It is not as ambitious as the St. Patrick's Day Parade but just as lively, and the floats with Apollo, Dionysus, and Helen of Troy are something to behold. You might see some musical instruments familiar from Greek vases, but the general accompaniment is more up-to-date pop, slightly watered down to accommodate the tempo of the procession.

April
At Easter time the Bronx and Brooklyn Botanical Gardens, the Channel Gardens in Rockefeller Center, and even little Gramercy Park are a sight to behold with their beds of Easter lilies and other spring flowers. Lots and lots of people promenade on Fifth Avenue for the Easter Parade, perhaps not quite as extravagant as Hollywood would have you believe, but it is still the place to show the world your new spring outfit.

At Madison Square Garden, for about two months, there is the Ringling Bros. and Barnum & Bailey Circus with three rings, famous animal tamers, highwire artists, many animals, and clowns.

At the beginning of the month, the Annex Antiques Fair and Flea Market arrives at Sixth Avenue and 26th Street and remains there until the end of October; for information, call 675-4289.

May

During the early part of the month, the Brooklyn Heights Promenade Fine Arts Show takes place, a good time to wander about the lovely streets with the most beautiful houses in New York, admire the Manhattan skyline from a fine vantage point, and at the same time see what the local talent has to offer. At the World Trade Center there is a Spring Flower Show in the lobby of Number One; call 466-7377 for information.

One weekend in the middle of the month is set aside for the Ninth Avenue International Festival, between 37th and 57th streets. Here are the famous food markets, and they put on a fantastic and fattening show, bringing the hungry and the curious in the thousands to sample their fares, from Greek dolmades and spinach pies, Italian salami and cheese, Milo's fish fried for you on the spot, to Philippine and Puerto-Rican delicacies.

June

From the end of May until about the middle of June, New York's Bohème celebrates the Feast of San Leonardo, otherwise known as the Washington Square Park Art Show, in Washington Square Park. It's well worth a visit, even if your hopes of discovering the next Picasso may be dashed very quickly.

One Sunday in the middle of the month is reserved for the 52nd Street Festival, and the whole street from the East River to the Hudson is one huge block party. Everything from antiques to zeppolli and from Polynesian dancers to jazzbands can be observed on one street. The papers print programs and maps a few days before.

During the second week of June you must go to SoHo, where the Festa di San Antonio takes place in honor of St. Anthony, who has a shrine on Sullivan Street. If you cannot be here in September for the Feast of San Gennaro, you must try to catch this one. On this one day, Fifth Avenue between 86th and 105th streets is closed to traffic and given over to pedestrians. All the museums along there remain open late and you can rub shoulders with quite a cross section of New Yorkers.

July and August

These are "New York is a Summer Festival" months, an institution by now but originated by John Lindsay's government many years ago. It means a bewildering choice of (mostly free) open-air performances, such as plays by the New York Shakespeare Festival in Central Park or operas, concerts, and jazz, pop, and rock performances in Central and Prospect parks; Lincoln Center also has out-of-doors concerts and shows then.

Independence Day is celebrated appropriately: Macy's sponsors "Fireworks on the Hudson," a spectacular half-hour show from barges in the Hudson River (79th to 125th streets).

During the first week in July there is a Harbor Festival at the southern tip of Manhattan Island with just about everything maritime you can imagine: regattas, skydiving, international life-boat races, a canoe cavalcade, and such un-maritime activities as fireworks, music, and dancing thrown in for good measure.

Toward the end of July, if you have any energy left, you will find a spirited Festa Italiana on Bleecker and Carmine streets and a very lively Salsa en el Barrio, a Puerto-Rican street festival on Lexington Avenue between 107th and 108th streets. Last, but by no means least, July brings the Newport Jazz Festival to New York (call 787-2020), usually in the middle of a heat wave. But that does not stop anyone from swinging along happily, and you will have a hard time choosing from the many tempting sessions.

For a week in the middle of August, Harlem celebrates its Harlem Week with art exhibitions, parties, and parades culminating on Harlem Day, the last day.

If it is hot, and it is bound to be, you might want to get out of Manhattan. If you take the Staten Island Ferry and go to the Richmondtown Restoration in Staten Island you might catch their country fair; for information, call 351-1611.

September
The most important event of the month is the Festa di San Gennaro, patron saint of Naples and Little Italy. It is the oldest of New York's *feste,* and it is celebrated for a week around the 19th with eating and drinking, dancing, and bazaar-hopping. A statue of the saint in flowing robes (to which you may pin dollar notes) is carried through the streets as the high point of the festivities. If you get claustrophobic you can always catch your breath in a side street; for information, call 226-9546.

And if you find yourself on Fifth Avenue one September Saturday or Sunday afternoon and come across a parade with slightly German accents, you have before you the Steuben Parade, named after the German general who fought for George Washington in the War of Independence.

If you are interested in sailing, you might want to watch the Governor's Cup Race in New York Bay; for information call 269-2710.

On the East Side of Manhattan, in Carl Schurz Park, there is an outdoor art show in the middle of the month, and while there, you can take a look at the official residence of New York's mayor, Gracie Mansion.

October
On the 5th, or the nearest Sunday, the Polish have their Pulaski Day Parade up Fifth Avenue from 26th to 52nd streets;

the highlight of it is the pretty costumes.

Around the 10th of the month, on or near Columbus Day, Italians celebrate the feast of their famous compatriot with a parade along Fifth Avenue from 44th to 86th streets.

November
At the beginning of the month the best horses and riders meet, along with many other prominent folk, for the famous and beautiful National Horse Show in Madison Square Garden.

In honor of this important American holiday, Macy's organizes the famous Thanksgiving Day Parade. This is more than a parade; it really is a gigantic street festival, with dancing Mickey and Minnie Mouse, the Rockettes from Radio City Music Hall (also dancing, naturally), famous faces from screen and politics, and the first Santa Claus of the season. The parade moves down Central Park West from 77th Street to 59th Street, and then down Broadway to 34th Street.

December
Christmas decorations are in place by the 1st of the month. Behind Prometheus in Rockefeller Center a gigantic Christmas tree is put up and carols are sung there on several afternoons before Christmas. And for two Sundays Fifth Avenue becomes a pedestrian mall from 57th Street to 34th Street filled with last-minute shoppers, choirs, dance groups, trampolines, slides, and the usual sprinkling of eccentrics.

Concert halls and churches resound with music, and so do many street corners. The Metropolitan Museum puts up the beautiful tree in its Medieval Sculpture Hall and decorates it with at least a hundred figures from an eighteenth-century Neapolitan nativity.

And if you don't mind considerable crush, you could take the subway to Times Square on New Year's Eve and watch — along with many not-too-sober fellows human beings — the huge lit ball announce the New Year. Or you can watch the fireworks the city offers every year on the Sheep Meadow in Central Park.

Children's Clothes

see SHOPPING.

Children's Entertainment

Barnes & Noble Sales Annex, Fifth Avenue at 18th Street; 675-5500. Puppet shows.

Big Apple Circus, 1 East 104 Street; 369-5110. Shows June-Sept.

Bill Baird's Marionette Theater, 59 Barrow Street; 989-7060.

Courtyard Playhouse, 39 Grove Street; 765-9540.

First All Children's Theater, 37 West 65 Street; 873-6400.

Henry Street Settlement Family Theater, 466 Grand Street; 766-9334.

Swedish Collage Marionette Theater, Central Park at 81 Street; 988-9093.

Theater of the Riverside Church, 490 Riverside Drive (121 Street); 864-2829.

Town Hall Theater for Children, 123 West 43 Street; 489-0120.

Children's Museums

Many of New York's museums would be suitable for children, so also see Museums. The following are specially set up for children.

Brooklyn Children's Museum, 145 Brooklyn Avenue, Brooklyn; 735-4400.

Manhattan Laboratory Museum, 314 West 54 Street; 765-5904. A small children's museum concentrating on scientific matters.

Metropolitan Museum of Art, Junior Museum, Fifth Avenue at 81 Street; 535-7710.

Staten Island Children's Museum, 15 Beach Street, Staten Island; 273-2060.

Climate and Clothing

"Everybody talks about the weather, but nobody does anything about it." — Mark Twain

The weather in New York can play havoc with your plans: either you are creeping along in summer humidity or icy winds and snowstorms chase you off the winter streets. Yet although the weather is just as unpredictable here as elsewhere, **autumn** is considered the best time to visit New York. Ideally, the elusive Indian Summer occurs between mid-September and mid-November with warm daytime temperatures, cool nights, and clear air. But even then you might be surprised by a sudden shift in the weather, so be prepared.

The best clothing to bring is that which can be layered. You can put more on if you need it and remove a layer when it is warm. Most of the better restaurants expect men to wear jackets and ties, even at lunchtime; but they often lend customers both.

Concert Halls

Brooklyn Academy of Music, 30 Lafayette Street, Brooklyn; 783-2434.

Brooklyn Museum, Eastern Parkway and Washington Avenue, Brooklyn; 639-5000. Sunday afternoon concerts in the sculpture garden.

Carnegie Hall, 57 Street and Seventh Avenue; 247-7549. Over eighty years old and still going strong, with terrific accoustics. Also here is Carnegie Recital Hall.

Frick Collection, 1 East 70 Street; 288-0700. On Sundays in winter there are good chamber music concerts.

Juilliard School Theater, 144 West 66 Street; 799-5000. This famous school gives about two hundred performances a year, from small chamber music groups to complete operas and symphony orchestra performances.

Lincoln Center for the Performing Arts, Broadway and 63 Street; 765-5100.

Alice Tully Hall; 362-1911. Small-group performances, including the Chamber Music Society of Lincoln Center.

Avery Fisher Hall; 874-2424. Home of the New York Philharmonic and host to other orchestras.

Metropolitan Opera; 799-3100. The Metropolitan Opera Company is here, as are visiting ballet troupes and other opera companies.

New York State Theater; 877-4727. George Balanchine's famous New York City Ballet Company is here, as are the New York City Opera and visiting companies.

Madison Square Garden, 4 Penn Plaza; 564-4400. Mostly sports events and rock concerts, but occasionally some serious music.

Metropolitan Museum of Art, Fifth Avenue at 82 Street; 879-5500. Museum has an excellent concert series, given usually in the Grace Rainey Rogers Auditorium; occasionally medieval music is played in the Medieval sculpture hall.

Museum of the City of New York, Fifth Avenue and 103 Street; 534-1674. Sunday-afternoon concerts between October and May.

New York City Center, 131 West 55 Street; 246-8989. Ballet and light opera.

92nd Street YM-YWHA, Kaufman Concert Hall, 92 Street and Lexington Avenue; 427-6000. The Y has very good, often unusual music series of chamber music and opera.

Radio City Music Hall, 1260 Sixth Avenue (50 Street); 246-4600. Huge Art Deco temple which has become less important for its entertainment offerings. With the largest Wurlitzer organ ever built, a line of thirty-six Rockettes, and a seasonal program.

Town Hall, 123 West 43 Street; 427-6000. A variety of concerts held there.

Cooking Schools

There are a number of schools, but we have listed a few of the best.

Diana Kennedy's Mexican Cooking, 513 East 82 Street; 737-8669.

John Clancy's Kitchen Workshop, 325 West 19 Street; 243-0958. Baking, Continental fish and chicken cookery.

Le Cordon Bleu de Paris, 155 West 68 Street; 873-2434. French cuisine.

Madame Grace Chu's Chinese Cooking Classes, 370 Riverside Drive; 663-2182.

Madhur Jaffrey's Cooking Classes, 101 West 12 Street; 924-6287. Indian cooking.

Scuola Italiana de Cucina, America-Italy Society, 667 Madison Avenue; 838-1560. Northern Italian.

Dance

Brooklyn Academy of Music, 30 Lafayette Street, Brooklyn; 636-4100.

Harlem Performance Center, 2349 Seventh Avenue (129 Street); information c/o Harlem Cultural Council, 862-3000.

New York City Center, 131 West 55 Street; 246-8989.

Metropolitan Opera House, Lincoln Center; 580-9830.

New York State Theater, Lincoln Center; 877-4700.

Daycare

Babysitters Guild; 682-0227.

Babysitters Association; 865-9348.

Cornell Nursing School Babysitting Service; 472-8393.

Part-Time Child Care; 879-4343.

Excursions

If your stay in New York is long enough, you may want to consider a trip to one of the outlying areas, even beyond the other boroughs. We give you a few suggestions for easy-to-arrange trips.

Long Island

One ideal place to visit is Long Island, jutting out from Manhattan eastward into the Atlantic Ocean. Of course Brooklyn and Queens are also part of Long Island, but nowadays when most people speak of the island, they mean Nassau and Suffolk counties.

Although they have a character and history all their own, Nassau and Suffolk (less so) are the home of many people who during the day work in Manhattan and who commute in to the city on the infamous Long Island Railroad. In addition, the beaches of Long Island — from Long Beach all the way out to Montauk — are the playground of Manhattanites. The Hamptons and Fire Island are especially known as the summer resort of well-to-do New Yorkers tired of cement and glass.

Both Nassau and Suffolk have historical, cultural, and natural areas worthy of visit, especially if you have access to a car (see Rentals — Cars). But if you are limiting yourself to public transportation, you will find several lovely trips offered by the Long Island Railroad as well.

And if you are in New York during the summer and wish to beat the heat, try a trip to **Jones Beach**. Here the miles and miles of marvelous beach are littered with people, but if you don't mind walking a little you can easily find a less crowded spot. Walters Bus Line leaves from 56 Street and Second Avenue; 397-2626. You can also take the Long Island Railroad from Pennsylvania Station; RE 9-4200. The train fare includes the short bus trip and locker when you get there.

Upstate

North of New York City is also a fascinating area, full of historical sites and lush, elegant homes. The Hudson River Valley is often compared with the Rhine Valley in Germany because of its steep cliffs and shores dotted with mansions. Two such trips are listed below.

Caramoor, Katonah, New York; (914) 232-4206. Caramoor is a villa with twenty-three rooms imported intact from Europe (one contains the bed of Pope Urban VIII). It sits in lovely gardens and has a Venetian open-air theater with concerts and opera performances on summer Saturday afternoons and evenings. You can go for just a visit on Saturdays from 10 to 4. To get there, you can either take the Harlem Line from Grand Central Station to Katonah and then continue by taxi, or by car you take the Saw Mill River Parkway to Route 35, turn right and right again at the first stop light onto Route 22, then take Route 22 as far as Route 127.

Hudson River Cruise to Bear Mountain State Park, Hudson River Day Line; 279-5151. Take this cruise up the Hudson River (all-day trip) and view this elegant and dramatic river. The boat leaves from Pier 81 at the foot of West 41 Street and travels up to the state park, stopping at the U.S. Military Academy at West Point and Poughkeepsie. Return home the same day, usually with a lovely suntan.

Connecticut

Nearby **Connecticut** is a lovely state, very much a part of New England yet close to the city. There is a new excursion offered on an old railroad line that enables travelers to connect with a steam train and boat tour of the Connecticut River Valley — all in one day.

Take Amtrak Train 192 from Pennsylvania Station to Old Saybrook, Connecticut, then catch the Valley Railroad Shuttle (a 1914 coach with diesel locomotive) to Essex. In Essex you transfer to a vintage Valley Railroad steam train that chugs its way up the valley to Deep River. At Deep River, you board a sixty-five-foot steam launch for a cruise upstream to East Haddam. The return trip connects back with the steam train and the shuttle. These trips run from May to October. For information, call (203) 767-0103.

Farther Away

We couldn't begin to list all the possible places to visit on an overnight, let alone a three- or four-day trip. However, one place that always interests tourists is **Niagara Falls**. If you want to really enjoy the tremendous waterfalls, you are best staying a few days. At night the falls are floodlit and during the day you can go on guided tours that take you very close — a raincoat can be borrowed from the trip organizers. If you go up by car, take the New York State Thruway to exit 50, then continue to Route 190. You can also take a Greyhound Bus, but the night trip, which is the shortest, will take eleven hours. The bus leaves from Port Authority Bus Terminal; for information call 594-2000.

Gay Scene

For complete information, consult the *Gayellow Pages*.

Information

Lesbian Switchboard, 243 West 20 Street; 741-2610.

Gay Switchboard; 777-1800.

National Gay Task Force, 80 Fifth Avenue (14 Street); 741-5800.

Bookstores

Djuna Books, 154 West 10 Street; 242-3542.

Oscar Wilde Memorial Bookshop, 15 Christopher Street; 255-8097.

Womanbooks, 201 West 92 Street; 873-4121.

The following general bookstores have strong gay sections:

Book-Friends, 457 Third Avenue (33 Street); 689-8746.

East Side Bookstore, 34 St. Marks Place; 777-7240.

Idle Hour Bookstore, 59 Greenwich Avenue; 924-6517.

Marloff Paperback, 10 Sheridan Square; 924-5864.

New Morning, 169 Spring Street; 966-2993.

New Yorker Bookshop, 250 West 89 Street; 799-2050.

St. Mark's Bookshop, 13 St. Mark's Place; 260-7853.

Three Lives & Co., 131 Seventh Avenue South (10 Street); 741-2069.

Libraries

Gay History Archive; 674-4198. By appointment only.

International Homophile Research Library, 348 West 14 Street; 242-6616. By appointment.

Lesbian Herstory Archives; 874-7232. By appointment only.

Muhlenberg Branch of New York Public Library, 209 West 23 Street; 924-1585.

Counseling Services/ Legal Aides

Identity House, 544 Sixth Avenue (15 Street); 243-8181. Free peer counseling.

Gay and Lesbian Community Services of New York, 110 East 23 Street; 533-2619.

Lambda Legal Defense and Education Fund, 22 East 40 Street; 532-8197.

Social and Political Groups

Chelsea Gay Association, 164 West 21 Street; 691-0057.

Gay Women's Alternative, c/o Universalist Church, 4 West 76 Street; 532-8669.

National Gay Task Force, 80 Fifth Avenue (14 Street); 741-5815.

West Side Discussion Group; 242-1212.

Women's Bars and Discos

Ariel, 53 West 19 Street; 929-9328. Warm and friendly.

Bonnie & Clyde's, 82 West Third Street; 674-0959. Fast action.

Dapper and Friends, 350 East 81 Street; 535-9260. Intimate and sensuous disco.

Deja Vu, 85 Washington Place; 473-8895.

Dutchess, 70 Grove Street; 242-1408. Young and sometimes political.

The Club, 277 Bleecker Street; 242-2228. Disco.

Paula's, 64 Greenwich Avenue; 243-9200. Mixed.

Peeches, 1201 Lexington Avenue (82 Street); 650-0067. Disco upstairs, dressy bar downstairs.

Men's Bars and Discos

Andre's, Eighth Avenue at 125 Street. The biggest and most popular gay bar in Harlem.

Badlands, 388 West Street; 741-9236. Lots of leather.

Barbary Coast, 54 Seventh Avenue; 243-9678. With a feeling of San Francisco.

Boots and Saddles, 76 Christopher Street; 929-9684. A local Western bar.

Camp David, 1007 Lexington Avenue (38 Street); 650-0673. Dancing at a popular bar.

Chaps, 1558 Third Avenue (82 Street); 860-9829. Very friendly.

Cowboy and Cowgirl; 244 East 53 Street; PL 3-1000. Fast action.

Dakota, 550 Third Avenue (37 Street); 725-9853.

Half Breed, 168 Amsterdam Avenue (68 Street); 874-9782.

Harry's, 1422 Third Avenue (81 Street); 249-6991. Very popular.

Ice Palace 57, 57 West 57 Street; 838-8557. Extremely popular disco.

Julius, 159 West 10 Street; 929-9672. A young crowd at this Village stand-by.

Keller's, 384 West Street; 243-1907. The city's oldest gay bar.

Nickel Bar, 127 West 72 Street; 362-1485.

Ramrod, 394 West Street; 929-9718.

Ty's, 114 Christopher Street; 741-9641.

Wildwood, 308 Columbus Avenue (75 Street); 874-8325.

Restaurants

Unless otherwise noted, these serve both lesbians and gay men. Some also are mixed gay and straight.

Beau Geste, 239 Third Avenue (22 Street); 475-9724.

Black Sheep, 342 West 11 Street; 741-9772.

Bonnie's Restaurant, 82 West Third Street; 673-9551. Mostly women.

Fedora's, 239 West 4th Street; 252-9691.

Le Bistroquet, 90 Bedford Street; 242-8301.

Omnibus Restaurant, 263 West 12 Street; 243-8704.

Peechstreet Dining Club, 408 East 64 Street; 888-1608. Women only.

Trilogy, 135 Christopher Street; 242-6753.

Twentynine Palms Restaurant, 129 Lexington Avenue (28 Street); 686-8299.

Under the Trees, 314 Bleecker Street; 929-9811.

Holidays

Note that on Christmas eve and New Year's eve many people work; some only until noon. Shops are generally open on Sundays and some holidays.

January 1 — New Year's Day
February 12 — Lincoln's Birthday
February 22 — Washington's Birthday
(not always celebrated on this date)
March/April — Easter Sunday
March/April — Passover
May 30 — Memorial Day (not always celebrated on this date)
July 4 — Independence Day
September (first Monday) — Labor Day
September/October — Rosh Hashanah
September/October — Yom Kippur
October 12 — Columbus Day (not always celebrated on this date)
November 11 — Veteran's Day
November (fourth Thursday) — Thanksgiving Day
December 25 — Christmas Day

Hotels

Do not come to New York without a hotel reservation. Although there are many hotels of all types, it is sometimes quite difficult to find a room. The Convention and Visitors Bureau (2 Columbus Circle) has put together a comprehensive list of hotels with prices, so we are only listing a small selection below.

Once settled in your room, you usually don't leave your key or card with the desk, but rather take it with you. When you are in your room, you should always lock yourself in and not open the door unless you have made absolutely sure you know who it is who wants to get in. Your more valuable possessions had best reside in the hotel safe.

Hotel Abbey-Victoria, Seventh Avenue and 51 Street; 246-9400. A thousand rooms with bath and TV. It is a busy place with a lot of tourists and business people. They have cars to the airport, and to and from Wall Street in the mornings and evenings.

Algonquin Hotel, 59 West 44 Street; 840-6800. Site of the famous round table of New York "literati" (Robert Benchley, Dorothy Parker, et al) in the twenties. There is a good after-theater buffet; the bar is famous and its original decor tends to feed the fires of nostalgia.

Allerton House, 130 East 57 Street; 753-8841. For women only, a slightly anachronistic phenomenon, but not without its advantages. You should inquire about their weekly rates.

Barbizon for Women, 140 East 63 Street; 838-5700. Quiet and elegant, exclusively for women. Grace Kelly used to live here.

Biltmore Hotel, East 43 Street at Madison Avenue; 687-7000. Large but in a convenient area. The clock in the lobby is famous.

Hotel Carlyle, 35 East 76 Street; 744-1600. Deluxe accommodations.

Hotel Carter, 250 West 43 Street; 947-6000. Convenient to Broadway theaters. The staff will get theater tickets, too, if you ask in enough time; there is a coffee shop which is not bad for small meals. Air conditioning. Ask about their "Visit-U.S." rates.

Chelsea Hotel, 222 West 23 Street; 243-3700. La vie de Bohème in New York, and that implies a certain sloppiness. However, the building dates from 1833 and is a landmark. Andy Warhol filmed his *Chelsea Girls* in it; William Burroughs wrote *Naked Lunch* in it; and Mark Twain, Sarah Bernhardt, Tennessee Williams, and Jane Fonda, among many others, have at one time or other lived in it.

Hotel Earle, 103 Waverly Place; 777-9515. Good locale for people who want to spend a lot of time in the Village or SoHo.

Gorham Hotel, 136 West 55 Street; 245-1800. A well-situated, reasonable hotel, with friendly staff. Air conditioning.

Gramercy Park Hotel, 21 Lexington Avenue (23 Street); 475-4320. Some rooms have a view of the park. If you ask, you can have the key to it.

Grand Hyatt Hotel, 90 East 42 Street; 883-1234. Where the old Hotel Commodore used to be, right near Grand Central Station. Also very expensive and posh.

Helmsley Palace Hotel, 455 Madison Avenue (50 Street); 888-7000. The latest, and most expensive hotel in New York. Built into the old (landmark) Villard houses.

International House, 500 Riverside Drive (122 Street); 678-5000. Visitors with student identification can live here economically but not exactly in a central location. Rooms are available only during the summer months when the university is on vacation. Some of the rooms have lovely views; none have private bath or air conditioning.

Pickwick Arms, 230 East 51 Street; 355-0300. Fantastic location, popular with U.N. diplomats and Europeans. The rooms are not big, but prices are very good; ask about their weekly rates.

Pierre Hotel, 61 Street and Fifth Avenue; 838-8000. Deluxe, elegant hotel in the European tradition. Upper floors have rooms that overlook Central Park.

Plaza Hotel, Fifth Avenue between 58 and 59 streets; 759-3000. Tenderly cared for survivor of Edwardian glory, it is the most beautiful, but easily one of the most expensive places to put your head down in New York. The best rooms are on the northern side, with a view of Central Park.

Royalton Hotel, 44 West 44 Street; 730-1344. Very good location in midtown, inviting foyer, respectable rooms with air conditioning and TV.

Stanhope Hotel, 995 Fifth Avenue (81 Street); 288-5800. First class, without charging first-class prices. Elegant and cozy. On the ground floor is a restaurant which at lunch time is the meeting place of the museum set. In summer, the sidewalk café is one of the nicest places to be — across from the Metropolitan Museum.

Hotel Tudor, 304 East 42 Street; 986-8800. Near the U.N. and popular with diplomats. Rooms with air conditioning and TV.

United Nations Plaza Hotel, First Avenue and 44 Street; 355-3400. Modern skyscraper with a nice swimming pool on the 27th floor and tennis courts on the 38th floor.

Hotel Wales, 1295 Madison Avenue (90 Street); 876-6000. If you want to be on the Upper East Side and the Stanhope and others in that class are a bit too rich for your blood, try this. It has been renovated recently and attracts an amusing artsy-crafty crowd. If you want a room with a view, you have to write early; ask about weekly rates.

YMCA-Vanderbilt Branch, 224 East 47 Street; 755-2410. Despite the *M* in YMCA, women get rooms here too. A large, friendly place with neat rooms at a reasonable cost. Air conditioning is extra and baths are on the floor but have to be shared. There is a swimming pool, a gymnasium, a sauna, washing machines, a cafeteria, and a library. If you want to reserve, send the price of one night's stay to the residence director. You might inquire about their three- to seven-day rates.

YMCA-William Sloane House, 356 West 34 Street; 760-5860. Very popular with students and Europeans. The rooms are simple; inquire about weekly rates. The location is convenient for the Port Authority Bus Terminal, the markets on Ninth Avenue, and Chelsea.

Westside Y, 5 West 63 Street; 787-4400. Fantastic location (across from Lincoln Center), friendly atmosphere, but for students only. In fact a number of rooms are set aside for men only and for women as long as they stay a full semester. The Y has three gymnasiums, two swimming pools, a sauna, and a cafeteria. Write to the residence director.

Ice Cream

The city has become enamoured with ice cream, and there are ice cream parlors springing up everywhere. Here are a few.

Agora, 1550 Third Avenue (87 Street); 860-3425. A real ice cream parlor.

Baskin-Robbins, 979 First Avenue (51 Street); 223-9391. Also many other branches throughout the city.

Fay & Allen's Food Works, 1241 Third Avenue (71 Street); 794-1101.

Haagen-Dazs, 1188 First Avenue (62 Street); 288-5200.

Hicks, 16 East 49 Street; 688-5552. A real ice cream parlor.

Peppermint Park, 1231 First Avenue (66 Street); 879-9484.

Rumpelmayer's, 50 Central Park South; 755-5800. A favorite ice cream parlor.

Information

Important Telephone Numbers

Police emergency: 911

First aid: 911 or 0 (for Operator)

Doctor: New York Medical Society, 679-1000

Dentist: Emergency Dental Service, 759-9606

Drug abuse: Addiction Service Agency, 433-2020

Pregnancy tests and abortion advice: Margaret Sanger Center, 677-6474

Poison: 340-4494

Rape: 233-3000

Helpful Telephone Numbers

Time: 976-1616

Weather: 976-1212

Travel Information (subways, buses): 330-1234

Parks, special events information: 755-4100

Convention and Visitors Bureau: 397-8222

Lost and Found: If you have lost something in a taxi, the nearest police precinct will keep things for forty-eight hours; after that they go to Central Lost and Found (374-4925). If you remember the name, number, or fleet of your taxi driver, call 825-0416. If you have lost something in the subway or on a bus call 625-6200 or 330-4484.

Drugstores, open all night: Kaufman's, Lexington Avenue at 50 Street; 755-2266. Many drugstores are open twenty-four hours a day; look in the yellow pages of the telephone directory under "Pharmacies" for one listed near you.

General Information: 999-1234. If you call this number between 10 AM and 3:30 PM you can find out what the daily specials are in the supermarkets, where there is a block party or street market going on, or what special exhibits are on

view at the museums. At other hours you will be told about the weather, news, and traffic conditions.

New York Convention and Visitors Bureau: 397-8222. This office is located at 2 Columbus Circle (59 Street) and is open Monday through Saturday from 9 AM to 6 PM. The Information Center at Times Square (Broadway and 43 Street) is open everyday from 9 AM to 6 PM.

Other Useful Telephone Numbers

Big Apple Report (traffic): 976-2323

Children's Story: 976-3636

Dial-a-joke: 976-3838

Dial-a-prayer: 246-4200

Dr. Joyce Brothers: 976-1919

Dow Jones Report: 976-4141

Good Looks Line: 976-2626

Horoscope: 976-3636

Jazzline: 421-3592

Lottery: 976-2020

OTB (horse racing): 976-2121

Sports: 976-1313

Maps

Especially useful are *New York in Flash-maps* ($2.50) and *Hagstrom's Pocket Atlas* ($5.95). Both are available at various bookstores as well as at Rand McNally, 10 East 53 Street.

Limousines

Cream Limousine, Ltd., 37-04 24 Street, Long Island City; 784-2666.

Cooper Rolls-Royce Limousines, 132 Perry Street; 929-0094.

London Towncars, Inc., 40-13 23 Street, Long Island City; 988-9700.

Interservice Limousine Inc., 38-62 13 Street, Long Island City; 729-6994.

Money

Most banks in New York (and there is one at practically every street corner) are open weekdays from 9 to 3, at least one evening a week, and often on Saturday mornings. You can cash traveler's checks at any bank with ease; cashing a personal check is usually more difficult. You can change money at the airport, at the East Side Air Terminal, or Grand Central Station, as well as at most commercial banks. It is a good idea to bring traveler's checks in dollars if you are coming from another country. Eurochecks, in contrast to U.S. traveler's checks, will not be accepted at stores or restaurants.

Terminology for Foreigners

dollar: often referred to as "buck" — 100 cents; the Susan B. Anthony dollar is relatively new and not widely circulated.

half-dollar: 50 cents

quarter: 25 cents

dime: 10 cents

nickel: 5 cents

penny: 1 cent

Movie Theaters

New Yorkers love to go to the movies, and there are hundreds of opportunities to do so. Check the newspapers and magazines for up-to-date listings. The *New Yorker* gives intelligent capsule reviews of most current films. Listed below are a number of revival houses as well as a few theaters that show new and avant-garde work.

Anthology Film Archives, 80 Wooster Street; 226-0010. Here movies are art and not entertainment. The Archives has a collection of about five hundred films.

Bleecker Street Cinema, 144 Bleecker Street; 674-2360. If you missed it when it first came out you can catch it here.

Carnegie Hall Cinema, Seventh Avenue at 57 Street; 757-2131. Here you can see two old movies for the price of one new one. Sometimes the programming is quite clever, such as showing the 1966 version of *The Merry Wives of Windsor* with the 1967 *Falstaff* (with Orson Welles). Admission is reduced for members.

Film Forum, 15 Vandam Street; 989-2994. Visitors are welcome to occupy some of the fifty-five seats in this renovated loft where the fare is strictly experimental and avant-garde.

Millenium Film Work Shop, 66 East 4 Street; 673-0090. Avant-garde; shorts.

Museum of Modern Art, 11 West 53 Street; 956-7078. There are several showings a day of films from the museum's large and famous collection. Tickets are limited and are free with admission to the museum.

New Yorker 1 and 2, 2409 Broadway (90 Street); 580-7900. Often old French or Italian movies; a Woody Allen retrospective; but also *Mary Poppins*. Sometimes current films are shown in one of the theaters.

Public Theater, The Little Theater, 425 Lafayette Street; 598-7171. This is where to catch foreign films that don't make it to the East Side.

Quad Cinema, 34 West 13 Street; 255-8800. The Quad is really four theaters showing a mixture of the recent and the recently old.

Thalia, Broadway and 95 Street; 222-3370. The most famous revival house; shows the classics of all nations; but also features special series and new works.

Whitney Museum of American Art, 945 Madison Avenue (73 Street); 794-0630. A special series allows unknown film-makers to find an audience for their work. Tickets are available in the lobby.

Museums

Most museums in New York are open from 10 AM to 5 PM Tuesday through Saturday and from noon to 5 PM on Sunday. Admission is charged in almost all of them. Since opening hours and admission fees can change without warning, it is advisable to telephone in advance.

There are usually good floor plans and comprehensive schedules listing all events such as concerts, lectures, and special films available at the information desk. It is often possible to rent cassettes with a guided tour of the museum or of a special exhibition, often with two pairs of earphones. And if you want to tackle the museum scene in depth, you can call the Institute of Fine Arts of New York University and borrow an art student as your guide. Call the academic office: 988-5550.

Most museums have extensive gift shops (Brooklyn's has the best things for the smallest prices) and fair restaurants (the Metropolitan's encircles a lovely pool reflecting bronze dancers).

Art

American Crafts Museum, 44 West 53 Street; 397-0600. With exhibitions like "Made with Paper," in which there was the most wonderful lampshade of white paper cups, or "The Art of Dyeing," this small museum has contributed much to a new appreciation of crafts and has given impetus to the decorative arts movement.

Asia House Gallery, 112 East 64 Street; 751-3210. In a small, elegant glass palace (by Philip Johnson) the Asia Society organizes some of the most wonderful exhibitions of Asian art in the city.

Brooklyn Children's Museum, 145 Brooklyn Avenue, Brooklyn; 735-4400.

Brooklyn Museum, Eastern Parkway and Washington Avenue, Brooklyn; 638-5000. Well known for its Egyptian, pre-Columbian, and primitive collections, it also has a community center with exhibits of local artists. The gift shop alone is worth the trip.

Bronx Museum of the Arts, Grand Concourse and 161 Street, Bronx; 681-6000. Contemporary and modern art.

Cloisters, Fort Tryon Park; 923-3700. The medieval branch of the Metropolitan Museum. A real cloister, with herb gardens, tapestries (noted are the Unicorn Tapestries), and sculpture.

Cooper-Hewitt Museum of Decorative Arts and Design, 2 East 91 Street; 860-6868. A branch of the Smithsonian Institution. Housed in Andrew Carnegie's sturdy and gracious mansion, the museum has a famous collection of textiles. Exhibits here are related to design in every form — from fancy cars to mustard pots.

Frick Collection, 1 East 70 Street; 288-0700. In the little Louis XVI palace (built around 1913) you can see how rich New Yorkers lived in the early twentieth century. Frick's fabulous collection of masterpieces by European sculptors, painters, and artisans is beautifully displayed in well-proportioned rooms scented with fresh flowers. The glass-covered atrium with fountain and plants is a welcome oasis in a noisy city. Concerts and lectures are presented throughout the year.

Jacques Marchais Center of Tibetan Art, 338 Lighthouse Avenue, off Richmond Road, Lighthouse Hill, Staten Island; 987-3478. Lovely gardens and a well-respected collection.

International Center of Photography, 1130 Fifth Avenue (94 Street); 860-1783. The works of famous masters and contemporary wielders of the camera (even beginners) are exhibited here.

Japan House, 333 East 47 Street; 832-1155. Japanese art and artifacts are on display here.

Jewish Museum, 1109 Fifth Avenue (92 Street); 860-1888. This is one of the most beautiful and comprehensive collections of Judaica in America. On display are ceremonial objects, sculpture, and painting. Special exhibits are often held here.

Metropolitan Museum of Art, Fifth Avenue and 82 Street; 535-7710. The museum's collections of Egyptian, Greek, and Roman art are justly famous, as well as the arms and armor hall, the medieval court, and the new American Wing. Don't miss the Temple of Dendur housed in its own wing, complete with reflecting pool.

Museum of American Folk Art, 49 West 53 Street; 581-2474. Imaginative exhibits featuring the art of the Shakers, or quilts, or weather vanes, or carved and painted saints figures from New Mexico.

Museum of Modern Art, 11 West 53 Street; 956-7070. A million people visit the 30,000 modern art masterpieces here each year. In the summer the sculpture garden is a favorite spot for New Yorkers. Notable, too, are the extensive film archives.

New Muse Community Museum, 1530 Bedford Avenue, near Eastern Parkway, Brooklyn; 774-2901. Black people's contribution to Brooklyn's development.

Pierpont Morgan Library, 29 East 36 Street; 685-0008. The library of J. Pierpont Morgan, built to house his extensive collection of manuscripts, rare books, and art works. On view are a variety of the library's holdings including a Gutenberg Bible.

Project Studio One, 21-01 46 Road, Long Island City, Queens; 233-1096. Saved from demolition, this old school now houses exhibitions on a regular basis.

Solomon R. Guggenheim Museum, 1071 Fifth Avenue (89 Street); 860-1313. In Frank Lloyd Wright's snail shell it is best to take the elevator to the top and then slowly walk down the spiral ramp. That way you not only have the works of art arranged in the gentle curves before you, but you can look across and up and down at the others. There are 200 Kandinskys and many works by Paul Klee, Franz Marc, Marc Chagall, and other modern artists. The Thannhauser Collection, in its special wing, provides a useful historical background.

Storefront Museum, 162-02 Liberty Avenue, Jamaica, Queens; 523-5199. A new cultural center and theater for black artists.

Studio Museum in Harlem, 2033 Fifth Avenue (125 Street); 427-5959. Works of established and upcoming black artists.

Staten Island Children's Museum, 15 Beach Street, Staten Island; 273-2060.

Whitney Museum of American Art, 945 Madison Avenue (75 Street); 794-0663. You can trace the development of modern American art — from the early beginnings of the "eight" to the height of Pop. The bulk of their permanent collection is twentieth-century American art, some of which is usually on display.

Historical

American Museum of Immigration, in the Statue of Liberty National Monument, Liberty Island; 732-1236. Photographs, religious objects, and oral-history tapes relate the story of immigration to the United States.

City Island Historical Nautical Museum, 190 Fordham Street, east of City Island Avenue, Bronx; 885-1292. Memorabilia and artifacts relating to City Island's history as a seaport.

Fort Wadsworth and Military Museum, Bay Street, near the Verrazano-Narrows Bridge, Staten Island; 447-5100. The oldest manned military installation in the U.S. and a museum of military memorabilia.

Garibaldi/Meucci Museum, 420 Tompkins Avenue, Rosebank, Staten Island; 442-1608. An old farmhouse, with objects dating back to the mid-1800s.

Museum of the American Indian, Audubon Terrace, Broadway at 155 Street; 283-2420. Here you will find the world's largest collection of Indian artifacts from North and South America — among them wampum belts, masks, intricate beadwork, ritual objects, and the personal belongings of such legendary chiefs as Red Cloud, Sitting Bull, and Crazy Horse.

Museum of the City of New York, Fifth Avenue at 103 Street; 534-1672. Decorative arts, furniture, paintings, toys, and costumes — all depicting the history and life of New York City.

Museum of the Long Island Historical Society, 128 Pierrepont Street, Brooklyn; 624-0890. Books, manuscripts, paintings, and artifacts of Brooklyn and the rest of Long Island. Housed in a red brick building that is also architecturally intriguing.

Museum of Bronx History, Bainbridge Avenue and 208 Street, Bronx; 881-8900. Fascinating displays highlight the contributions of people from the Bronx.

National Maritime Historical Museum, 2 Fulton Street, Fulton Ferry Landing, Brooklyn; 858-1348. Exhibits on a nautical theme.

New York Historical Society, 170 Central Park West (76 Street); 873-3400. In this well-restored building you can see a notable collection of portraits, engravings, furniture, and toys, as well as interesting special exhibits concerning the history of New York.

Queens Museum, New York City Building, Flushing Meadow-Corona Park, Flushing, Queens; 592-2405. A full program of changing exhibitions and a permanent collection that includes a 15,000-square-foot scale model of New York City.

Schomberg Center for Research in Black Culture, 103 West 135 Street; 862-4000. The world's largest collection of materials on black history.

South Street Seaport Museum, 16 Fulton Street; 766-9020. Restored ships, buildings, and shops make up this unusual indoor/outdoor museum.

Scientific

American Museum of Natural History, Central Park West at 79 Street; 873-4225. Don't miss the dinosaurs! Other special exhibits include the hall of gems and minerals; the wonderful dioramas depicting life on the African veldt; and the new Hall of Asian Peoples.

Hayden Planetarium, Central Park West at 81 Street; 873-8828. With the help of a Zeiss projector model no. VI, you may just grasp astronomy. In the Guggenheim Space Theater you can experience "astrovision," which one might call a slide show, but thanks to special tone and light effects the illusion is perfect.

Hall of Science, Flushing Meadows-Corona Park, Flushing, Queens; 699-9400. Numerous science exhibitions as well as a planetarium, radio station, and full-sized orbital space vehicles.

Manhattan Laboratory Museum, 314 West 54 Street; 765-5904. Science museum for children.

New York Aquarium, Surf Avenue at West 8 Street, Coney Island, Brooklyn; 266-8500. Indoor and outdoor tanks are home for seals, penguins, sea lions, turtles, and other marine creatures.

Museum of Holography, 11 Mercer Street; 925-0526. Laser-beam light makes three-dimensional images.

Staten Island Institute of Arts and Sciences, 75 Stuyvesant Place, St. George, Staten Island; 727-1135. In addition to art exhibits, this museum is strong on natural science and archaeology.

Miscellaneous

Black Fashion Museum, 155 West 126 Street; 666-1320. The designs of black fashion designers and their influence upon fashion as a whole.

Firefighting Museum, Home Insurance Company, 59 Maiden Lane, Fifteenth Floor; 530-6800. An outstanding collection of firefighting memorabilia including historical records.

Museum of Broadcasting, 1 East 53 Street; 742-7684. The museum concentrates on the first fifty years of radio and television (starting in 1926). For a fee you can hear or see a program of your choice from their collection.

Museum of Colored Glass and Light, 72 Wooster Street; 226-7258. Glass sculptures with special light effects.

New York City Transit Exhibition,

Boerum Place and Schermerhorn Street, Brooklyn; 330-3060. The history of the world's most complex mass transportation system: memorabilia, photographs, equipment, and artifacts.

Police Academy Museum, 235 East 20 Street, Second Floor; 477-9753. Historical items and police memorabilia largely about New York's finest.

Songwriters Hall of Fame, 1 Times Square (at West 42 Street and Broadway), Eighth Floor; 221-1252. Tinkle Fats Waller's ivories or admire the breakfast tray on which Otto Harbach wrote "Smoke Gets in Your Eyes."

Newspapers and Magazines

Space prohibits listing all the papers and magazines that are available in New York. Wide selections are to be found at most newsstands. The best places for foreign papers and magazines are **Hotalings** (in Times Square) and **Rizzoli** (712 Fifth Avenue).

Daily Newspapers

Many people are surprised that there are only three major daily newspapers in New York: the *New York Times*, the *Daily News*, and the *New York Post*.

New York Times. Fairly liberal and with brilliant columnists — including James Reston, Anthony Lewis, Tom Wicker, and Russell Baker. On Sundays the *Times* weighs a good five pounds, and at least two of them are pure reading matter. On Fridays there is a useful entertainment guide; Wednesday's Living Section deals with foods and wines.

Daily News. The largest circulation in the U.S. Its bent is conservative; and its readership lower middle class.

New York Post. The principal afternoon paper and quite liberal. Most people buy it for the closing prices on the stock exchanges and the satire of Art Buchwald.

Weekly Newspapers

Village Voice. Not the progressive and rebellious paper it used to be, this is now aimed at a more affluent readership and goes beyond the confines of lower Manhattan. Still has good listings of galleries and off-beat entertainment.

Soho News. Came in a long time ago to fill the void left when the *Voice* turned establishment. Now this too is becoming more trendy than off-beat, with good columns on food, art, and other New York matters.

Other Newspapers

Wall Street Journal. Read by all business types, whether they work on Wall Street or not, this newspaper excels in its coverage of business but also features good special-feature articles.

Women's Wear Daily. A specialized paper concentrating on fashion and the garment industry, this paper has expanded to cover food and wine and some other social matters.

Weekly Magazines

New Yorker. Famous world-wide at least for its cartoons, it is still number one from a literary point of view, without being too forbiddingly intellectual.

New York Magazine. Indispensable for all who wish to know what is "in" or "out" in New York. Now merged with the old *Cue Magazine*, it features extensive listings of theater, concerts, galleries, etc.

Other Magazines

The following are mentioned earlier in the book and will be of interest. You can find them at newsstands with large selections.

Latin NY

Carribeat

Amsterdam News

Nightlife

see also BARS AND PUBS.

Cabarets, Nightclubs, and Dinner/Dancing

Applause, 360 Lexington Avenue (40 Street); 687-7267. The waiters and waitresses perform. Reservations recommended.

Balalaika, 300 East 24 Street; 532-9297. A Russian nightclub; kosher food is available. Attractive, cozy setting. Reservations necessary on weekends.

Ballroom, 458 West Broadway; 473-9367. Bright, pleasant place. You can have dinner and listen to singers of various types. Reservations necessary.

Big Julie's, 148 East 65 Street; 759-7454. Midnight-blue Art Deco room with a lot of chrome. Good food and entertainment. Reservations recommended.

Café Pierre, Pierre Hotel, 2 East 61 Street; 838-8000. Sophisticated dining; dancing to a trio. Reservations recommended.

Catch a Rising Star, 1487 First Avenue (77 Street); 794-1906. An improvisation club featuring singers and comics; lots of fun.

Club Ibis, 151 East 50 Street; 753-3884. Floor show Las Vegas-style. Dancing. Reservations recommended.

Copacabana, 10 East 60 Street;

281

755-6010. Not a bad place if you want to see what other tourists do when they come to New York. Disco dancing is featured.

Cotton Club, 666 West 125 Street; 663-7980. Recently reborn and catching on.

Dangerfield's, 1118 First Avenue (61 Street); 593-1650. This popular club specializes in American food and comedy. Reservations recommended.

Dionysos, 304 East 48 Street; 758-8240. A Greek nightclub; entertainment includes a belly dancer. Reservations required on weekends.

Edwardian Room, at the Plaza Hotel, Fifth Avenue at 58 Street; 759-3000. Elegant dinner and dancing in sumptuous surroundings. The room has a view of Central Park. Reservations recommended.

El Morocco, 307 East 54 Street; 752-2960. Insiders call it Elmo's. A posh nightclub; reservations required.

Improvisation, 358 West 44 Street; 765-8268. Well-known comic audition club; informal and crowded.

La Chansonette, 890 Second Avenue (47 Street); 752-7320. French cuisine, a floor show, and dancing. Reservations recommended.

Le Club, 416 East 55 Street; 355-5520. Expensive and quite elegant; meeting place of the less freaky café society.

Once Upon a Stove, Valentine Room, 325 Third Avenue (24 Street); 683-0044. Crammed with antiques (for sale), entertainment is upstairs on the second floor under crystal chandeliers; Victorian atmosphere; good food.

Rainbow Room, 30 Rockefeller Plaza, Sixty-Fifth Floor; 757-9090. Dining and dancing with one of the best views of New York. Sophisticated atmosphere; good dance orchestra. Jacket and tie required. Reservations recommended, required on weekends.

Red Blazer Too, 1576 Third Avenue (88 Street); 876-0440. American food and music, sometimes jazz. On Sundays a jazz brunch is featured. Informal.

Roseland, 239 West 52 Street; 247-0200. *The* place for serious dancing in New York. Two orchestras, bar, restaurant. It's okay to go by yourself, if you're a good dancer you'll find partners. On Wednesday and Thursday after 11 PM and Friday and Saturday after midnight it turns disco.

Stork Club, 112 Central Park South; 581-7080. The famed New York supper club; continental menu; disco after 11 PM. Jacket and tie required; reservations necessary.

Top of the Gate, 160 Bleecker Street; 982-9292. Theater cabaret; no food served (bar only). Reservations recommended.

Disco and Pop Rock Clubs (including Roller Disco)

Apollo Theater, 253 West 125 Street; 749-1800. No longer showing sleazy movies, this has returned to offering live entertainment.

Bond International Casino, Times Square (Broadway and 45 Street); 944-5880. One of the latest discos.

Bottom Line, 15 West 4 Street; 228-7880. Big-name rock stars and showcase performers; food and drink are served. Reservations recommended.

CBGB, 315 Bowery; 982-4052. Punk rock bands; crowded.

Electric Circus, 100 Fifth Avenue (15 Street); 989-7457. Circus theme, funhouse mirrors, and pinball machines at this popular disco. Good sound systems.

Empire Roller Disco, 200 Empire Boulevard (near Bedford Avenue), Brooklyn; 462-1570. Skate rental is included in the admission charge.

Hippopotamus II, 405 East 62 Street; 486-1566. Continental cuisine; disco dancing to a live band after 10 PM. Reservations recommended.

Hurrah's, 36 West 62 Street; 586-2636. Informal disco featuring live and recorded punk and rock music.

Les Mouches, 260 Eleventh Avenue (26 Street); 695-5190. Restaurant, cabaret, and disco (after 11 PM). A sophisticated place; pleasant atmosphere, good lighting. Reservations recommended.

Loreli, 231 East 86 Street; 348-4991. An uptown spot for dance-rock.

Max's Kansas City, 213 Park Avenue South; 777-7871. An old standby for popular music. Dinner is served.

Mudd Club, 77 White Street; 227-7777. Avant-garde, the club is underground; recorded music, though sometimes there are live bands.

New York, New York, 33 West 52 Street; 245-2400. Modern, slick disco with light show, laser beams, fog machines, and so forth. Restaurant and bar.

Regine's, 502 Park Avenue (59 Street); 826-0990. Restaurant and disco frequented by New York's café society. Expensive. Jackets and ties required for men; evening dress required for women. Reservations recommended.

Ritz, 11 Street between Third and Fourth avenues; 228-8888. A hip, new spot for rock-disco. This is an old Art Deco Latin ballroom. Dance-rock is interspersed with live acts; video.

Trude Heller Now, Sixth Avenue and 9 Street; 254-8346. Art Deco surroundings; disco; live cabaret.

Village Disco Roller Rink, 15 Waverly Place; 677-9690. Roller disco; skate rental plus admission charge.

Xenon, 124 West 43 Street; 221-2690. Pinball machines, laser beams, and spaceships lend a futuristic air to this popular disco.

Blues, Country, and Folk Music

Folk City, 130 West 3 Street; 254-8449. Folk music and showcase performers at this established club. Informal and fun.

Kenny's Castaways, 157 Bleecker Street; 473-9870. Restaurant featuring Irish food; folk music and jazz in the evenings.

Lone Star Cafe, Fifth Avenue and 13 Street; 242-1664. Country and western music; chili and other specialties including beer from Texas; informal and popular.

Other End, 149 Bleecker Street; 673-7030. American food; showcase performers featuring local talent; and game room; casual. The Cabaret next door (at 147) features well-known rock, folk, and jazz performers.

Tramps, 125 East 15 Street; 777-5077. Various folk and blues artists perform here nightly. Pub atmosphere; bar and restaurant.

Jazz

For general information the Universal Jazz Coalition is very useful; they can be reached at: 924-5026.

All State Café, 250 West 72 Street; 874-1883. Cozy, rustic sort of pub with jazz background.

Boomer's, 340 Bleecker Street; 243-0245. Special groups.

Bradley's, 70 University Place; 228-6440. Dark wood panelling and the best pianists and bassists available.

Cookery, 21 University Place; 674-4450. Modern decor; varied menu. Owner Bunny Jacobson, New York's greatest jazz aficionado, fills the place with intesting performers. Alberta Hunter, the famous blues singer, sings weeknights except in the summer.

Eddie Condon's, 144 West 54 Street; 265-8277. Well-known restaurant with traditional jazz and blues. Jam night is on Tuesdays.

Environ, 476 Broadway; 431-5786. Recently very popular.

Jazzmania Society, 14 East 23 Street; 477-3077. One of the top jazz lofts.

Jimmy Ryan's, 154 West 54 Street; 664-9700. This famous bar features Dixieland jazz. Bar only, no food.

Ladies Fort, 2 Bond Street; 677-9728. Another jazz loft.

Kitchen Center for Video and Music, 484 Broome Street and 59 Wooster Street; 925-3615. A multipurpose performance space, including jazz.

Knickerbocker Saloon, 33 University Place; 228-8490. Popular restaurant and bar featuring well-known musicians.

Library, 2475 Broadway; 799-4860. An uptown favorite with students.

Marvin Gardens Restaurant, 2274 Broadway (73 Street); 799-0579. Quiet and cozy.

Michael's Pub, 211 East 55 Street; 758-2272. Traditional jazz is featured in this comfortable restaurant. Top artists perform.

Mikell's, 760 Columbus Avenue (98 Street); 864-8832. One week of jazz alternating with one week of soul.

Storyville, 41 East 58 Street; 755-1640. Features top artists like Gerry Mulligan; restaurant serves American food.

Studio RivBea, 440 Tenth Avenue (36 Street); 244-8773.

Sweet Basil, 88 Seventh Avenue South; 242-1785. Mainstream jazz, usually by well-known performers. Restaurant has a varied menu; surroundings are pleasant.

Village Gate, 160 Bleecker Street 475-5120. Top-name artists only. Reser vations recommended.

Village Vanguard, 178 Seventh Avenue South; 255-4037. The world's most celebrated jazz basement.

West End Café, 2911 Broadway (115 Street); 666-8750. Swing. Bar and res taurant; popular.

Observation Points

see SIGHTS WORTH SEEING.

Opera

see CONCERT HALLS.

Post Offices and Telephones

The two largest post offices are:

General Post Office, Eighth Avenue and 33 Street. Open weekdays 8 AM to 6 PM Saturdays 8 AM to 2 PM, Sundays 9 AM to 5 PM.

Grand Central Post Office, Lexington Avenue and 45 Street. Open weekdays 8 AM to 6 PM, Saturdays 8 AM to 2 PM, Sundays 11 AM to 3 PM.

Local Post Offices: generally open from 9 AM to 5 PM weekdays and until noon on Saturdays. These branches are located all over the city; to find the one nearest you, look in the telephone book under United States Government, Postal Information.

Postal Rates

Airmail letters to Europe and South America are 40¢ per ½ ounce; postcards (standard size) are 21¢; aerograms are 22¢. Letters within the United States, to Canada, or Mexico are 15¢; postcards are 10¢.

Telegrams

To send a telegram (or night letter) call Western Union: 962-7111.

Telephone Calls

A **local call** from a pay phone costs 10¢ (a dime or two nickels).To make a **long-distance call** you may dial direct (but have exact change). Instructions are usually posted on each telephone. **Overseas calls** can often be made directly (either from your hotel of from someone's house) by dialing 011, the country code, the area code, and the number.

Telephone Information

To locate a telephone number, dial 411 (in Manhattan). If you are in Manhattan and want a number in another borough, dial 555-1212. If you want information for a number outside of New York City, dial 1, then the area code + 555-1212. Telephone information, from a pay phone, is free of charge.

Religious Services

There are 4,000 places of worship in New York — from the largest neo-Gothic cathedral in the world (St. John the Divine) to a Buddhist shrine in Chinatown. Consult the newspapers, especially on weekends, for times of services and other information.

Rentals — Cars, Bicycles, Roller Skates, Boats

Car Rentals

Car rentals are very popular with New Yorkers, so it is a good idea to book in advance. **Hertz, Avis,** and **National** are the largest agencies with numerous outlets all over the city. You will find them in the telephone directory or in the telephone yellow pages under Automobile Leasing and Renting. For a compact car, you pay roughly $20 to $30 a day. You can get weekly rates and rates with unlimited mileage, depending upon your needs. In all cases you pay for your gasoline. For information and maps, travel tips, etc. you might contact **Mobil Touring Service,** 150 East 42 Street; 883-4242; or **Exxon Travel Service,** 1251 Sixth Avenue (51 Street); 398-3000. See also LIMOUSINES.

Bicycles

Central Park Loeb Boathouse, on East Drive in the Park at about 75 Street. Rentals are about $1.50 an hour or $5 a day, with a $5 deposit (usually) and identification.

Gene's Bicycle Shop, 77 Street and Second Avenue; 249-9218.

Angelo's Bicycle Service, 462 Columbus Avenue (83 Street); 662-2525.

Roller Skates

You can usually rent skates at the roller discos as well.

Le Petit, 213 West 58 Street; 581-4960.

Rowboats/Sailboats

If you would like to row on the lake in Central Park you can get the boats at the

Loeb Boathouse (see Bicycles, above) as well. They cost $1.50 per hour for four people and a deposit of at least $10 is required.

If you want, you can rent a sailboat for up to 35 people. The *Petrel* can take you on a cruise of any duration but also offers shorter, scheduled trips such as the Lunch Sails from noon to 12:45 for $3.50, leaving from the Battery. If you want to be alone, it will cost you upwards of $150 per hour. Information, 825-1976.

Repairs/Restorations

New Yorkers may appear to be more attracted to the new things in life, but the city abounds in little shops that serve only to repair those favorite old items.

Antiques

All-Art Restorers, 140 West 57 Street; 489-6937.

Antique Furniture Restorations, Inc., 421 East 76 Street; 737-6270.

Han Dynasty Restoration Studio, 220 Fifth Avenue; 532-0337.

Oriental Antique Restorers, 118 East 59 Street; 751-3299.

Veterans Caning Shop, 550 West 35 Street; 868-3244.

Artwork

Baldaccini Renzo, 110 Madison Avenue (87 Street); 861-5010.

Irwin Braun, Inc., 315 East 62 Street; 593-1467.

China and Glassware

Hess Repairs, 200 Park Avenue South; 260-2255.

Mr. Fixit, 1300 Madison Avenue; 369-7775.

Clocks and Watches

Antique Clock Restoration Services 166 East 61 Street; 421-9640.

Clock Doc, 18 Lexington Avenue (2: Street); 475-9509.

E. Greenberg, 9 East 47 Street; 759 6630.

International Clock Repair Co., 13C West 42 Street; 354-6118.

Joseph Fanelli Clocks & Things, 100 Second Avenue (53 Street); 755-8766.

Sutton Clock Shop, 139 East 61 Street 758-2260.

Dolls

Brown Iris Antiques, 253 East 57 Street; 593-2882.

Manhattan Doll Hospital, 4245 Broadway (181 Street); 927-5225; or 176 Ninth Avenue (21 Street); 989-5220.

New York Doll Hospital, 787 Lexington Avenue (61 Street); 838-7527.

Electric Appliances

Appliance & Shaver World, 118 East Fordham Road (Bronx); 364-3862.

Lenox Fit-It Shop, 277 Lenox Avenue; 662-4943.

Furniture

Abraham Arts Center, 38 East 19 Street; 228-1890.

Artbench, 254 East 89 Street; 427-3770

Berkshire Woodfinishing Shop, Inc., 521 West 26 Street; 244-8230.

Steiner Zoltan, 37 West 20 Street; 242-8686.

Varsas, 45 East 20 Street; 777-8599.

Handbags

Aaron Willet, 303 East 51 Street; 759-1955.

Alligator on the Rug, Inc., 1057 Madison Avenue (80 Street); 794-1500.

Artbag Creations, Inc., 735 Madison Avenue (64 Street); 744-2720.

Henri Betrix, Inc., 669 Madison Avenue; 838-8120.

Lester Bags, 669 Madison Avenue (61 Street); 838-5653.

Modern Leather Goods Repair Shop, Inc., 11 West 32 Street; 279-3263.

Occhicone, 834 Lexington Avenue; 980-3295.

Jewelry

American Watch Service, 106 West 29 Street; 695-7321.

B. Harris & Sons, 25 East 61 Street; 755-6455.

Constance Jewelry, 40 East 45 Street; 697-5810.

Louis Fried & Son, Inc. 1188 Third Avenue (69 Street); 861-5500.

Kars Jewelry, 218 East 14 Street; 473-5875.

M. Haberman & I Jewelers, Inc., 380 Lexington Avenue (42 Street); 697-5270.

Norel Jewelry, 72 Bowery; 966-0566.

Rissin's Jewelry Clinic, 4 West 47 Street; 575-1098.

Luggage

Aeroplane Luggage Co., 4114 13 Avenue (Brooklyn); 344-0900.

Carnegie Luggage Inc., 1388 Sixth Avenue (56 Street); 586-8210.

John Gerardo Inc., 30 West 31 Street; 695-6955.

Igor Barkagan Luggage Repair Shop, 506 Amsterdam Avenue (85 Street); 724-8715.

Leeds Luggage Shops, Inc., 33 West 46 Street; 582-2860.

Martins Custom Repair Shop, 217 East 83 Street; 737-2694.

Superior Repair Center, 2 West 32 Street; 564-2267.

Musical Instruments

Accent Guitars, 159 West 48 Street; 869-3985.

Accordion-o-Rama, 874 Broadway; 777-4780.

Art-Shell Inc., 167 West 48 Street; 869-8337.

Bell Eddie Guitar Headquarters, Inc., 251 West 30 Street; 594-8124.

Biardinelli Band Instruments Co., 151 West 46 Street; 575-5959.

Guitar Lab Repair Shop, 165 West 48 Street; 765-7738.

Havivi Violins, 140 West 57 Street; 265-5818.

Luthier Rosenthal Rare Violins, 50 East 42 Street; 697-4333.

Traegers Bass Shop, 115 Christopher Street; 989-2517.

Photographic Equipment

Chap Camera Repair Service, 15 West 47 Street; 765-0843.

Professional Camera Repair Service, 37 West 47 Street; 246-7660.

Swiss Camera & Optic Service, 308 Fifth Avenue; 594-6340.

West Side Camera, Inc., 2400 Broadway (88 Street); 877-8760.

Windsor Camera Exchange, Inc., 146 West 72 Street; 362-3275.

Picture Frames

Julius Lowy Frame & Restoring Co., 511 East 72 Street; 535-5250.

Silver

B & D Polishing and Plating Co., 1575 York Avenue; 988-4240.

Hess Repairs, 200 Park Avenue South; 260-2255.

Umbrellas

Gloria Umbrella Manufacturing Co., 39 Essex Street; 475-7388.

Uncle Sam Umbrella Shop, 161 West 57 Street; 247-7163.

Weaving/Fabric Repair

Ace Weaving Service, 123 East 34 Street; 683-8953.

Berhir Karekin Ltd., 1125 Madison Avenue (84 Street); 838-3763.

French American Re-Weaving Co., 37 West 57 Street; 753-1672.

Karlton Weavers, 168 Fifth Avenue (21 Street); 255-9530.

New York Art Weaving Co., 17 East 37 Street; 685-9113.

Restaurants

All the restaurants listed here are open every day for lunch and dinner, unless otherwise noted. In all cases, it is a good idea to phone ahead for reservations.

Downtown

LOWER MANHATTAN

Cheese of All Nations, 153 Chambers Street; 732-0752. A cheese shop with a restaurant upstairs where you can taste the various cheeses right away.

Fraunces Tavern, 54 Pearl Street; 269-0144. Of historic interest, with a museum upstairs in what was once Washington's headquarters. Open Monday to Friday only.

Market Dining Rooms and Bar, 5 World Trade Center, Concourse; 938-1155. American food in recreated market atmosphere. Lunch not served on weekends; Sunday brunch.

Oliver Eatwell, 54 Pine Street; 425-3062. Crowded at lunch time.

Sloppy Louis's, 92 South Street; 952-9657. Seafood; bring your own wine. Open Monday to Friday only; closes at 8 PM. You sit at long, scrubbed tables among workers from the docks or Wall Street bankers. Good bouillabaisse.

Sweet's, 2 Fulton Street; 825-9786. No reservations; crowded at lunch time; open Monday to Friday; closes at 8:30 PM. In a row of historic buildings, this is a good fish restaurant but tends to be expensive.

CHINATOWN

BoBo, 201½ Pell Street; 267-8373. Cantonese; bring your own wine. Try their shrimps in seaweed.

456, 2 Bowery; 964-5853.

Phoenix Garden, 46 Bowery; 962-8934.

Say Eng Look, 1 East Broadway; 731-0796. Shanghai specialties.

Silver Palace, 50 Bowery; 964-1204.

Wo Hop, 17 Mott Street; 233-9632. Bring your own wine; inexpensive.

Wo Ping, 24 Pell Street; 732-0847. Bring your own wine; inexpensive.

LITTLE ITALY

Angelo's, 146 Mulberry Street; 966-1277. Closed Mondays.

Benito's, 174½ Mulberry Street; 226-9007.

Il Cortile, 125 Mulberry Street; 226-6060.

Puglia, 189 Hester Street; 226-8912.

Umberto's Clam House, 129 Mulberry Street; 431-7545.

Vincent's Clam Bar, 119 Mott Street; 226-9683. Clams, mussels, shrimp — all first class.

SoHo

Ballato, 55 East Houston Street; 226-9683. A nondescript exterior hides the good things within.

Cupping Room Café, 359 West Broadway; 925-2898. A good place for pastries and coffee.

Oh-Ho-So, 395 West Broadway; 966-6100. Good Cantonese food, marvelous decor.

Raoul's, 180 Prince Street; 966-3518. French food, at this downtown clique's restaurant. Atmosphere is exciting, food is good. Dinner only.

SoHo Charcuterie, 195 Spring Street; 226-3545. French; on Sundays only brunch is served. With an inviting counter and good food to take out as well.

WPA, 152 Spring Street; 226-3444. Marvelous black Art Deco interior; fun for Sunday brunch.

GREENWICH VILLAGE

Caffé Reggio, 119 Macdougal Street; 475-9557. A touch of Italy; open late for coffee and pastry.

Chumley's, 86 Bedford Street; 243-9729. Bar with good American food.

Claudio's, 289 Bleecker Street; 242-4889. Seafood. Lunch Saturday and Sunday, dinner every day. Good Northern Italian cuisine.

Coach House, 110 Waverly Place; 777-0303. Elegant American food; very expensive. Dinner only; closed Monday.

Dardanelles, 86 University Place; 242-8990. Good Armenian food, reasonable and pleasant.

Elephant and Castle, 68 Greenwich Avenue; 243-1400. Omelettes are featured; open 9 AM to midnight, every day. Busy and popular.

Front Porch, 253 West 11 Street; 675-8083. Casual, simple, and cozy with hanging plants. Stresses soups, casseroles, and homemade desserts.

Gottlieb's, 343 Bleecker Street; 929-7800. Continental.

Hisae's Place, 35 Cooper Square; 228-6886. Good Japanese continental food in generous portions. Dinner only.

Il Ponte Vecchio, 206 Thompson Street; 473-9382. Italian. Dinner only, closed Tuesday.

Joe's, 79 Macdougal Street; 764-1838. Good Italian food, cozy room in front, while back is more formal.

Lady Astor's, 430 Lafayette Street; 228-7888. French food in Victorian elegance.

Mary's, 42 Bedford Street; 741-3387. Home-style Italian cooking.

Minetta Tavern, 113 Macdougal Street; 475-3850.

Monte's, 97 Macdougal Street; 674-9456.

O Henry's, 345 Sixth Avenue; 242-2000. Steakhouse; a Village institution with sawdust on the floor and waiters in white butcher's aprons and straw boaters.

One Fifth, 1 Fifth Avenue; 260-3434. Furnished from a '30s oceanliner (*S.S. Coronia*). American food; piano music; weekend brunch.

Phebe's Place, 361 Bowery; 473-9008. Burgers and other American dishes. Recently enlarged and more "uptown" but still a hangout for actors in the neighborhood.

Peacock Caffé, 24 Greenwich Avenue; 242-9395. Espresso and pastries.

Starthrower Café, 2 Bank Street; 924-9450. Bare brick walls and bentwood chairs; an eclectic menu in the new style. Lunch except Sunday; closed Monday.

Tavola Calda da Alfredo, 285 Bleecker Street; 924-4789. Italian. Closed Wednesday.

Trattoria da Alfredo, 90 Bank Street; 929-4400. Italian; bring your own wine. Lunch except Sunday; closed Tuesday.

Ye Waverly Inn, 16 Bank Street; 243-9396. One of the oldest restaurants in the Village; American food. With a garden and fireplace. Lunch weekdays only, dinner every day.

East Side
FROM 14 TO 59 STREETS

Box Tree, 242 East 50 Street; 758-8320. French; expensive and elegant. Good appetizers and desserts. Lunch not served on weekends.

Brasserie, 100 East 53 Street; 751-4820. French (largely Alsatian); open 24 hours and very popular.

Cafe Nicholson; 323 East 58 Street; 355-6769. French. Delightful decor and good but limited food.

Edwardian Room, Plaza Hotel, 59 Street and Fifth Avenue; 759-3000. Continental menu; dancing. Dinner only.

Four Seasons, 99 East 52 Street; 754-9494. Elegant and famous. Closed Sunday.

Irish Pavilion, 130 East 57 Street; 759-9041. Shop in front, restaurant in back; continental with Irish specialties. Closed Sunday.

La Bibliotheque, 341 East 43 Street; 689-5444. Good view; opposite the U.N., it attracts diplomats for lunch. French cuisine.

La Côte Basque, 5 East 55 Street; 688-6525. Formal and French. Closed Sunday.

La Grenouille, 3 East 52 Street; 752-1495. Deluxe French restaurant; closed Sunday.

Le Cygne, 53 East 54 Street; 759-5941. Deluxe French restaurant; lunch not served on Saturday. Closed Sunday.

Lutece, 249 East 50 Street; 752-2225. Deluxe French restaurant; generally rec-

ognized as the best in New York; lunch not served on weekends; closed Sunday.

Mimosa, 153 East 33 Street; 685-2595. Continental, light food; bright and friendly. Very reasonable.

Nanni's, 146 East 46 Street; 697-4141. Northern Italian; closed Sunday and in August.

Oak Room, Plaza Hotel, 59 Street and Fifth Avenue; 759-3000. Continental cuisine. Lunch weekdays only, dinner every day.

Oyster Bar and Restaurant, Grand Central Station, 42 Street and Vanderbilt Avenue, lower level; 532-3888. Seafood; variety of fresh oysters featured; closed weekends.

Palace, 420 East 59 Street; 355-5150. Very expensive. Lunch not served on weekends. Closed Sunday.

Palm, 837 Second Avenue (45 Street); 687-2953. Lunch not served on weekends. Closed Sunday.

ABOVE 59 STREET

Carlyle Restaurant, Hotel Carlyle, 76 Street and Madison Avenue; 744-1600. Bar features murals by Ludwig Bemelmans. Open for breakfast, lunch, and dinner daily.

Casa Brazil, 406 East 85 Street; 288-5284. Brazil night is Wednesday when *feijoada* (with all the trimmings) is served. Limited continental menu the rest of the week. Bring your own wine. Dinner only; closed Sunday.

David K's, 1115 Third Avenue; 371-9090. Two stone lions guard the entrance. Dim Sum is featured at this Chinese restaurant.

Garden of Delights, 1192 Lexington Avenue; 861-0088. Good Middle Eastern food; dinner only.

Greek Village, 1016 Lexington Avenue; 744-9359. Reasonable Greek food.

Hoexter's Market Restaurant, 1442 Third Avenue (82 Street); 472-9322. Dinner only.

Il Monello, 1460 Second Avenue (76 Street); 535-9310; solid Northern Italian; almost campy decor. Lunch weekdays only; closed Sunday.

J. G. Melon, 1291 Third Avenue (74 Street); 744-0585. American food, good hamburgers.

La Petite Ferme, 973 Lexington Avenue (71 Street); 249-3272. French; closed Sunday.

La Famille, 2017 Fifth Avenue (124 Street); 722-9909. Good home cooking for when you are all the way uptown.

Le Refuge, 309 East 83 Street; 861-4505. Nouvelle cuisine and very popular.

Le Plaisir, 969 Lexington Avenue (70 Street); 734-9430. Closed Sunday.

Le Relais, 712 Madison Avenue (63 Street); 751-5108. French; closed Sunday.

Maxwell's Plum, 64 Street and First Avenue; 628-2100. Very popular bar and restaurant featuring continental food. The setting is more important than the food. Weekend brunch.

Mortimer's, 1057 Lexington Avenue (72 Street); 861-2481. Continental food; a meeting place.

Pancho Villa's, 1501 Second Avenue (78 Street); 650-1455. Mexican food; glassed-in sidewalk café.

Pinocchio, 170 East 81 Street; 650-1513. Northern Italian; dinner only; closed Monday.

P. J. Clarke's, 915 Third Avenue (55 Street); 759-1650. American food, good hamburgers; often very crowded; Sunday brunch.

Sichuan Pavilion, 322 East 44 Street; 986-3775. Szechuan (Chinese) cuisine in large but quiet rooms.

Sixty-Five Irving Place, 65 Irving Place; 673-3939. Nouvelle cuisine.

Sumptuary, 400 Third Avenue (30 Street); 889-6056. Continental menu; cozy with greenery. Lunch on weekdays only; closed Sunday and Monday.

Z, 117 East 15 Street; 254-0960. Plain Greek food; small garden; closed Monday.

West Side

FROM 14 TO 59 STREET

Act I, 1 Times Square; 695-1880. Good view, popular with tourists. Closed Sunday.

Barbetta, 321 West 46 Street; 246-9171. Northern Italian food at moderate prices. Closed Sunday.

Cabana Carioca, 123 West 45 Street; 581-8088. Brazilian food at realistic prices.

Cafe de France, 330 West 46 Street; 974-9452.

Café in the Cradle, 27 West 38 Street; 221-6466. Vegetarian Middle Eastern food. Crowded at lunchtime; closed Sunday.

Charley O's Bar and Grill, 33 West 48 Street; 582-7141. Irish saloon; weekend brunch. Open 24 hours.

Crepe Suzette, 313 West 46 Street; 581-9717.

El Tenampa, 304 West 46 Street; 586-8039. Cozy pub.

Empire Diner, 210 Tenth Avenue (24 Street); 243-2736. Simple American food; open 24 hours, and very popular.

Hurley's, 1240 Sixth Avenue (50 Street); 765-8981. Next to Radio City Music Hall.

Joe Allen's, 326 West 46 Street; 581-6464. Theater crowd; steaks are featured; open until 2 AM.

La Bonne Soupe, 48 West 55 Street; 566-7650. Other branches.

La Caravelle, 33 West 55 Street; 586-4252. Deluxe French restaurant; prix fixe lunch, a la carte dinner. Closed Sunday and in July.

Landmark Tavern, 626 Eleventh Avenue; 757-8595. Traditional food (including steak-and-kidney pie) in an English pub setting; Sunday brunch; open until midnight.

Magic Pan Creperie, 1409 Sixth Avenue (58 Street); 765-5080. Two levels, with a nonsmoking section.

Orsini's, 41 West 56 Street; 757-1698. Italian cuisine; closed Sunday.

Paddy's Clam House, 215 West 34 Street; 244-9123. Fish and shellfish in the midst of 34 Street hustle.

Patsy's, 236 West 56 Street; 247-3491. Italian menu; closed Monday.

Pearl's, 38 West 48 Street; 586-1060. Chinese food; lunch not served Sunday. Sometimes frequented by the famous.

Raga, 57 West 48 Street; 757-3450. Indian cuisine; lunch served weekdays only. Pre-theater buffet offered.

Rainbow Room, 30 Rockefeller Plaza, Sixty-Fifth Floor; 757-9000. Dining and dancing with a sensational view; varied menu; dinner served daily.

Restaurant Español, 318 West 23 Street; 691-0590. Spanish food in a friendly atmosphere.

Russian Tea Room, 150 West 57 Street; 265-0947. Russian specialties; a separate vodka menu lists exotic drinks; Sunday brunch.

Sea Fare of the Aegean, 25 West 56 Street; 581-0540. Good fish dishes with a Greek accent.

Shezan, 8 West 58 Street; 371-1414. Indian cuisine; lunch served weekdays only; closed Sunday.

ABOVE 59 STREET

Anita's Chili Parlor, 287 Columbus Avenue (74 Street); 595-4091. Chili and other Mexican foods to take out or eat in.

Café des Artistes, 1 West 67 Street; 877-3500. Continental menu; famed Howard Chandler Christy murals cover the walls.

Cafe La Fortuna, 69 West 71 Street; 724-5846. Open late for pastries and espresso.

Green Tree Hungarian Restaurant, 1034 Amsterdam Avenue (111 Street); 864-9106. A favorite of students.

Ruskay's, 323 Columbus Avenue (76 Street); 874-8391. Stylish Art-Deco surroundings; varied menu; weekend brunch; open from noon until 5 AM.

Saloon, 1920 Broadway (61 Street); 874-1500. Convenient to Lincoln Center; continental cuisine; sidewalk cafe; weekend brunch.

Tavern on the Green, 40 West 67 Street (in Central Park); 873-3200. Popular with tourists; Continental menu; very expensive. Garden room at Christmastime is lovely.

Teacher's Pub, 2248 Broadway (82 Street); 787-3500. A hangout for Westsiders.

Terrace, 400 West 119 Street (atop Butler Hall, Columbia University); 666-9490. French food; closed Monday; lunch on weekdays only. With a view across the Hudson.

Top of the Park; 60 Street and Central Park West; 333-3800. Wonderful view.

For Sunday Brunch

Brunch is served in hundreds of restaurants in New York. A few are listed below.

Algonquin Hotel, 59 West 44 Street; 687-4400.

Café des Artistes, 1 West 67 Street; 877-3500.

Hors d'Oeuverie, Windows on the World, World Trade Tower #1; 938-1111. Jacket required. International brunch served noon to 2:30 PM.

J. G. Melon, 1291 Third Avenue (74 Street); 744-0585.

Maxwell's Plum, 64 Street and First Avenue; 628-2100.

One Fifth, 1 Fifth Avenue; 260-3434.

Palm Court, Plaza Hotel, 59 Street and Fifth Avenue; 759-3000.

Rainbow Room, 30 Rockefeller Center; 757-8970.

WPA, 152 Spring Street; 226-3445. Continental food served in a '30s surrounding.

Vegetarian

Many "regular" restaurants also offer vegetarian meals.

Four Steps to Nature, 4 Waverly Place; 673-5955.

Great American Health Bar, 15 East 40 Street, 532-3232; also at: 76 Beaver Street, 344-7522; and at 35 West 57 Street, 355-5177.

Healthworks, 148 East 57 Street, 838-8370; other branches at: 804 Madison Avenue, 472-9300; 1345 Sixth Avenue, 586-1980; 12 East 36 Street, 686-0401; and in the Citicorp Market (53 Street and Lexington Avenue), 838-6221.

Sta-Well Nutrition Center, 16 West 40 Street; 398-0800.

Whole Wheat 'n' Wild Berrys, 57 West 10 Street; 677-3410. Closed Monday; weekend brunch.

World Health Center, 2320 Broadway (86 Street), 874-0988; also at 1431 Third Avenue; 628-9413.

With a Garden, Terrace, or View

Barbetta, 321 West 46 Street; 246-9171. Italian food; lovely garden. Closed Sunday.

Emilio's, 307 Sixth Avenue; 929-9861.

Lion's Rock, 316 East 77 Street; 988-3610. Continental restaurant with lovely garden; Sunday brunch.

Top of the Sixes, 666 Fifth Avenue (53 Street); 757-6662. Rooftop restaurant with American menu; closed Sunday.

Windows on the World, 1 World Trade Tower, 107 floor; 938-1111. The most spectacular view in New York; continental fare; jacket and tie required. Dinner only; weekend noon buffet.

Open-Air Cafés

Some time ago, New York grabbed hold of the sidewalk café idea, fashioned after those in Paris and Rome, and now there are many such spots in Manhattan. Unfortunately, some restaurants have found it necessary to encase their cafés in glass, but you can still sit out-of-doors in the following spots.

Back Porch, 488 Third Avenue; 685-3828. Relaxed spot, a bit out of the way.

Buffalo Roadhouse, 87 Seventh Avenue South, 242-9028. Fairly new Village spot.

Café de la Paix (St. Moritz), 50 Central Park South; 755-5800. Expensive, with a view of the park.

Café du Parc (Stanhope Hotel), Fifth Avenue at 81 Street; 288-5800. Across from the Metropolitan Museum.

Caffe Biondo, 141 Mulberry; 226-9285. New, in Little Italy.

Caffe Primavera, 51 Spring Street; 226-8421. Old favorite in Little Italy.

Curtain Up, 402 West 43 Street; 564-7272. In the Theater District.

Doral Park Avenue Hotel Cafe, 70 Park Avenue (38 Street); 687-7050. Small but inviting.

Le Figaro Cafe, 186 Bleecker Street; 677-1100. Typical Village spot — just like you would have imagined.

Fiorello's Roman Cafe, 1900 Broadway; 595-5330. Convenient to Lincoln Center.

Gleason's Public House, 400 Columbus Avenue (79 Street); 874-8726. Across from the Museum of Natural History.

Lincoln Center Fountain Cafe, in the Plaza. Filled with expectant opera and concert goers.

La Maganette Cafe, 825 Third Avenue (50 Street); 759-5677. Low-keyed.

Riveria Cafe, 225 West 4 Street; 242-8732. Village hangout.

Rocking Horse Cafe, 224 Columbus (70 Street); 724-7816. Singles gathering spot.

Ruskay's Restaurant, 323 Columbus Avenue (75 Street); 874-8391. Art Deco and charming.

Saloon, 1920 Broadway (64 Street); 874-1500. A touch of Europe, but here the waiters pass by on roller skates.

Trattoria, 200 Park Avenue (45 Street); 661-3090. In the Pan Am Building.

For People Watching

In addition to the celebrities, these spots have decent food.

Café des Artistes, 1 West 67 Street; 877-3500. Romantic and quiet restaurant.

Regine's, 502 Park Avenue; 826-0990. More subdued than many of the other discos.

Russian Tea Room, 150 West 57 Street; 265-0947. The stars come late and prefer the booths in the front.

Sardi's, 234 West 44th Street; 221-8440. Always a top spot.

Coffee Shops and Delicatessens

There are various coffee-shop chains located all over New York such as Chock-full-of-Nuts, Hickory House, and so on. There's a coffee shop on almost every corner; follow your instinct about going in.

Excelsior Coffee Shop, 45 West 81 Street; 877-0746.

Heidi's Coffee Shop, 8 West 56 Street; 586-3040.

Delicatessens are a New York specialty. They are called "delis" by their patrons.

Fine and Shapiro, 138 West 72 Street; 877-2874. Kosher; great sandwiches; reserve for parties of 6 or more.

Madison Avenue Restaurant, 1175 Madison Avenue (86 Street); 369-6670. Superior sandwiches, desserts.

Ratner's Dairy Restaurant, 138 Delancy Street; 677-5588. Kosher, dairy restaurant; wonderful blintzes.

Second Avenue Kosher Delicatessen and Restaurant, 156 Second Avenue

(10 Street); 677-0606. Best kosher deli in the city; great chopped liver and pastrami. Open till midnight every day.

Stage Deli, 834 Seventh Avenue (53 Street); 245-7850. Popular with theater people; good sandwiches, home-cooked meals. Open from 6:30 AM till 2:30 AM.

Wolf's Sixth Avenue Delicatessen, 101 West 57 Street; 586-1110. Good sandwiches, soups.

Restaurants with Children's Menus

Cattleman, 5 East 45 Street; 661-1200. On weekends a special menu for children is offered; a clown entertains.

O'Neal Brothers, 296 Columbus Avenue (75 Street); 399-2355. Children can play with pinball machines while waiting for their hamburgers or ham and eggs.

Pelican, 200 West 70 Street; 585-8067. Fish and chips are very popular; lobsters can be watched as they wander around in their tank.

Vegetaria, 64 Charles Street; 243-7979. A special children's menu is available.

In Brooklyn

Dar Lebnan, 155 Atlantic Avenue; 625-7998. Bring your own wine; convenient for BAM.

Gage and Tollner, 372 Fulton Street; 875-5181. A Brooklyn institution for seafood and other traditional dishes.

Gargiulo's, 2911 West 15 Street; 266-0906. Large and famous for its hearty Italian cuisine.

Hubert's, 148 Hoyt Street; 858-0400. French-inspired cuisine; guest chef program at certain times of the year; Sunday brunch. Closed Monday.

Nathan's Famous, Surf and Stillwell Avenues; Coney Island. The original, going since 1916.

Peter Luger, 178 Broadway; 387-7400. A great old steakhouse, with an original 1887 polished oak bar.

Pâté Vite, 178 Atlantic Avenue; 855-2650. Small and lovely bistro.

River Café, 1 Water Street; 522-5200. Great view of Manhattan. Continental-international menu. Outdoor dining in good weather. Sunday brunch.

Son of Sheik, 165 Atlantic Avenue; 625-4023.

Shopping

We've tried to give you a practical listing — one that reflects a diversity of tastes and pocketbooks. You won't find this to be a comprehensive listing at all; if a particular store isn't listed here that you wish to visit, then check the telephone book for the address or telephone number. What we've given you is just a starting point.

Most stores in New York are open from 10 or 11 AM to 5 or 6 PM, Monday through Saturday. Some stores close one day a week; others are open on Sunday. Check with the store first if you have any doubts as to hours.

Antiques

MARKETS

These markets are clusters of shops or stalls gathered together under one roof. Usually they are open all year, many on Sunday as well.

Antiques Market, 137 Ludlow Street; 674-9805.

Collectors Market, 252 Bleecker Street; 255-0175.

Manhattan Art & Antiques Center, 1050 Second Avenue (56 Street); 355-4400.

New Fulton Market, Fulton and Front Streets; 349-7174.

Soho Canal Flea, 369 Canal Street; 966-6820.

SHOPS

You will find whole nests of antique shops as well as junk shops in the thirties on Third and Second Avenues, around University Place, and on Columbus Avenue around 80 Street.

America Hurrah, 316 East 70 Street; 535-1930. Very pretty quilts, perhaps the nicest around; countrified furniture and objects.

Ann Phillips Antiques, 899 Madison Avenue (72 Street); 535-0415. Eighteenth- and nineteenth-century Americana.

Bob Pryor, 1023 Lexington Avenue (73 Street); 688-1516. Brass objects; glass and china; a good selection of small and easily transportable items.

Israel Sack, 15 East 57 Street; 753-6562. Here you will find the crème de la crème of American furniture.

Justin G. Schiller, 36 East 61 Street; 832-8231. Antique children's books.

Karekin Beshir Galleries, 1126 Madison Avenue (82 Street); 838-3763. A very beautiful collection of antique Persian, Turkish, Caucasian, Chinese, and French rugs.

Kover King, Inc., 120 West 44 Street; 581-6910. Antique postcards, among them collector's items.

Magnificent Doll, 209 East 60 Street; 753-7425. Everything from wooden Pinocchios and bored-looking courtesans to a Jumeau dating from 1860 and dressed in her original costume; both old and new.

Patina Antiques, 334 Bleecker Street; 929-3170.

Pierre Deux, 369 Bleecker Street; 243-7740. Take a look, if you happen to be in the neighborhood.

S. J. Shrubsole, 104 East 57 Street; 753-8920. Very good silver and jewelry.

Speakeasy Antiques, 797 Broadway (10 Street); 533-2440. From the twenties.

Army/Navy Surplus

These shops are great for army-style clothing and camping gear.

Hudson Army and Navy Store, 105 Third Avenue (15 Street); 475-9568. Easy on the eyes and the money bag.

Kaufman's Surplus, 319 West 42 Street; 757-5670. Also 623 Broadway, corner of Houston Street; 673-3535.

Richard's, 233 West 42 Street; 947-5018. Much like the above, but they also sell working clothes and deep-sea fishing equipment.

Unique Clothing Warehouse, 716-720 Broadway (near New York University); 674-1767. Old and new stuff.

Weiss & Mahoney, Inc., 142 Fifth Avenue (19 Street); 675-1915. Not just surplus, but also flags, trophies, camping equipment, military badges, and vacuum-packed — that is to say, for eternity — food.

Art Supplies

Materials for the artist are sold throughout the city, but listed here are two of the leading shops.

New York Central, 62 Third Avenue (11 Street); 473-7705.

Sam Flax, 25 East 28 Street; 620-3040. Also with uptown branch.

Bakeries

Here are some of the city's finest, along

with some specifically mentioned in the White Pages of this book.

Bonte Patisserie, 1316 Third Avenue (75 Street); 535-2360.

Delices La Cote Basque, 1032 Lexington Avenue (74 Street); 535-3311.

Dumas Patisserie, 116 East 60 Street; 688-0905.

Damascus Bakery, 195 Atlantic Avenue, Brooklyn; 855-1456.

Just Desserts, 443 East 75 Street; 535-4964.

Leske's, 7612 Fifth Avenue, Brooklyn; 680-2323.

Louis Lichtman, 532 Amsterdam Avenue (86 Street); 873-2373.

Miss Grimble, 51 Greenwich Avenue; 989-1836. Also other locations.

Olsen's, 5722 Eighth Avenue, Brooklyn; GE9-6673.

One Smart Cookie, 70 Seventh Avenue, Brooklyn; 636-5288.

Well-Bred Loaf, 1742 Second Avenue (90 Street); 534-6951.

William Greenberg, 1100 Madison Avenue (82 Street); 744-0304.

Bargains — Discount Stores

The majority of these stores are noted for bargains in women's wear, however Chambers Street is good for all sorts of bargains and Reade and Duane streets are also worth visiting.

A. Altman, 182 Orchard Street; 982-7722.

Bernard Krieger & Son, 316 Grand Street; 226-4927.

Bolton's, 43 East 8 Street; 475-6626. Other locations as well.

Lace-up Shoe Shop, 119 Orchard Street; 475-8040.

Loehmann's, 9 West Fordham Road, Bronx; 295-4100. Other branches in Brooklyn and Queens.

M. Friedlich, 196 Orchard Street; 254-8899.

Sam Popper, 85 Orchard Street; 226-9752.

Trieste General Merchandise, 568 Twelfth Avenue (44 Street); 246-1548. Everything from heavily discounted luggage to tins of Nivea.

Bath Accessories

Here's an assortment of stores offering a variety of bath-related items.

Caswell-Massey, 518 Lexington Avenue (48 Street); 755-2254. Oils, lotions, soaps.

Crabtree & Evelyn, 1310 Madison Avenue (91 Street); 289-3923. Soaps.

Sherle Wagner, 60 East 57 Street; 758-3300. Elegant fixtures.

Bookstores

This listing includes both the large chain stores and small, specialized shops dealing in very limited selections. The specialized shops are where New York is at its best.

Argosy, 116 East 50 Street; 753-4455. Old maps from $1 to $900, drawings and lithographs depicting New York, Americana, first editions, books about medicine.

Barnes and Noble, 105 Fifth Avenue (18 Street); 255-8100. Annex across the street and uptown branch at 600 Fifth Avenue (50 Street). New York's oldest university bookseller.

Batcave Comic Book Store, 120 West 3 Street; 674-8474. A wide selection for collectors.

Books & Co., 939 Madison Avenue (74 Street); 737-1450. First editions (new), autographed, plus a wide selection of art and photography books as well as fine literature.

Brentano's, 586 Fifth Avenue (47 Street); 757-8600. Aside from books, Brentano's sells amusing jewelry (reproductions), gadgets, and paperbacks in the basement.

China Books and Periodicals, 125 Fifth Avenue (20 Street); 677-2650. Books dealing with Chinese communism.

Cinemabilia, 10 West 13 Street; 989-8519. Books about the movies.

Complete Traveler, 199 Madison Avenue (36 Street); 679-4339. Travel books on all parts of the world.

Djuna Books, 154 West 10 Street; 242-3642. Books by and about women.

Doubleday Bookshop, 724 Fifth Avenue (57 Street); 397-0550. Also as 673 Fifth Avenue (53 Street). A general store, with a large number of titles; records and cassettes are also sold.

Drama Book Shop, 150 West 52 Street; 582-1037. Books on the theater and copies of plays.

Eeyore's Books for Children, 2252 Broadway (80 Street); 362-0634. The leading store in the city for children's books.

Four Continent Book Corporation, 149 Fifth Avenue (20 Street); 533-0250. Books and folk art from other countries.

Gotham Book Mart and Gallery, 41 West 47 Street; 757-0367. A famous literary spot with small press books, privately printed poetry, and magazines in many languages. Gotham sold the first U.S. copy of James Joyce's *Ulysses* in the twenties.

Jaap Rietman Artbooks, 167 Spring Street; 966-7044. Good should you be gallery-hopping in SoHo and need background material.

Madison Avenue Bookstore, 833 Madison Avenue (70 Street); 535-6130. The Upper East Side set buy here. Its window is decorated by Tiffany's famous window-dresser.

Military Bookman, 170 East 92 Street; 348-1280. If military history is your thing, this is the place to go.

Murder Ink®, 271 West 87 Street; 362-8905. Detective novels, but the cream of the crop. There is even a lending library, with such goodies as thrillers written by a former art critic of the *New York Times* under a pseudonym. Murder Ink® organizes marvelously creepy outings — for instance a weekend in a slightly musty fin-de-siècle hotel in the country entitled "In the Dead of Winter," during the course of which someone gets "murdered" and the amateur detectives have a field day finding the murderer; or a series of "Sinister Sundays" where crime buffs meet to discuss the horrors of their avocation.

Oscar Wilde Memorial Bookshop, 15 Christopher Street; 255-8097. Books by and about homosexuals; New York's exclusively gay bookstore.

Quinion Books, 541 Hudson Street; 989-6130. Devoted primarily to cookbooks and books on drama.

Rizzoli International Bookstore, 712 Fifth Avenue (56 Street); 397-3700. Elegant, very European shop with books, records and magazines in many languages and a small gallery with works by new artists or some lithographs by established ones. The atmosphere is very pleasant and you might come across familiar faces. There is a branch at Union Square (860 Broadway), 397-3750.

Samuel Weiser, 470 Broadway (8 Street); 777-6363. Books on the occult.

Scribner's, 597 Fifth Avenue (49 Street); 486-4070. Publisher and Bookseller. Hemingway and Thomas Wolfe (among many others) were coddled here. There is a very knowledgeable sales staff and a well-arranged stock. The façade of the building is famous.

SoHo Books, 307 West Broadway; 925-4948. Open until midnight; readings; very good atmosphere.

Strand Bookstore, 828 Broadway (12 Street), 473-1452. Buys and sells used books (among them brand new review copies) and browsing is not only permitted but *de rigueur*. Prices are fantastic: a few years ago you could buy a complete 1958 *Encyclopedia Britannica* for $100 — in perfect condition.

Supersnipe Comic Book Art Euphorium, 1617 Second Avenue (84 Street); 879-9628. The favorite spot for comic book collectors.

Thousand Eyes Film Bookshop, 144 Bleecker Street (in Bleecker Street Cinema lobby); 677-7408. A large supply of books and magazines concerned with movies and moviemaking, as well as tapes, 15,000 photographs, and posters. Open Fridays and Saturdays from 2 PM to 10 PM, Sundays from 2 PM to 7 PM.

Urban Center Books, 457 Madison Avenue (51 Street); In a wing of the recently restored Villard Houses, this new store has 1,400 books on architecture and urban design.

Wittenborn Art Books, 1018 Madison Avenue (8 Street), Second Floor; 288-1558. Chock full of good things: posters are on the ceiling because the shelves are full to bursting. You can find just about everything to do with art and architecture — from obscure avant-garde leaflets to expensive special editions with original illustrations not only by Picasso and Braque, but promising new artists as well.

Womanbooks, 201 West 92 Street; 873-4121. Here you will find everything to do with women. Periodicals, records, and nonsexist children's books are sold. There is a corner for listening to records, a lending library, and a sofa on which

to drink coffee and peruse the latest magazines.

Boutiques

Many European designers have shops in New York or have boutiques within the department stores. American designers (of both *haute couture* and *prêt-à-porter*) have their own shops, boutiques in the department stores, or just sell their lines to various shops. For women.

Ann Taylor, 3 East 57 Street; 832-2010. Youthful, tailored sportswear.

Bea Entes, 109 University Place (12 Street); 982-3388. Fantastic Art Deco shop — clothes, jewelry, and objects — and you can haggle.

Betsey, Bunky and Nini, 746 Madison Avenue (64 Street); 744-6716. Diaphanous concoctions, mostly made of silk chiffon and to order, but cotton shirts as well, from $50.

Capezio, 755 Seventh Avenue (50 Street); 245-2130. There are also branches in the Village and on the East Side.

Charivari, 2307 Broadway (83 Street); 873-1424. Stylish, young clothes, not too cheap.

Design Observations, 280 Columbus Avenue (73 Street); 799-2986. The latest popular spot.

Fiorucci, 125 East 59 Street; 751-1404. Slightly mad, very funny place; good for unusual souvenirs.

French Connection, 1211 Madison Avenue (87 Street); 348-4990. Also 1411 Broadway (39 Street); 869-0934. There are other branches as well. Sells imported and local clothes at vastly reduced prices.

Honeybee, 7 East 53 Street; 688-3660. Young, amusing things.

Horsefeathers, 41 East 78 Street;

628-8254. Jackets and coats made of silk, taffeta, or cotton, filled with down and quilted.

Lady Madonna, 793 Madison Avenue (67 Street); 988-7173. The maternity clothes are so pretty that one is tempted to buy them pregnant or not.

Miso Clothes, 416 West Broadway; 226-4955. Beautiful, expensive things.

Olivia of Norway, 7721 Fifth Avenue, Brooklyn; Good if you are in the borough.

Regenesis Mastectomy Boutique, 18 East 53 Street; 593-2782. Clothes and underwear for women who have had a mastectomy.

Rubicon Boutique, 849 Madison Avenue (68 Street); 861-3000.

Skin Clothes, 801 Lexington Avenue (62 Street); 752-4605. Evening clothes and costumes; indeed they say they can equip you with just about anything you might need in the way of outrageous getups.

Stewart Ross — Stone Free, 754 Madison Avenue (64 Street); 744-3870. Also 105 West 72 Street; 362-9620. Very stylish, sporty clothes made only from natural fibers. Shoes in the earth-shoe style. For men too.

Strawberry, 110 Fifth Avenue (18 Street); 691-6480. Also other branches. Not really chic, not really young, but inexpensive clothes.

Turtlegreen, 1006 Lexington Avenue (18 Street); 535-7756. Well-made skirts, dresses, and blouses; some imports, amusing fashion jewelry, scarves, and belts.

Upper Mad, 1260 Madison Avenue (90 Street); 369-5005. Marvellous hand-painted jackets.

Victoria Falls, 147 Spring Street; 226-5099. Very beautiful old dresses, lace blouses, etc. Expensive.

Ceramics, China, Glass and Pottery

The china and glass departments of the various department stores usually have good selections. In addition, we list some specialty stores.

Baccarat, 55 East 57 Street; 826-4100.

Ginori Fifth Avenue, 711 Fifth Avenue (55 Street); 752-8790.

Jenny B. Goode, 1194 Lexington Avenue (81 Street); 794-2492. A mixed bag of merchandise, including pottery and china.

Pottery Barn, 117 East 59 Street; 741-9132. And branches elsewhere. A very nice shop, with kitchen utensils, china, mats, boxes, etc.

Pottery Plus, 1453 Third Avenue (82 Street); 535-8943. Calls itself New York's ceramics supermarket, with its large selection.

Plummer McCutcheon, in Hammacher-Schlemmer, 145 East 57 Street; 421-1600.

Royal Copenhagen, 573 Madison Avenue (56 Street); 759-6457.

Stephen Anson, 1058 First Avenue (57 Street); China on a New York taxicab theme.

Steuben Glass, 715 Fifth Avenue (56 Street); 752-1441.

Cheese

The gourmet sections of the large department stores such as Macy's and Bloomingdale's sell a wide variety of cheese. Here also are some specialty shops.

Cheese of All Nations, 153 Chambers Street; 732-0752.

Cheese Unlimited, 1529 Second Avenue (79 Street); 861-1306.

Cheese Village, 3 Greenwich Avenue; 924-6816.

Children's Clothing

Glad Rags, 1007 Madison Avenue (78 Street); 988-1880. Very popular with both mothers and children.

Morris Brothers, 85 Street and Broadway; 724-9000. A good source for genuine Oshkosh overalls.

Small Business, 101 Wooster Street; 966-1425. Hand-painted tee-shirts, crocheted bikinis, embroidered jackets and shirts.

Stone Free Kids, 124 West 72 Street; 362-8903. Recycled denim jackets, a large selection of Absorba.

Wendy's Store, 1046 Madison Avenue (79 Street); 861-9230. Very original, funny tee-shirts, baby quilts, pretty cotton dresses; not cheap.

Chocolates and Candies

Bloomingdale's Au Chocolate, 59 Street Entrance; 223-6650.

Candy Kisses, 58 Greenwich Avenue; 929-7133.

Godiva Chocolatier, 701 Fifth Avenue (54 Street); 593-2845.

Krön Chocolatier, 764 Madison Avenue (65 Street); 288-9259.

Perugina, 636 Lexington Avenue (54 Street); 688-2490.

Sweet Temptations, 128 West 57 Street; 757-5318.

Teuscher Chocolates, 25 East 61 Street; 751-8482.

Coffee and Tea

Coffee beans and special blends of loose teas are sold in many gourmet food stores, as well as the department stores. Listed here are some shops devoted exclusively to these goods.

McNulty's Tea and Coffee Co., 109 Christopher Street; 242-5351.

Sensuous Bean, 228 Columbus Avenue (70 Street); 724-7725.

Simpson & Vail, 53 Park Place; 344-6377. Teas only.

Cosmetics

The department stores have filled their ground floors with counters where all the large cosmetics producers can offer their wares. In addition, New Yorkers go a few other places as well.

Boyd Chemists, 655 Madison Avenue (60 Street); 838-6558.

Face Factory, 754 Lexington Avenue (59 Street); 838-0295. Also at 41 East 42 Street; 687-2079.

"I" Natural Cosmetics, 737 Madison Avenue (64 Street); 734-0664. These products are made with more natural ingredients and include papaya cleansing cream, strawberry fluff, avocado moisturizer.

Merle Norman Cosmetic Studio, 955 Eighth Avenue (56 Street); 265-5010.

Department Stores

Like everything else in New York, stores come in a variety of sizes and cater to a variety of tastes — from the very chic Henri Bendel (which is not really a department store) to Macy's (which *is* one, down to the basement). Below we have tried to describe some of them.

B. Altman & Co., 34 Street and Fifth Avenue; 689-7800. One of the original Fifth Avenue emporia in the heart of Murray Hill. You can buy designer dresses and shoes, but the stress is on sensible clothes. The housewares, china, and linen departments are well worth a visit. The whole store is much quieter than Bloomingdale's, and the sales help very friendly. The accessories on the ground floor are worth investigating as well.

Bergdorf Goodman, 58 Street and Fifth Avenue; 753-7300. Here you will find elegant women buying their Chanels and Givenchys; they get from one luxurious floor to the next in an elevator — there is no such vulgar thing as an escalator.

Bloomingdale's, 59 Street and Lexington Avenue; 223-7111. Bloomingdale's is New York's real emblem, don't let anyone try to persuade you that it is not so. When the Queen of England came to New York she did not go to City Hall but to Bloomie's.

Gimbels, 33 Street and Broadway; 564-3300. Also Gimbels East, 86 Street and Lexington Avenue; 348-2300. The main store is very much a traditional department store; the uptown branch is for a younger set.

Henri Bendel, 10 West 57 Street; 247-1100. Here you will find the most beautiful women in New York, whether they live around the corner or have just arrived from London or Paris. It is very important to pronounce "Henri" like "Henry," and under no circumstances to put the stress on the second syllable in Bendel. Bendel's used to have the most beloved, diminutive doorman in New York, called Buster, who knew everybody and was heartily envied by every man in town. To everybody's disappointment he retired recently, but you can buy a small rag doll — supposedly look-alike — if you're feeling sentimental.

Lord and Taylor, 39 Street and Fifth Avenue; 391-3344. A good place for youthful, reasonably priced clothes; a designer salon specializes in American labels.

Macy's, Herald Square (Seventh Avenue and Broadway, between 34 and 35 Street); 695-4400. Macy's says that it is the largest department store in the world and that may well be true, as you will find out when you try to get from one end to the other.

Ohrbach's, 5 West 34 Street; 695-4000. A moderate-priced store with dependable although predictable styles. Good bargains.

Saks Fifth Avenue, 50 Street and Fifth Avenue; 753-4000. The Saks customer is a little staid, no matter how young or old she is. Here she will find the "bargains" she likes so much, a great deal of expensive quality goods, and cruisewear for the trip south in the winter.

Ethnic Specialties

In no other city can you find such a concentration of different kinds of goods from all over the world. Here are some examples of what makes New York tops!

Ashanti Bazaar, 872 Lexington Avenue (65 Street); 535-0740. Things woven, knitted, and dyed by hand, not only African.

Azuma, 666 Lexington Avenue (56 Street); 752-0599. Also branches elsewhere. A potpourri of things from the Orient, India, and so on.

Cepelia, 63 East 57 Street; 751-0005. Polish goodies, including their wonderful carved boxes.

Chor Bazaar, 801 Lexington Avenue (62 Street); 838-2581. Items from Afghanistan and India.

Grecophilia, 132 West 72 Street; 877-2566. Greek clothes.

Greek Island, 215 East 49 Street; 355-7542. Everything from Greece.

Irish Pavilion, 130 East 57 Street; 759-9041. With goods for sale in front and a small cafe in the rear.

Merchants of Oyo, 130 East 3 Street; 674-8281. Masks from Mali and Tansania, wall hangings from Egypt, jewelry.

Norsk, 114 East 57 Street; 752-3111. Norwegian silver, rugs, and jewelry.

Sahadi, 187 Atlantic Avenue, Brooklyn; 624-4550. Goods, spices, and jewels from the Arabian countries.

Sermoneta, 740 Madison Avenue (64 Street); 744-6551. Ponchos, espadrilles, lovely cotton blouses and dresses, wool jackets and coats — mostly made in South America and India.

United Nations Giftshop, General Assembly Building; 754-1234. Goods from all over the world.

Drugstores

These are located throughout the city and you should have no trouble locating one. Listed below are a few that are special.

Cambridge Chemists, 702 Madison Avenue (62 Street); 838-1884.

Caswell-Massey, 518 Lexington Avenue (48 Street); 755-2254. Exotic soaps, snuff, and after-shave lotion.

Kaufman Pharmacy, 557 Lexington Avenue (50 Street); 755-2266. Never closes.

Kiehl's, 109 Third Avenue (13 Street); 475-3400. Essences, vitamin oils, herbs, and a large selection of honeys.

Fabrics

Probably the best spot to buy all-purpose fabric is Macy's, however other shops offer less common items in likewise less comprehensive surroundings.

Fabric Warehouse, 406 Broadway; 966-0470.

La Provence de Pierre Deux, 353 Bleecker Street; 675-4054. Lovely provençal prints from France.

Laura Ashley, 714 Madison Avenue (63 Street); 371-0606. Tiny, delicate prints from England.

Liberty of London, 229 East 60 Street; 888-1057. London's famous fabric house

has a branch now in New York.

Silk Surplus, 843 Lexington Avenue (64 Street); 879-4708. Specializes in silk.

Furniture

The department stores have large selections of furniture, and antique stores carry used and antique items. Below are a few specialty stores that feature inexpensive furniture for everyday use.

Bon Marche, 74 Fifth Avenue (13 Street); 924-5060.

Conran's, Citicorp Building, 160 East 54 Street; 371-2225.

W & J Sloane, 414 Fifth Avenue (38 Street); 840-1000.

Housewares and Cooking Utensils

Macy's and Bloomingdale's have strong departments in this area, but here are a few more alternatives.

Bazaar de la Cuisine,1003 Second Avenue (53 Street); 421-8028.

Bridge Kitchenware, 212 East 52 Street; 688-4220.

Manhattan Ad Hoc Housewares, 842 Lexington Avenue (64 Street); 752-5488.

Professional Kitchen, 18 Cooper Square; 254-9000.

Well-Tempered Kitchen, 2080 Broadway (72 Street); 595-8077.

Zabar's, 2245 Broadway (80 Street); 787-2000.

Gourmet Foods and Spices

Balducci's, 422 Sixth Avenue (10 Street); 673-2600.

Casa Moneo, 210 West 14 Street; 929-1644. Spanish products.

Caviarteria, 870 Madison Avenue (71 Street); 861-1210.

Chinese American Trading, 91 Mulberry Street; 267-5224.

Dean & DeLuca, 121 Prince Street; 254-7774.

E.A.T., 1064 Madison Avenue (80 Street); 879-4017.

Fredricksen & Johannesen, 7719 Fifth Avenue, Brooklyn; 745-5980. Scandinavian products.

H. Roth, 1577 First Avenue (81 Street); 734-1110.

Les Trois Petits Cochons, 17 East 13 Street; 255-3844. Pâtés and terrines.

Maison Glass, 153 East 53 Street; 832-1530.

Molinari Brothers, 776 Ninth Avenue (52 Street); 582-5048.

Jefferson Market, 455 Sixth Avenue (10 Street); 675-2277.

Manganaro Foods, 488 Ninth Avenue; 563-5331.

Murray's Sturgeon Shop, 2429 Broadway (91 Street); 724-2650.

Paprikas Weiss, 1546 Second Avenue (80 Street); 288-6903.

Silver Palate, 274 Columbus Avenue (73 Street); 799-6340.

Word of Mouth, 1012 Lexington Avenue (72 Street); 734-9483.

Zabar's, 2245 Broadway (80 Street); 787-2000.

Jewelry

Fifth Avenue, of course, is lined with all the great and famous jewelers in the world. Take a look, even if you can't purchase anything to take home with you. We list these, along with a few others of less renown.

Artwear, 409 West Broadway; 431-9405. Pretty, imaginative things.

Buccellati, 703 Fifth Avenue (57 Street); 755-4975.

Bulgari, Pierre Hotel, Fifth Avenue and 61 Street; 486-0086.

Cartier, 653 Fifth Avenue (52 Street); 753-0111.

C'est Magnifique, 124 Macdougal Street; 475-1613. Buy jewelry here or have it repaired. Glass eyes are made into brooches.

Fortunoff, 124 East 57 Street; 758-6660. Virtually a supermarket for jewelry.

Fred Leighton, 763 Madison Avenue (66 Street); 288-1872. Antiques.

Gallery 10, 138 West 10 Street; 989-9138. Interesting modern jewelry.

Harry Winston, 718 Fifth Avenue (56 Street); 245-2000.

Jewelry Workshop and Gallery, 150 Spring Street; 226-5303. Classic and cloissone are most popular here.

Tiffany's, Fifth Avenue at 57 Street; 755-8000. The most famous; don't miss the windows.

Van Cleef & Arpels, 744 Fifth Avenue (57 Street); 644-9500.

Leather Goods and Luggage

Crouch & Fitzgerald, 400 Madison Avenue (48 Street); 755-5888.

Gucci, 689 Fifth Avenue (54 Street); 826-2600.

Leather Man, 111 Christopher Street; 243-5339. Custom-made leather jackets, etc.

Mark Cross, 645 Fifth Avenue (51 Street); 421-3000.

T. Anthony, 722 Madison Avenue (66 Street); 879-2730. Made-to-order luggage.

Magic and Metaphysical

Astrological Consultant Center, 45 East 51 Street; 833-0020.

Flosso-Hornmann Magic Company, 304 West 34 Street; 279-6079. America's oldest magic emporium.

Mad Monk, 500 Sixth Avenue (13 Street); 242-6678.

Lou Tannen's, 1540 Broadway (45 Street); 541-9550. America's largest purveyor of magical things.

Samuel Weiser, 740 Broadway (8 Street); 777-6363. The best books on the occult.

Very Mysterious Store, 324 East 9 Street; 473-9582.

Warlock, 35 West 19 Street; 242-7182.

Men's Apparel

A. Sulka, 711 Fifth Avenue (55 Street); 980-5200. Custom shirts.

Bancroft Haberdashers, 1250 Sixth Avenue (RCA Building); 245-6821. Also other branches. Greatest selection of Arrow shirts.

Barney's, Seventh Avenue and 17 Street; 929-9000. Largest store of its kind; something for everyone at varying prices.

B & B Lorry's, 521 Fifth Avenue (43 Street); 599-9730. High quality at discount prices.

Brooks Brothers, Madison Avenue and 44 Street; 682-8800. The classic haberdasher.

Burberry's, 9 East 57 Street; 371-5010. English raincoats.

Charivari, 2339 Broadway (84 Street); 873-7242. Chic.

DeNoyer, Inc., 219 East 60 Street; 838-8680. Ties.

Dunhill Tailors, 65 East 57 Street; 355-0060. Custom and ready to wear.

Gucci, 699 Fifth Avenue (54 Street); 826-2600. Shoes with status.

J. J. Hats Center, 1276 Broadway (32 Street); 244-8860. Wide selection.

Miller's, 123 East 24 Street; 691-1000. Riding apparel.

Oxford Handkerchief Co., 51 Orchard Street; 226-0878. Designer shirts.

Paul Stuart, Madison Avenue and 45 Street; 682-0320. Not too conservative; sometimes quite daring.

Roger's Peet, 479 Fifth Avenue (41 Street); 682-8170. Moderate.

Sr. David, 779 Madison Avenue (66 Street); 628-3213. Also 821 Madison Avenue (68 Street); 737-2422. Many imports.

Ted Lapidus, 1010 Third Avenue (60 Street); 751-7251.

Wallach's, 555 Fifth Avenue (46 Street); 687-0106. Also other branches. Moderate prices.

Musical Instruments and Sheet Music

Charles Hansen Educational Music and Books, 1860 Broadway (61 Street); 246-4175.

G. Schirmer, Inc. (at Brentano's), 4 East 49 Street; 752-3800.

Jos. Patelson Music House, 160 West 56 Street; 582-5840. Good textbooks.

Sam Ash, 160 West 48 Street; 245-4778.

Sohmer & Co., 31 West 57 Street; 753-9235.

Steinway and Sons, 109 West 57 Street; 246-1100.

Terminal Music Supply, 166 West 48 Street; 245-5249. Instruments at a good discount.

Wurlitzer Music Stores, 130 West 42 Street; 221-5780. Organs.

Needlework and Needlework Supplies

Alice Maynard, 133 East 65 Street; 535-6107. Designs.

Design Point, 15 Christopher Street; 929-0550. Custom designs.

Erica Wilson, 717 Madison Avenue (63 Street); 832-7290. Supplies and kits.

Sunray Yarn Co., 349 Grand Street; 475-0062. Inexpensive supplies.

Party Goods

Hallmark Card and Party Basket, 464 Madison Avenue (51 Street); 838-0880.

Paper House, 741 Madison Avenue (64 Street); 737-0082. Also branches elsewhere.

Party Bazaar — Dennison's, 390 Fifth Avenue (36 Street); 695-6820.

Photography and Equipment

Berkey K & L Custom Service, 222 East 44 Street; 661-5600. Developing and enlarging; cheap film.

Berkey Photo, 132 Fourth Avenue (near Union Square); 673-8400. Good camera repair.

Nikon House, 620 Fifth Avenue (50 Street); 586-3907.

Swiss Camera & Optic Service, 308 Fifth Avenue; 679-6844.

Willoughby's, 110 West 32 Street; 564-1600.

Picture Frames

Frame-it-Yourself, 85 Fourth Avenue (10 Street); 673-2214.

Granick Frames, 52 West 56 Street; 246-2869.

Kulicke Frames, 43 East 10 Street; 677-3772.

Make A Frame, Ltd., 1300 Third Avenue (75 Street); 988-8455.

Prints and Posters

L'Affiche Galerie, 145 Spring Street; 966-4620.

Non Sequitur, 329 Columbus Avenue (76 Street); 874-4202. After 1910.

Oestreicher's Prints Inc., 43 West 46 Street; 757-1190. The daddy of them all.

Postermat, 16 West 8 Street; 982-2946.

Poster Originals Ltd., 924 Madison Avenue (73 Street); 861-0422. Contemporary American posters.

Smolin Prints, 1215 Lexington Avenue (82 Street); 876-1464. Prints, posters, and buttons of the "I Like Ike" kind.

Records and Tapes

Discophile, 26 West 8 Street; 473-1902. If you are a collector and knowledgeable too, you will be well taken care of here.

House of Oldies, 267 Bleecker Street; 243-0500. You may find things you thought no longer existed, sometimes at a price.

King Karol, 1500 Broadway (43 Street); 869-0230. Also four more branches, distributed across the city. They claim that they have everything in stock.

Rizzoli, 712 Fifth Avenue (56 Street); 397-3700. Upstairs on the balcony you will find imported as well as American records, and most of them you may listen to, a practice not usually found in other New York record shops.

Sam Goody, 1290 Sixth Avenue (51 Street); 246-8730. Also 666 Third Avenue (42 Street); 986-8480. Their selection is large and generally a little cheaper than the other shops.

Record Hunter, 507 Fifth Avenue (42 Street); 697-8970. Usual new records, sometimes at reduced prices, as well as an assortment of Oriental, African, and Latin American pressings.

Shoes

FOR WOMEN

Chandler's, 695 Fifth Avenue (54 Street); 688-2140. Moderate.

Ferragamo, 717 Fifth Avenue (56 Street); 759-3822. Imported.

Goody Two Shoes, 33 Greenwich Avenue (10 Street); 243-9827. Whimsical.

I. Miller, 734 Fifth Avenue (57 Street); 581-0062.

La Maria, 43 East 57 Street; 759-8588. Avant-garde.

Maud Frizon, 210 East 60 Street; 753-8978. Very expensive.

Olof Daughters of Sweden, 459 Sixth Avenue (57 Street); 929-7957. Clogs.

Shoes, Etc., 59 Fourth Avenue (9 Street); 242-0490. Pappagallo and Klein shoes at discount.

Shoe Steal, 116 Duane Street; 964-4017. Wide and narrow widths.

Tree-Mark, 27 West 35 Street; 594-0720. Wide-calf boots.

FOR MEN

Benedetti Custom Shoes, 530 Seventh Avenue (30 Street); 221-9830.

Botticelli, 666 Fifth Avenue (53 Street); 582-2984. Expensive Italian shoes.

Gucci, 699 Fifth Avenue (54 Street); 826-2600.

McCreedy & Schreiber, 37 West 46 Street; 582-1552. Also another branch on 59 Street.

St. Mark's Leather Co., 37 St. Mark's Place; 982-3444. Frye boots.

Specialty Stores

What makes shopping in New York so special are these shops devoted to individual themes. Some are self-evident.

Ballet Shop, 1887 Broadway (63 Street); 581-7990.

Barone, 414 West Broadway; 431-9460. A neopunk boutique.

Cat Cottage, 254 West 81 Street; 580-7622. Souvenirs for cats.

Chess Mart, 240 Sullivan Street (3 Street); 473-9564. Boards and pieces.

Cinemabilia, 10 West 13 Street; 989-8519. Everything about the movies.

Collector's Cabinet, 153 East 57 Street; 355-2033. Collectibles of all sorts.

Erotic Baker, 73 West 83 Street; 362-7557. X-rated goodies.

Eve's Garden, 246 East 51 Street; 755-0148. A very elegant sex shop.

Go Fly a Kite, 1434 Third Avenue (81 Street); 988-8885. Beautiful kites of all kinds.

Hunting World, 16 East 53 Street; 755-3400. Rings and bracelets from elephant hair; safari needs.

Hammacher-Schlemmer, 147 East 57 Street; 937-8181. A gadget-lover's paradise.

Left Hand, 140 West 22 Street; 675-6265. Kitchen utensils, scissors, spoons, etc., for the left-handed person.

Lucidity, 775 Madison Avenue; 861-7000. Large and small items made from Lucite, sometimes with a simple but very beautiful design.

Mini Mundus, 1030 Lexington Avenue (73 Street); 288-5855. Doll's houses and other miniatures. World famous.

Mythology, 370 Columbus Avenue (77 Street); 874-0774. Amusing little stuff, including artistic rubber stamps.

Old Friends, 202 East 31 Street; 532-8234. Old and new Disney figures and Disney memorabilia.

Only Hearts, 281 Columbus Avenue (73 Street); 724-5608. A variety of items, all based on a theme of hearts. A year-round Valentine shop.

Pleasure Chest, 152 Seventh Avenue (10 Street); 242-4372. The most unusual of sex shops.

Props & Practicals, 150 West 52 Street; 765-4487. Broadway gifts.

Pop/eye, 130 Thompson Street; 777-1646. Oversized versions of every-day items, such as pencils, paper clips, etc.

P.S. I Love You, 2264 Broadway (81 Street); 874-4663. Hearts.

Tender Buttons, 143 East 62 Street; 758-7004. Buttons of all sizes and styles.

Untitled, 159 Prince Street; 982-2088. Museum art postcards.

Unicorn City, 55 Greenwich Avenue; 243-2017. Items involving unicorns.

Welcome to New York, 26 Carmine Street; 242-6714. Postcards, posters, and objects concerning old New York.

Sporting Goods

The department stores have general selections, but some of the following offer more extensive inventories.

Athlete's Foot, 170 West 72 Street; 874-1003. Also other branches. For the runner.

Castello Fencing Equipment, 836 Broadway (12 Street); 473-6930. One of the best shops in existence.

Herman's World of Sports, 135 West 42 Street; 730-7400. Also other branches. They have absolutely every-thing.

M. J. Knoud, 716 Madison Avenue (61 Street); 738-1434. The best in riding out-fits, as well as golf equipment.

Morsan's, 747 Third Avenue (46 Street); 758-2855. Comprehensive selection and especially good for camping and skiing equipment.

Princeton Skate & Ski Chalet, 379 Fifth Avenue (35 Street); 684-0100.

Racquet Shop, 289 Madison Avenue (40 Street); 685-1954.

Tennis Lady, 765 Madison Avenue (64 Street); 535-8601. Equipment and clothing.

Second-Hand Clothes and Thrift Shops

Second-hand dresses and antique cloth-ing are stylish in New York, so these businesses are always crowded. The thrift shops also offer period clothing, but less frequently. You will find several more thrift shops around Third Avenue and 80 Street, and you will be surprised at the quality of goods.

Abet-Rent-A-Fur, 307 Seventh Avenue (27 Street); 989-5757. A good place to go if you are here in the winter and cold.

Bogie's Antique Furs and Clothing, 201 East 10 Street; 260-1199. Venerable furs and other garments, such as air force jackets.

Cherchez, 864 Lexington Avenue (64 Street); 737-8215. Beautiful old white linen, in many shapes.

Encore Resale Dress Shop, 1132 Madi-son Avenue (84 Street); 879-2850. Rumor has it that Jackie O. takes her old Halstons to this place; they do sell very good things and those that are too much out of fashion, or too long or too short, are not accepted in the first place.

Gently Worn Inc., 351 Columbus Ave-nue (77 Street); 873-6927.

Harriet Love, 412 West Broadway; 966-2280.

Lydia, 21 East 65 Street; 861-8177. The most beautiful creations and therefore expensive.

Memorial Sloane Kettering Thriftshop, 350 Third Avenue (52 Street); 421-6900. A veritable emporium.

Palma, 90 Thompson Street; 966-1722. Old clothes in good repair and not too expensive.

Ritz Thrift Shop, 107 West 57 Street; 265-4559. The best deals in used furs.

Shady Lady, 2205 Broadway (80 Street); 799-2523.

Tobacco

Alfred Dunhill of London, 620 Fifth Avenue (50 Street); 684-7600.

Gilbert's Pipeline, 122 East 42 Street; 687-6907.

Nat Sherman Cigars, 71 Fifth Avenue (55 Street); 751-9100.

Stationery and Writing Paper

Letter paper is not expensive here. You can go to Bendel's or Tiffany's, but you won't save much money. If you need reasonably large quantities, you might try these.

Folio 72, 888 Madison Avenue (72 Street); 879-0675.

Public Stationery and Printing Corp., 5 Hanover Square; 344-5440.

Toys

Childcraft Center, 155 East 23 Street; 674-4754. Also 150 East 58 Street; 753-3196. Many toys made of wood.

F.A.O. Schwartz, 745 Fifth Avenue (58 Street); 644-9400. The largest and best-known toy store.

Gingerbread House, 9 Christopher Street; 741-9101.

Play It Again, 129 East 90 Street; 876-5888. Used toys.

Rappaport's Toy Bazaar, 1381 Third Avenue (78 Street); 679-3383. A wide selection of toys at reasonable prices.

Second Childhood, 283 Bleecker Street; 989-6140.

Toy Chest, 226 East 83 Street; 988-4320. Used toys.

Wines and Liquors

Astor Place Wine and Liquor, 12 Astor Place; 674-7500.

Morrell & Co., 307 East 53 Street; 688-9370.

Sixty-Seven Liquor Shop, 179 Columbus Avenue (67 Street); 724-6767.

Sherry Lehmann, 679 Madison Avenue (61 Street); 838-7500.

Sights Worth Seeing

Almost every corner of New York has a sight worth seeing, but we've tried to narrow down your choices somewhat with this listing. For additional information, see the White Pages of this book. See also THINGS TO DO.

Bridges

Brooklyn Bridge, City Hall Park in Manhattan to Cadman Plaza in Brooklyn. Many people consider it the most beautiful bridge in the world. It was built in ten years by a German immigrant and his son. To walk across it leisurely and see the incomparable skyline of lower Manhattan through a filigree of steel cables is unforgettable.

George Washington Bridge, from West 179 Street in Manhattan to Fort Lee, New

Jersey. At one time, it was the longest bridge in the world.

Churches

Abyssinian Baptist Church, 132 West 138 Street; 862-7474. The oldest black church in New York; where Adam Clayton Powell, former pastor and Congressman, began his career.

Judson Memorial Church, 55 Washington Square; 477-0351. Built in 1892 and an example of Italian Renaissance design. John LaFarge did the stained-glass windows.

Plymouth Church of the Pilgrim, Orange Street, Brooklyn Heights, Brooklyn. Henry Ward Beecher was the first minister when the church was founded in 1847.

Riverside Church, Riverside Drive and 122 Street; 749-7000. The huge tower nowadays contains offices, schoolrooms, and Quaker meeting places, you but can still climb it.

St. Andrew's Church, 4 Arthur Kill Road, Richmondtown, Staten Island. Founded in 1708, the church was chartered in 1713 by Queen Anne. During the Revolution it was headquarters and hospital for British troops.

St. Bartholomew's Church, Park Avenue, between 50 and 51 Streets. An ornate Romanesque Byzantine church in the midst of midtown Manhattan. The mosaics and alabaster windows are spectacular.

St. John the Divine, 112 Street and Amsterdam Avenue; 678-6888. With its 10,000 seats it is the largest church in the world. The neo-Gothic construction has been in progress since 1892 and still is not complete.

St. Patricks Cathedral, Fifth Avenue at 50 Street; 753-2261. A white marble Gothic cathedral patterned after the one at Cologne. Note the fine bronze doors.

St. Paul's Chapel, Broadway and Fulton Street; 732-5564. Manhattan's oldest building has been a church ever since it was built in 1766. A good example of Georgian style.

St. Peter's Church, Citicorp Center, Lexington Avenue at 54 Street. Nestled under the stilts supporting the Citicorp Building, this chapel is the only one in America designed entirely by a well-known artist — sculptor Louise Nevelson.

Trinity Church, Broadway and Wall Street; 285-0800. Like a tiny toy among the skyscrapers, this lovely church is an oasis for Wall Street workers. The old churchyard has stones for Alexander Hamilton and Robert Fulton.

Historic Sights

Of course many places we cite as historic are also architectural gems and vice versa.

IN MANHATTAN

Dyckman House, 204 Street and Broadway. The last typical Dutch Colonial farmhouse on Manhattan. Built in 1783, this building replaced an earlier one of 1748, which was destroyed by the British.

Federal Hall National Memorial, 26 Wall Street; 264-8711. Built in 1703, this was the place that John Peter Zenger was tried for libel. It was also first Capitol and where George Washington was inaugurated.

Fraunces Tavern Museum, 54 Pear Street; 425-1776. Built in 1719, this was where the Sons of Liberty met to protest the tyrannical oppression of the English.

Hamilton Grange National Memorial, 287 Convent Avenue; 283-5154. In 1801 Alexander Hamilton built his home here; the house remained in the family until the 1830s.

Morris-Jumel Mansion, West 160 Street and Edgecombe Avenue; 923-8008. Manhattan's oldest residence, built in 1765. First used as Washington's headquarters, it later was a tavern and also a farm.

IN THE BRONX

Bartow-Pell Mansion, Shore Road in Pelham Bay Park; 885-1461. Outstanding example of Greek Revival style, built in 1836.

Edgar Allan Poe Cottage, Grand Concourse and Kingsbridge Road; 881-8900. The last home of the poet and writer; where he wrote "Annabel Lee."

Mott Haven Historic District, Alexander Avenue between 138 and 142 Streets. Churches, a public library, police station, and townhouses make this a section as old as the Civil War.

Valentine-Varian House, 3266 Bainbridge Avenue and East 208 Street; 881-8900. Built in 1758, this is a typical farmhouse linked with the history of the area.

Van Cortlandt Mansion, Van Cortlandt Park, North of 242 Street and Broadway; 546-3323. A Georgian-style house built in 1748. Used as headquarters by George Washington.

IN BROOKLYN

Lefferts Homestead, Prospect Park; 965-6511. Built between 1778 and 1783, this is a beautiful Dutch house typical of the period.

IN QUEENS

Bowne House, 37-01 Bowne Street, Flushing; 359-0528. One of the oldest houses in the city; built in 1661, it remained a home until 1945. Don't miss the kitchen.

Friends Meeting House, 137-16 Northern Boulevard, Flushing; 762-9743. The oldest house of worship in the county,

dating to 1694.

Hunters Point Historic District, 45 Avenue between 21 and 23 Streets, Astoria. Examples of Italian and French architecture of the late nineteenth century.

Kingsland Homestead, 143-35 37 Avenue, Flushing; 939-0647. Built in 1774, this Dutch Colonial-English house is the only example of its era.

Town Hall, 137-35 Northern Boulevard, Flushing; 961-1111. Early Romanesque building dates back to mid-nineteenth century, when it was used for political and cultural activities.

Weeping Beech Tree, 37 Avenue between Parsons Boulevard and Bowne Street, Flushing. Planted in 1849 and still growing.

IN STATEN ISLAND

Billiou-Stillwell-Perine House, 1476 Richmond Road, Dongan Hills. Original part of the house was built in 1662.

Conference House, 7455 Hylan Boulevard; 984-2086. Built in the 1680s, this is made of stone brought from Holland as ballast in sailing vessels. Furnished with authentic eighteenth-century furnishings.

Richmondtown Restoration, 302 Center Street; 351-9414. An area being restored to show examples of an American village during the seventeenth-, eighteenth-, and nineteenth centuries.

Voorlezer's House, Richmondtown Restoration (see above). This is the original Little Red School House, built in 1695 and now part of the restoration village.

Architectural Gems

As usually happens when you try to classify things, we've included some extraordinary examples of period architecture under categories other than this one. These listed below are of interest especially for their architectural details and most do not function also as museums, churches, or historical sites.

Chrysler Building, Lexington Avenue and 42 Street. Certainly one of New York's most beautiful skyscrapers, this 1,048-foot building is topped with a stunning Art Deco design.

Citicorp Center, Lexington Avenue at 54 Street. One of New York's newest skyscrapers, this building is in large part dedicated to food. Notice how the top of the building slants toward the sun; that's for eventually setting up a solar heating system.

City Hall, Broadway and Park Row. A little jewel of a mixture of French Renaissance brought up to date with Georgian. The Governor's Room on the second floor can be visited on weekdays.

Federal Reserve Bank, 33 Liberty Street. Many countries keep their gold here, in this adapted Italian Renaissance building which is one of the most imposing in the financial world. If you want to visit, call 791-6130 ahead of time. The bank has a good map of the southern tip of Manhattan.

Grant's Tomb, Riverside Drive at 122 Street; 666-1640. The mausoleum of the Civil War victor is situated on a little hill in Riverside Park and is reminiscent of Napoleon's tomb in the Invalides in Paris. The interior is rather stark, indeed tomblike, of cold white marble; outside, a South American artist and the children from nearby Harlem have created a wonderful, if incongruous ceramic border.

E. V. Haughwout Building, 488-492 Broadway, corner of Broome Street. Erected in 1857, this building's prefabricated cast-iron panel wall and passenger elevator were milestones in the development of the skyscraper.

Flatiron Building, Broadway and Fifth Avenue at 23 Street. Daringly high and incredibly slender, this triangular sky scraper of 1902 demonstrates what the imagination can offer for New York's limited space.

Gracie Mansion, East End Avenue at 88 Street. Erected in 1799–1801 for Archibald Gracie, this is still occupied as a home — since 1942 the official residence of the mayor.

Grand Central Terminal, East 42 Street between Vanderbilt and Lexington avenues. Completed in 1913, this is one of the great buildings of the nation — a symbol of the city. The architects solved staggering engineering and people-circulation problems through the extensive use of ramps, while the French Beaux-Arts decoration makes the building artistically magnificent.

Lever House, 390 Park Avenue, between 53 and 54 streets. This glass-walled building appears weightless. A good example of the then-new trend in skyscrapers.

Mercedes-Benz Showroom, 430 Park Avenue, corner of 56 Street. Designed by Frank Lloyd Wright, this seems a bit crowded now but remains an interesting application of a practical use.

Seagram Building, 375 Park Avenue, between 52 and 53 streets. Designed by Mies van de Rohe and Philip Johnson, this is considered still to be one of New York's finest examples of modern-day skyscraper art.

Union Carbide Building, 270 Park Avenue, between 47 and 48 streets. A 53-story tower with gray glass and black panels.

Woolworth Building, 233 Broadway, between Park Place and Barclay Street. Impressive skyscraper built in 1913, noted for its dramatic accent and Gothic crown.

Sights with a View

These particularly give you a good overview of the city.

Empire State Building, Fifth Avenue and 34 Street; 736-3100. There are two observatories: on the 86th and 102nd floors. The latter is glass-enclosed and on a clear day you can see for 60 miles.

RCA Building, in Rockefeller Center, 30 Rockefeller Plaza; 489-2947. The observation deck on the 70th floor is large, with benches on the south side and a perfect perspective, since you are looking at the Empire State Building 15 blocks away.

World Trade Center, 2 World Trade Center; 466-7377. From the observation deck on one of the 110-story towers you have a magnificent view — on clear days for a radius of a hundred miles.

The World in Microcosm

New York has a little bit of almost every culture. Besides the many ethnic restaurants and shops in the city, there are many cultural centers.

EUROPEAN

French Cultural Services, 972 Fifth Avenue; 570-4443. Special exhibitions in a lovely building.

Goethe House, 1014 Fifth Avenue; 744-8310. Films and exhibitions.

Scandinavian Foundation, 127 East 73 Street; 879-9779. A reading room with Norwegian, Swedish, and Danish newspapers, plus exhibits of art.

Spanish Institute, 684 Park Avenue; 628-0420. Sculpture exhibitions, language courses.

ASIAN

China Institute, 125 East 65 Street; 744-8181. Exhibits, courses, and publications in this fascinating building.

Jacques Marchais Center for Tibetan Art, 338 Lighthouse Avenue (Staten Island); 987-3478. A temple-like museum.

Japan House, 333 East 47 Street; 832-1115. Art exhibitions, films, and garden in an exciting modern Japanese building.

Ukrainian Museum, 203 Second Avenue; 228-0110. Galleries display crafts and there are also workshops.

AMERICAS

Center for Inter-American Relations, Park Avenue at 68 Street; 249-8950. Modern-day culture exhibits including those from Colombia and Peru.

Hispanic Society, Broadway and 155th Street; 926-2234. Exhibits of art, pottery, grillwork.

AFRICA

African-American Institute, 833 United Nations Plaza; 949-5666. Exhibitions of the works of artists from various countries.

OTHER

Alternative Museum, 17 White Street; 966-4444. Changing exhibits of varying types from all parts of the world.

Other Sights Worth Seeing

Lincoln Center for the Performing Arts, Broadway and 63 Street; 877-1800. Gigantic, still controversial building complex, with the Metropolitan Opera, Avery Fisher Hall, several theaters, a library, and a museum for dance and theater history. Guided tours of the whole complex, as well as a look behind the scenes.

New York Public Library, Fifth Avenue and 41 Street. Not only with a comprehensive collection of books and exhibition halls, but also with a gallery of nineteenth-century paintings and collections of rare books or books of special interest. Legend has it that the two lions guarding its wide stairs only roar when a virgin goes by. At Christmastime, they wear wreaths around their necks.

New York Stock Exchange, 20 Broad Street, between Wall Street and Exchange Place; 623-5168. During the week you can observe the frantic goings-on below through glass-enclosed gallery windows, while an automatic narration gives you an explanation of the action.

New York Times, 229 West 43 Street; 556-1234. Here you can see how a newspaper is put together — from scratch. You have to make an appointment for a tour in advance.

Rockefeller Center, 49 Street to 52 Street, Fifth Avenue to Sixth Avenue; 489-2947. A city within a city — city planning par excellence. Guided tours of this Art Deco marvel are given every forty-five minutes and the tour ends on the observation deck where you can stay and admire the marvelous view.

Statue of Liberty, Liberty Island; 732-1286. Ferries leave every hour on the hour from Battery Park, South Ferry (9 AM to 4 PM), with additional sailings every half-hour during the summer months. Take the ferry out to the island, then climb up the grand lady to her crown, where you'll have a magnificent view of the harbor. Also here is the American Museum of Immigration.

United Nations, First Avenue, 42 to 49 streets; 754-7713. The headquarters for world action. Tours are given every fifteen minutes daily from the lobby of the General Assembly building.

Sports

Arenas and Stadiums

Madison Square Garden, West 33 Street (Seventh Avenue); 564-4400.

Shea Stadium, Roosevelt Avenue and 126 Street, Flushing, Queens; 672-3000 or 421-6600.

USTA National Tennis Center, Flushing Meadow-Corona Park, Queens; 271-5100.

Yankee Stadium, 161 Street and River Avenue, Bronx; 293-6000.

Racetracks

Note: There are off-track betting (OTB) offices throughout the city.

Aqueduct, Rockaway Boulevard at 108 Street, Jamaica, Queens; 641-4700.

Belmont Park, Hempstead Turnpike and Plainfield Avenue, Elmont, Long Island; (516) 641-4700.

Meadowlands, East Rutherford, New Jersey; (201) 935-8500.

Roosevelt Raceway, Westbury, Long Island; (516) 222-2000.

Yonkers Raceway, Yonkers, New York; (914) 968-4200.

Gyms/Indoor Sports Facilities

Many gyms in the city are open to members only.

Fifth Avenue Racquet Club, 404 Fifth Avenue (37 Street); 594-3120. Excellent squash facilities.

Gym for Gymnastics, 305 East 47 Street; 753-3553.

92 Street YM-YWHA, 1395 Lexington Avenue; 427-6000. Good for paddleball.

McBurney YMCA, 215 West 23 Street; 741-9216. Good indoor track.

Kounovsky Physical Fitness Center, 25 West 56 Street; 246-6415.

Skateboard Palace, 71-17 Roosevelt Avenue, Jackson Heights, Queens; 779-5353. A skateboard track, stressing safety.

Theaters

On Broadway

Alvin, 250 West 52 Street; 757-8646.

Ambassador, 219 West 49 Street; 541-6490.

Anta, 245 West 52 Street; 246-6270.

Barrymore, 243 West 47 Street; 246-0390.

Belasco, 111 West 44 Street; 246-4490.

Bijou, 209 West 45 Street; 221-8500.

Biltmore, 261 West 47 Street; 582-5340.

Booth, 222 West 45 Street; 246-5969.

Broadhurst, 235 West 44 Street; 247-0472.

Broadway, 1681 Broadway (53 Street); 247-0472.

Brooks Atkinson, 256 West 47 Street; 245-3430.

Century, 235 West 46 Street; 354-6644.

Circle in the Square, 1633 Broadway (50 Street); 581-0720.

Cort, 138 West 48 Street; 489-6392.

Edison, 240 West 47 Street; 757-7164.

Eugene O'Neill, 230 West 49 Street; 246-0220.

46th Street, 226 West 46 Street; 246-0246.

Helen Hayes, 210 West 46 Street; 246-6380.

Imperial, 249 West 45 Street; 265-4311.

John Golden, 252 West 45 Street; 246-6740.

Little, 240 West 44 Street; 221-6425.

Longacre, 220 West 48 Street; 246-5639.

Lunt-Fontanne, 205 West 46 Street; 586-5555.

Lyceum, 149 West 45 Street; 582-3897.

Majestic, 247 West 44 Street; 246-0730.

Mark Hellinger, 237 West 51 Street; 757-7064.

Martin Beck, 302 West 45 Street; 246-6363.

Minskoff, 1515 Broadway (44 Street); 869-0550.

Morosco, 217 West 45 Street; 246-6320.

Music Box, 239 West 45 Street; 246-4636.

New Apollo, 234 West 43 Street; 921-8558.

Palace, 1564 Broadway (47 Street); 757-2626.

Playhouse, 359 West 48 Street; 541-9820.

Plymouth, 236 West 45 Street; 246-9156.

Royale, 236 West 45 Street; 245-5760.

St. James, 246 West 44 Street; 398-0280.

Shubert, 225 West 44 Street; 246-5990.

Trafalgar, 209 West 41 Street; 921-8000.

22 Steps, 200 West 48 Street; 541-6162.

Uris, 1633 Broadway (50 Street); 586-6510.

Vivian Beaumont, Lincoln Center (65 Street); 362-7616.

Winter Garden, 1634 Broadway (51 Street); 245-4878.

Off-Broadway

Below are some of the major theaters; consult a theater guide or the *New Yorker* or *Village Voice* for a more extensive listing.

American Place, 111 West 46 Street; 247-0393.

Cherry Lane, 38 Commerce Street; 989-2020.

Circle in the Square Downtown, 159 Bleecker Street; 254-6330.

Circle Repertory, 99 Seventh Avenue South; 581-1819.

Entermedia, 189 Second Avenue; 475-4191.

Manhattan Theater Club, 321 East 73 Street; 472-0600.

Phoenix, 221 East 71 Street; 730-0794.

Provincetown Playhouse, 133 Macdougal Street; 473-8779.

Public, 425 Lafayette Street; 677-6350.

Quaigh, Hotel Diplomat, 108 West 43 Street; 221-9088.

Spanish Theater Repertory, 138 East 27 Street; 889-2850.

Sullivan Street Playhouse, 181 Sullivan Street; 674-3838.

Theater de Lys, 121 Christopher Street; 924-8782.

Off-Off Broadway

These theaters come and go frequently, so check the latest listing in a newspaper or magazine. Here again we give you a selected listing.

AMAS Repertory, 1 East 104 Street; 369-8000.

Equity Library, 103 Street and Riverside Drive; 663-2028.

Impossible Ragtime, 120 West 28 Street; 243-7494.

Jean Cocteau Repertory, 330 Bowery; 677-0060.

Judson Memorial Church, 55 Washington Square South; 477-0351.

La Mama Etc., 74A East 4 Street; 475-7710.

National Black Theater, 9 East 125 Street; 427-5615.

Negro Ensemble Company, at St. Mark's Playhouse, 133 Second Avenue (11 Street); 674-3530.

New Federal Theater at Henry Street Settlement, 466 Grand Street; 766-9295.

New Heritage Repertory, 43 East 125 Street; 876-3272.

Open Space in Soho, 64 Wooster Street; 966-3729.

Performance Group, 33-35 Wooster Street; 966-3651.

SoHo Rep, 19 Mercer Street; 925-2588.

South Street, Pier 15, South Street Seaport Museum, Fulton and South streets; 724-4065.

Synesthetics, 61 Crosby Street.

Theater for the New City, 162 Second Avenue (11 Street); 254-1109.

Theater of the Riverside Church, 490 Riverside Drive (120 Street); 864-2929.

Thirteenth Street, 50 West 13 Street; 924-9785.

Top of the Gate, 160 Bleecker Street; 982-9292.

Truck and Warehouse, 79 East 4 Street; 228-8558.

Universalist Church, 76 Street and Central Park West; 873-3645.

Westside Community Repertory, 252 West 81 Street; 666-3521.

Wonderhorse, 83 East 4 Street; 691-8340.

WPA, 138 Fifth Avenue (19 Street); 691-2274.

Things to Do

If you are not quite in the mood for a museum and are stiff from looking up at skyscrapers, here are a few more suggestions for outings.

Astoria Studios, 35-11 35 Avenue, Long Island City, Queens; 392-5600. A thirteen-building complex used from 1919 to 1942 as a studio, has been reopened and revitalized.

Burlington House Mill, 1345 Sixth Avenue (54 Street); 333-3622. If you are interested in fibers and their origins, you can travel on a 150-foot-long conveyor belt through the history of textiles in America.

Hall of Fame for Great Americans, Bronx; 367-7300. Landmark structure houses bronze portrait busts of presidents, statesmen, scientists, artists, and humanitarians.

New York Experience, McGraw-Hill Building, 1221 Sixth Avenue (48 Street); 869-0345. A multisensory theater showing you a bit of New York's history and what else makes it special. Experience the fog as it rolls in over the East River, watch the lightning sizzle overhead, and crash into the Empire State Building; your seat swivels with the action.

Nostalgia Special and New York City Transit Exhibition, Boerum Place and Schermerhorn Street, Brooklyn. See page 280.

Roosevelt Island Tramway, 59 Street and First Avenue; 753-6626. Take this trip to Roosevelt Island in the East River and along the way you can view up and down the river.

Snug Harbor Cultural Center, Richmond Terrace, Staten Island; 448-2500. Former seamen's home includes twenty-six landmark buildings and eighty acres of parkland.

Staten Island Ferry, see page 221. Take one of the best rides in the city, and enjoy the remarkable view of the lower Manhattan skyline.

Tipping

Usually **15 percent** is minimum for taxis, restaurants, or room service. Allow 50 cents for your coat at times when you must check it. Figure $1 for porters at airports and stations, $2 if you have a lot of luggage; give 50 cents to $1 per suitcase for bellhops or porters at your hotel, depending upon the type of hotel.

Toilets

These are scarce items in New York — at least if you are looking for public conveniences. You can always resort to using a toilet in the subway, but you must pay the fare to get access and then you'll find them dirty and unattended.

When in need, go to a hotel or to a nearby department store or museum. Restaurants are less likely to allow you to use their facilities unless you also order a meal.

Tours and Sightseeing

By Boat

Around Manhattan Island, Circle Line, Pier 83, West 43 Street; 563-3200. One of the nicest excursions you can take in New York because the perspective is so different from the water. The trip takes about three hours, and tours begin at the end of March and run until November; in the summer they leave every forty-five minutes.

Ferry to the Statue of Liberty, Circle Line from the Battery; 269-5755. The brief ride also takes you to the American Museum of Immigration, also on Liberty Island. Boats leave Manhattan from 9 to 4 every hour.

Ferry to Staten Island, White Hall Terminal. Take the ferry at the tip of Manhattan and without question you'll have the cheapest boat trip in the world. You'll get to look at the greatest skyline in the world as well.

By Helicopter

Island Helicopters, Heliport, 34 Street and East River Drive; 895-5372. Daily from 9 to 6, unless weather is bad. Rides vary from six minutes to forty minutes.

By Bus

CITY BUS TOURS

You can tour parts of the city by New York City bus. There are two such tours, offered for only the cost of a token ($.60).

Culture Bus Loop I; 330-1234. Take the M41 on Saturdays, Sundays, and most holidays and get off at any one of the twenty-two stops. The bus runs from 10 to 6 and comes around every thirty-two minutes.

Culture Bus Loop II; 330-1234. This works like Bus Loop I, but the bus is B88, and you visit thirty-two stops in lower Manhattan and Brooklyn.

OTHER BUS TOURS

Crossroads Sightseeing, 701 Seventh Avenue (47 Street); 581-2828.

Gray Line of New York, Terminal at Eighth Avenue and 53 Street; 397-2600. Tours of varying lengths.

Manhattan Sightseeing Bus Tours, 150 West 49 Street; 245-6641.

New York Big Apple Tours, 162 West 56 Street; 582-6339. Especially for non-English speakers.

Penny Sightseeing Tours, 303 West 42 Street; 247-2860. Tours of Harlem.

Short Line-American Sightseeing International of New York, 168 West 46 Street; 246-5550. Vistacruiser service.

By Horse-Drawn Carriage

On the Plaza (near the Plaza Hotel) you will find a line of horse-drawn carriages. They are decorated with faded plastic flowers and their drivers often wear top hats. Tours go along the city's streets or into the park.

By Subway

Nostalgia Special; 330-3060. A special train leaves every Saturday and Sunday from April to November, from the 57th Street and Sixth Avenue station. It travels to Rockaway Park in Brooklyn and on the way it stops at the New York City Transit Exhibition in Brooklyn. This is an old-fashioned train from a bygone era and the ride takes four hours.

Other Types of Tours

Adventures on a Shoestring, 300 West 53 Street; 265-2663. Special trips that reveal another side of New York: talk to a lie detector expert, watch a heart surgeon operate, visit a painter in his studio, learn to dance the Flamingo, or try skiing.

Art Tours of Manhattan, 33 East 22 Street; 254-7682. Tours of SoHo, museums, galleries, artists' studios, and neighborhoods.

Backstage on Broadway, 228 West 47 Street; 575-8065. A tour behind the scenes of a Broadway theater, usually in the company of someone who is in the production. This group also takes you on a tour of the Waldorf Astoria Hotel, for instance, and its mile-long kitchen.

City Tour, 60 Lispenard Street; 226-4514. Enjoy neighborhoods and monuments with an architect-planner; tours of the city in a mini-bus.

Destination: New York, 122 East 42 Street; 986-2280. The insider way to see New York, with a native New Yorker.

Doorway to Design, 79 West 12 Street; 924-1919. Behind-the-scenes tour of the work of interior design with a decorating consultant.

Planners' New York Tours; 734-1366. Special tours of the city by urban planners.

Salt and Pepper Tours, 59 East 54 Street; 371-3459. Escorted night tours to introduce the excitement of the city.

Singer's Brooklyn; 875-9084. Lou Singer is Mr. Brooklyn, and if you go with him on Wednesdays or Saturdays at 10 AM (meeting place is Second Avenue between 41 and 42 streets), you will not only see houses and churches but the infamous Bedford-Stuyvesant quarter and the incredible rehabilitation taking place there.

Walking Tours and House Tours

Walking tours are scheduled frequently, but not always regularly. We suggest that you contact the following for their latest tours. In addition, the *New York Times* on Fridays lists talking tours for the upcoming weeks.

Friends of Cast-Iron Architecture, 44 West 9 Street; 982-7272. Trips through SoHo to see the magnificent factories-turned lofts.

Mayor's Office of Special Events, 42 Broadway; 248-8349. This office runs the newly begun tours of Gracie Mansion. These forty-minute tours through the eighteenth-century house and grounds go every Wednesday, from 10 to 4, April through October.

Municipal Art Society, 30 Rockefeller Plaza; 586-4761. Guided tours of notable buildings, including Grand Central Station and selected neighborhoods.

Museum of the City of New York; LE 4-1672. Tours of notable areas and buildings in knowledgeable company, arranged from April through October.

Traditions

Although appearing to prefer the new and different, New York is a city that cherishes many traditions. For some of those yearly events, see CALENDAR OF EVENTS. For other, more general traditions, see the various chapters of the white pages, pages 11–211.

Trains

---

see PUBLIC TRANSPORTATION and ARRIVAL IN NEW YORK, by train.

Veterinary Services

Should you travel with your pet and require the services of a veterinarian, try the following.

Animal Clinic of New York, 1623 First Avenue; 628-5580. By appointment only.

Animal Medical Center, 510 East 62 Street; 838-8100. Open 24 hours, 7 days a week.

Carnegie Animal Hospital, 1708 Second Avenue; 369-5665. Hours vary; call first.

For additional information, call the **Veterinary Medical Association of New York City,** 246-0057.

Weather

see CLIMATE AND CLOTHING.

Women's Interests

see white pages, pages 159–161; also GAY SCENE.

Photographic Credits

Black and White (numbers refer to pages)

Agentur Photo-Center, Braunschweig: 28, 52–53, 61, 116, 122–123, 158 r., 160 l.,
  173, 176 m.r., 195, 197, 198, 207 b., 208, 208–209 t. and b., 216 l., 217 l., 243,
  245 l., 252–253
Alexandra Roosevelt: 24, 142 b., 216 r.
Alfred Mayor, New York: 22, 50 l., 66, 76, 80, 81, 82, 85, 86–87, 90, 93, 136,
  164–165, 168, 176 m. l., 176 b., 192, 199, 200, 218, 222–223, 228, 245 t.
Archiv DuMont Buchverlag, Cologne: 94, 151 t.
Associated Press Photo, Frankfurt/M.: 128 l.
Bob Serating, New York: 117
Candida Höfer/Gerard Osborne: 201
Cowtesy: 13, 118, 120–121
Frick Collection, New York: 91
Gwen Phillips: 19 t., 27, 51, 139 b., 150, 209 u. l., 221
Heinz Held, Cologne: 14, 19 b., 21–22, 88, 92, 124, 126 l., 158 l., 176 t. r., 187 b.,
  191 l., 196, 220, 240 l.
J. Heilmeyer/Pea Fröhlich: 129, 130, 133, 134, 204
Keystone, Munich: 210–211
Laenderpress, Düsseldorf: 17, 25 r., 128 r., 160 r., 215, 217 r.
Klaus Lehnartz, Berlin: frontispiece, 16, 17 t., 25 l., 26, 56–57, 73, 78, 127, 141, 166,
  176 t. l., 180, 186 t., 187 t. l., 194, 219, 240 r., 251, 254–255
New York Convention and Visitor's Bureau: 10, 30–31, 54, 58, 75, 135, 170, 174,
  175, 178, 179, 182–183, 188, 190, 203, 207 t., 212, 230, 238, 242–243
Rizzoli International Bookstore, New York: 172
Rudi Herzog, Cologne: 18, 139 t., 142 t., 144–145, 156, 184, 226
Serge Cohen, Cologne: 152, 153
Tiffany & Co. Publicity Department, New York: 169
Thomas Gross, New York: 62, 64, 114, 151 b., 191 r., 206
Vista Point Verlag, Cologne: 140
Walter Vogel, Düsseldorf-Oberkassel: 146
Whitney Museum, New York: 233

Color (numbers refer to photo numbers)

Cafe Nicholson, New York: 30
Candida Höfer/Gerard Osborne: 8, 9, 11, 13, 14, 16, 17, 28, 29, 32, 46, 48, 55, 56
Colette: 49
Heinz Held, Cologne: 7, 18, 21, 22, 24–26, 34, 36, 39, 41, 53, 60, 61
Klaus Lehnartz, Berlin: 52, 57
Majella Brücher, Cologne: 27
Rudi Herzog, Wiesbaden: 51
Spectrum Colour Library, London: 23, 47
Thomas Gross, New York: 2, 4, 5, 6, 19, 40, 42, 44, 45
Vista Point Verlag, Cologne: 3, 10, 12, 15, 32, 33, 38, 59
Walter Vogel, Düsseldorf-Oberkassel: 1
ZEFA, Düsseldorf (Benser, Goebel, Scholz, Damm, Carle): front cover, 20, 37, 50, 58

Index

Note: Most references are to the white pages. For additional specific references the reader should consult the alphabetical listings in the appropriate sections of the Key to the City.

Horne, Philip, 83
horse-drawn carriages, 179
horseback riding, 157
horseracing, 157
hotels: entertainment at, 147, 162;
    tourist, 60, 63, 161, 272–274
House of Leather, 234
Hoving, Thomas, 89
Howe, Lord, 223
Hudson, Henry, 67
Hudson River, 67, 77, 90, 157, 185
Hunt, Richard Morris, 248
Hunter, Alberta, 149
Hunter Island Sanctuary, 185
Hunters Point Historic District, 216
Hurrah, 154

ice cream, 274
ice hockey, 157
immigrants, 15–16, 18, 72–73, 95,
    138–143, 147, 240–244, 248
Improvisation, 147
India House, 249
Indians (American), 67, 94, 248
information, 274–275
Institute of Arts and Sciences, 223
International Arrivals Building (Kennedy
    Airport), 77
Inwood Hill Park, 185
Irish, 15–16, 72–73
Isaacs-Hendricks House, 236
Istanbul Restaurant, 233

Jacques Marchais Center of Tibetan Art,
    223
Jamaica, 216
Jamaica Bay Wildlife Refuge, 185, 216
James Street, 243
Japan House Gallery, 93
jazz, 74, 131, 147, 149, 237
Jazzmania, 149
Jean Cocteau Repertory, 131
Jefferson, Eddie, 149
Jefferson Market, 237
Jefferson Market Courthouse, 237
Jets, 157
jewelry, 191
Jewish Museum, 93
Jezebel, 232
Jimmie Ryan's, 149
Jimmy Day's, 237
Joe Allen's, 143
Joe & Mike's, 199
Joffrey Ballet, 119
John Street Church, 250

Johnson, Philip, 79-80, 236
Judson Memorial Church, 79, 236
Jukes, Asbury, 154
Jumel Terrace, 84
Junior's Bakery, 138

Karp, Ivan, 201
Kaufman Surplus, 171
Kennedy Airport, 77, 113, 215
Kennedy Gallery, 94
Kenny's Castaways, 149
Kiehl Pharmacy, 171
King, Kenneth, 119
King, Woody, 133
King Street, 83
King's College, 70–71
Kings County, see Brooklyn
Kings Highway, 219
Kingsland Homestead, 216
Kitchen, 200
kitchenware shops, 137–138
Klais, Johannes, 81
Knickerbocker Saloon, 149
Knicks, 157
Knoedler Gallery, 94
Koch, Edward, 193
Koeppen, Wolfgang, 13, 225
kosher food, 244
Kounovsky Physical Fitness Center, 157
Kreiger & Son, 167
Krön, 229

La Guardia, Fiorello, 75
La Guardia Airport, 77, 215
La Mama theater, 130–131
Lace-Up Shoe Shop, 167
Ladies' Fort, 149
Lady Madonna, 171
Lauren, Ralph, 190
Le Corbusier, 79
leather, 234
Leather Man, 234
Left Hand shop, 171
Lerner, Alan Jay, 125
Lesbian Switchboard, 163
Leske's, 219
Lever Building, 75, 79
Lexington Avenue, 171
Liberty, Statue of, 95, 157–158, 248
Liberty Island, 248
libraries, 49, 73, 79, 117, 121, 159,
    236–237
Library (restaurant), 162
Lichtman Bakery, 137
Lietzmann, Sabina, 13

New York City Bus System

You can take buses up and down the major avenues and across the primary crosstown streets. Below we also show you three major diagonal routes that may prove most useful to tourists.

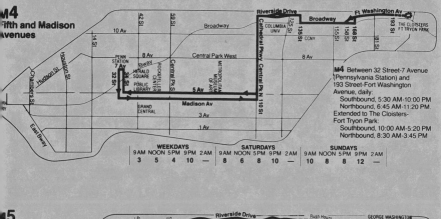

M4
Fifth and Madison Avenues

M4 Between 32 Street-7 Avenue (Pennsylvania Station) and 193 Street-Fort Washington Avenue, daily:
Southbound, 5:30 AM-10:00 PM.
Northbound, 6:45 AM-11:20 PM.
Extended to The Cloisters-Fort Tryon Park:
Southbound, 10:00 AM-5:20 PM
Northbound, 8:30 AM-3:45 PM

	WEEKDAYS				SATURDAYS				SUNDAYS			
9AM	NOON	5PM	9PM	2AM	9AM	NOON	5PM	9PM	2AM	9AM	NOON	5PM	9PM	2AM
3	5	4	10	—	8	6	8	10	—	10	8	8	12	—

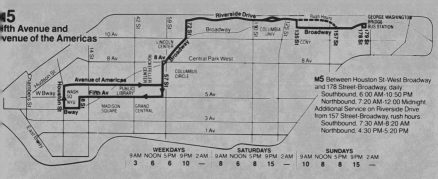

M5
Fifth Avenue and Avenue of the Americas

M5 Between Houston St-West Broadway and 178 Street-Broadway, daily:
Southbound, 6:00 AM-10:50 PM
Northbound, 7:20 AM-12:00 Midnight.
Additional Service on Riverside Drive from 157 Street-Broadway, rush hours:
Southbound, 7:30 AM-8:20 AM
Northbound, 4:30 PM-5:20 PM

	WEEKDAYS				SATURDAYS				SUNDAYS			
9AM	NOON	5PM	9PM	2AM	9AM	NOON	5PM	9PM	2AM	9AM	NOON	5PM	9PM	2AM
3	6	6	10	—	8	6	8	15	—	10	8	8	15	—

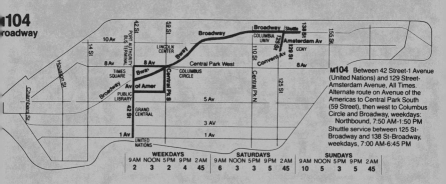

M104
Broadway

M104 Between 42 Street-1 Avenue (United Nations) and 129 Street-Amsterdam Avenue, All Times. Alternate route on Avenue of the Americas to Central Park South (59 Street), then west to Columbus Circle and Broadway, weekdays:
Northbound, 7:50 AM-1:50 PM.
Shuttle service between 125 St-Broadway and 138 St-Broadway, weekdays, 7:00 AM-6:45 PM

	WEEKDAYS				SATURDAYS				SUNDAYS			
9AM	NOON	5PM	9PM	2AM	9AM	NOON	5PM	9PM	2AM	9AM	NOON	5PM	9PM	2AM
2	3	2	4	45	6	3	3	4	45	10	5	3	5	45

Bus maps courtesy of New York City Transit Authority